Lecture Notes in Computer Science 12455

More information about this series at http://www.springer.com/series/7410

Robert Krimmer · Melanie Volkamer ·
Bernhard Beckert · Ralf Küsters ·
Oksana Kulyk · David Duenas-Cid ·
Mihkel Solvak (Eds.)

Electronic Voting

5th International Joint Conference, E-Vote-ID 2020
Bregenz, Austria, October 6–9, 2020
Proceedings

 Springer

Editors
Robert Krimmer (iD)
Tallinn University of Technology
Tallinn, Estonia

Tartu University
Tartu, Estonia

Bernhard Beckert (iD)
Karlsruhe Institute of Technology (KIT)
Karlsruhe, Baden-Württemberg, Germany

Oksana Kulyk
University of Copenhagen
Copenhagen, Denmark

Mihkel Solvak
University of Tartu
Tartu, Estonia

Melanie Volkamer (iD)
Karlsruhe Institute of Technology
Karlsruhe, Baden-Württemberg, Germany

Ralf Küsters
University of Stuttgart
Stuttgart, Germany

David Duenas-Cid (iD)
Tallinn University of Technology
Tallinn, Estonia

Kozminski University
Warsaw, Poland

ISSN 0302-9743   ISSN 1611-3349   (electronic)
Lecture Notes in Computer Science
ISBN 978-3-030-60346-5   ISBN 978-3-030-60347-2   (eBook)
https://doi.org/10.1007/978-3-030-60347-2

LNCS Sublibrary: SL4 – Security and Cryptology

This Springer imprint is published by the registered company Springer Nature Switzerland AG
The registered company address is: Gewerbestrasse 11, 6330 Cham, Switzerland

Preface

This volume contains papers presented at the 5th International Joint Conference on Electronic Voting (E-Vote-ID 2020), held during October 6–9, 2020. Due to the extraordinary situation provoked by the COVID-19 pandemic, the conference was held online during this edition, instead of at the traditional venue in Bregenz, Austria. The E-Vote-ID conference resulted from the merging of EVOTE and Vote-ID, and now totaling 16 years since the first E-Vote conference in Austria. Since that conference in 2004, over 1,000 experts have attended the venue, including scholars, practitioners, authorities, electoral managers, vendors, and PhD students. The conference collected the most relevant debates on the development of electronic voting, from aspects relating to security and usability through to practical experiences and applications of voting systems, also including legal, social, or political aspects, among others; turning out to be an important global referent in relation to this issue.

This year, the conference also consisted of the following tracks and sessions:

- Security, Usability and Technical Issues Track
- Administrative, Legal, Political and Social Issues Track
- Election and Practical Experiences Track
- PhD Colloquium, Poster and Demo Session (held on the day before the conference)

E-Vote-ID 2020 received 55 submissions, each of them being reviewed by three to five Program Committee members, using a double-blind review process. As a result, 14 papers were accepted for this volume, representing 25% of the submitted proposals. The selected papers cover a wide range of topics connected to electronic voting, including experiences and revisions of the real uses of e-voting systems and corresponding processes in elections.

We would also like to thank the German Informatics Society (Gesellschaft für Informatik) with its ECOM working group, and KASTEL for their partnership over many years. Further we would like to thank the Swiss Federal Chancellery for their kind support. Special thanks go to the members of the International Program Committee for their hard work in reviewing, discussing, and shepherding papers. They ensured the high quality of these proceedings with their knowledge and experience.

We are also thankful for the financial support receive through the European Union (H2020 Research and Innovation Programme, Grant Agreement No 857622).

October 2020

Robert Krimmer
Melanie Volkamer

The original version of the cover and book was revised: the seventh editor name has been updated. The correction to the book is available at https://doi.org/10.1007/978-3-030-60347-2_15

Organization

Program Committee

Marta Aranyossy	Corvinus University of Budapest, Hungary
Jordi Barrat i Esteve	eVoting Legal Lab, Spain
Bernhard Beckert	Karlsruhe Institute of Technology, Germany
Josh Benaloh	Microsoft, USA
Matthew Bernhard	University of Michigan, USA
Nadja Braun Binder	University of Zurich, Switzerland
Veronique Cortier	CNRS, Loria, France
Staffan Darnolf	IFES, Sweden
David Duenas-Cid	Tallinn University of Technology, Estonia and Kozminski University, Poland
Helen Eenmaa-Dimitrieva	University of Tartu, Estonia
Aleksander Essex	University of Western Ontario, Canada
Micha Germann	University of Bath, UK
J. Paul Gibson	Mines Télécom, France
Rosario Giustolisi	IT University of Copenhagen, Denmark
Kristian Gjøsteen	Norwegian University of Science and Technology, Norway
Nicole Goodman	University of Toronto, Canada
Rajeev Gore	The Australian National University, Australia
Ruediger Grimm	University of Koblenz, Germany
Rolf Haenni	Bern University of Applied Sciences, Switzerland
Thomas Haines	Queensland University of Technology, Australia
Toby James	University of East Anglia, UK
Robert Krimmer	University of Tartu and Tallinn University of Technology, Estonia
Ralf Kuesters	University of Stuttgart, Germany
Oksana Kulyk	IT University of Copenhagen, Denmark
Johannes Mueller	University of Luxembourg, Luxembourg
Magdalena Musial-Karg	Adam Mickiewicz University, Poland
Andras Nemeslaki	BME, Hungary
Stephan Neumann	Landesbank Saar, Germany
Hannu Nurmi	University of Turku, Finland
Jon Pammett	Carleton University, Canada
Olivier Pereira	UCLouvain, Belgium
Josep Mª Reniu	University of Barcelona, Spain
Peter Roenne	SnT, University of Luxembourg, Luxembourg
Mark Ryan	University of Birmingham, UK
P. Y. A. Ryan	University of Luxembourg, Luxembourg

Contents

Shifting the Balance-of-Power in STV Elections

Michelle Blom[1]([⊠]), Andrew Conway[2], Peter J. Stuckey[3],
and Vanessa J. Teague[4]

[1] School of Computing and Information Systems, University of Melbourne,
Melbourne, Australia
michelle.blom@unimelb.edu.au
[2] Silicon Econometrics Pty. Ltd., Melbourne, Australia
andrewelections@greatcactus.org
[3] Department of Data Science and AI, Monash University, Melbourne, Australia
Peter.Stuckey@monash.edu
[4] Thinking Cybersecurity Pty. Ltd., Melbourne, Australia
vanessa@thinkingcybersecurity.com

Abstract. In the context of increasing automation of Australian electoral processes, and accusations of deliberate interference in elections in
Europe and the USA, it is worthwhile understanding how little a change
in the recorded ballots could change an election result. In this paper
we construct manipulations of the ballots in order to change the overall
balance of power in an Australian Federal Senate election – the upper
house of Parliament. This gives, hopefully tight, over-estimations of the
Margin of Victory (MOV) for the party or coalition winning the Senate.
This is critical information for determining how well we can trust the
reported results, and how much auditing should be applied to the election process to be certain that it reports the true result. The challenge
arising in Australian Federal Senate elections is that they use a complicated Single Transferable Vote (STV) method for which it is intractable
to compute the true MOV, hence we must rely on greedy methods to
find small manipulations.

Keywords: Single Transferable Vote · Balance of power · Margin
of Victory

1 Introduction

In a climate of increasing public mistrust in all governmental activities, assurances that the results of elections are correct are critical for democracies to function well. One critical statistic that helps to define how trustworthy an election
result is, is the so called Margin of Victory (MOV), which indicates the minimal number of ballots that need to be modified to change the election result.
If the MOV is small, then we should invest considerable effort in auditing the
election processes, since the true result may differ if inevitable errors lead to

R. Krimmer et al. (Eds.): E-Vote-ID 2020, LNCS 12455, pp. 1–18, 2020.
https://doi.org/10.1007/978-3-030-60347-2_1

changes greater then that MOV. If the MOV is large we require less auditing to be assured that the election outcome is likely to be correct.

The Australian Federal Parliament consists of two houses: the House of Representatives, which defines the executive part of government responsible for making new laws; and the Senate, a house of review. For laws to be enacted they must pass both houses, so the controller of the Senate has significant influence on what legislation can be enacted. Australian politics is dominated by two "parties": the Labor Party (progressive); and the Liberal/National Party Coalition (conservative), an enduring coalition of two parties. Historically, one or other party has formed government. The Senate is more complicated as there is a greater number of smaller parties and independents. In some cases no party has held the balance of power in the Senate, though usually one or other party, with perhaps some agreements with minor parties, does.

Existing work [2] has examined how to compute the MOV for Australian House of Representatives elections, which makes use of Instant Runoff Voting (IRV). In this paper, we examine the much more challenging problem of *estimating* the MOV for Australian Federal Senate elections. The difficulty arises because the election uses Single Transferable Vote (STV) which is a complicated election methodology. Determining the MOV of an STV election is NP-hard [8]. While we can determine MOVs for small individual STV elections [3], these methods do not scale to the size of the elections that actually occur for the Australian Federal Senate.

An Australian Federal Senate election consists of a separate STV election in each of the six Australian states, and the two Australian territories. There are 76 seats in the Senate, with 12 seats awarded to each of the six states, and 2 to each of the two territories. In a regular election, 6 of the available 12 seats for each state, and both of the 2 seats for each territory, are up for re-election. In a double-dissolution election, all 76 seats are vacated. The party, or coalition of parties, that occupies the majority of seats in the Senate chamber (39 or greater) significantly influences the legislation that the government is able to pass. Legislation has to pass through both houses of Parliament (the lower and upper house) before it can become law. In the 2016 and 2019 Australian Federal elections, conservative politicians have formed the majority in both houses. This has limited the power of more progressive parties to shape legislation.

In this paper, we consider estimating the number of ballot changes required to change the outcome of such an election to give a particular coalition of parties the majority in the Senate. In 2016, we would have had to shift four Senate seats away from conservatives, to progressive candidates, to change the nature of the majority. In 2019, only two seats were required to change hands to achieve a progressive majority. We present a heuristic, combined with an integer program (IP), to compute an upper bound on the number of ballot changes required in order to award an additional n seats to a coalition of parties, $\mathbb{C}$. In other words, if a coalition $d \in \mathbb{C}$ was originally awarded N_d seats, we are interested in manipulations that would result in d being awarded $n + N_d$ seats. This implies that n seats are taken away from candidates outside of d.

An Australian Federal Senate election consists of a number of separate STV elections. Our approach is based on finding small manipulations of each individual s-seat STV election, that awards an additional $j = 1, \ldots, k$ seats to our desired coalition, where $k = \min(s, n)$. A knapsack problem is then solved to determine the combination of these manipulations that results in a combined n-seat shift to our coalition with the least number of required ballot changes. Existing work [1] considers the use of local search for finding small manipulations of a STV election that elects a specific, favoured candidate c to a seat. This paper moves beyond this to find an upper bound on the manipulation required to elect n additional candidates from a coalition of parties, across a set of individual STV elections responsible for allocating seats in a Senate.

We apply our method to data from the 2016 and 2019 Australian Federal Senate elections. In both elections, candidates from conservative parties form the majority in the elected Senate. We consider a coalition of more centrist or left-leaning parties, forming our desired coalition d. We then use our approach to find an upper bound on the number of ballots we would have to change, across each of the state and territory STV elections that form part of the Senate election as a whole, to shift enough seats to candidates in d to change the nature of the majority. In the 2016 and 2019 elections, we want to shift $n = 4$, and $n = 2$, seats respectively. Our local search algorithm is used to compute candidate manipulations that shift $j = 1, \ldots, \min(s, n)$ seats in each individual s-seat STV election. A simple integer program (IP) is then applied to the results to select a least cost combination of manipulations to apply in each state and territory. We have found that we can give a progressive coalition d a majority by changing 40,008 ballots in the 2016 election, and 27,635 ballots in the 2019 election.

2   Preliminaries

STV is a preferential system of voting in which voters rank candidates or parties in order of preference, and candidates compete for s seats. In Australian Senate Elections voters may cast their ballot in two ways. First, they may vote *above the line*. At the top of each ballot is a sequence of boxes, one for each party and group of independent candidates. To vote above the line, a voter ranks at least 6 of these parties and grouped independents. Alternatively, a voter may vote *below the line*. Under each of the above the line party boxes is a list of candidates belonging to that party or group. To vote below the line, a voter ranks at least 14 individual candidates in order of preference. STV elections for the Australian Senate can involve over 100 candidates.

Definition 1 (STV Election). *An STV election $\mathcal{E}$ is a tuple $\mathcal{E} = (\mathcal{C}, \mathcal{P}, \mathcal{B}, Q, s)$ where $\mathcal{C}$ is a set of candidates, $\mathcal{P}$ is the set of parties or groups to which candidates belong, $\mathcal{B}$ the multiset of ballots cast, Q the election quota (the number of votes a candidate must attain to win a seat – the Droop quota – Eq. 1), and s the number of seats to be filled.*

$$Q = \left\lfloor \frac{|\mathcal{B}|}{s+1} \right\rfloor + 1 \tag{1}$$

We will use a small running example to describe the concepts in this section, and our n-seat shifting approach. In this example, two 3-seat STV elections, $\mathcal{E}_1$ and $\mathcal{E}_2$, are held to elect a total of 6 candidates to a small Senate. In each election, four parties (A, B, C, and D) field 2 candidates, resulting in a total of 8 candidates. The candidates of $\mathcal{E}_1$ are denoted $a_{11}, a_{12}, \ldots, d_{11}$ and d_{12}, and those of $\mathcal{E}_2$, $a_{21}, a_{22}, \ldots, d_{21}$ and d_{22}. Tables 1a and 2a define the ballot profiles of $\mathcal{E}_1$ and $\mathcal{E}_2$, listing the number of ballots cast with a range of different *above the line* party rankings. For each ranking, we state the equivalent *below the line* ranking, indicating how the ballot would pass from candidate to candidate if they were eliminated in that sequence. During the election counting process, valid above the line votes are treated exactly as their below the line equivalent.

The counting of ballots in an STV election starts by distributing each ballot to the tally pile of its first ranked candidate. An above the line vote with a first preference for party p is given to the first candidate of that party listed on the ballot. Candidates are awarded a seat if the number of votes in their tally reaches or exceeds a threshold, called a *quota*. The value of the quota is based on the total number of ballots cast in the election, and the number of seats available (Eq. 1). The quotas of elections $\mathcal{E}_1$ and $\mathcal{E}_2$ are 137 votes $(1 + \lfloor 545 / (3 + 1) \rfloor = 137)$ and 188 votes, respectively.

Counting proceeds by electing candidates whose *tallies* (Definition 2) reach or exceed the quota, and distributing their *surplus* to the candidates that remain standing. A candidate's surplus is equal to the difference between their tally value and the quota. The non-exhausted ballots in an elected candidates tally pile are distributed to eligible candidates at a *reduced value*. Each ballot, starting with a value of 1, is reduced in value so that the sum of the value of the transferred ballots is equal to the surplus.

Definition 2 (Tally $t_i(c)$). *The tally of a candidate $c \in C$ in round i is the sum of the values of the ballots in c's tally pile. These are the ballots for which c is ranked first among the set of candidates still standing, S_i. Let $\mathcal{B}_{i,c}$ denote the subset of ballots sitting in c's tally pile, and $v_i(b)$ the value of ballot b, at the start of round i.*

$$t_i(c) = \sum_{b \in \mathcal{B}_{i,c}} v_i(b) \tag{2}$$

Table 1b shows that for $\mathcal{E}_1$, only the first listed candidate of each party have votes in their tallies after Round 1 of counting. This is because all voters have cast an above the line vote. The ballots sitting in a_{11}'s tally will pass to a_{12} when a_{11} is either elected or eliminated. Candidates a_{11} and b_{11} have a quota with tallies of 270 and 250 votes, and surpluses of 133 and 113 votes. They are elected to the first two available seats in Rounds 2–3 of counting. All 270 ballots in a_{11}'s tally pile are given to a_{12}, but they now have a combined value of 133 (each ballot now has a reduced value of 0.4926).

If no candidate has a quota, the candidate with the smallest tally is eliminated. In $\mathcal{E}_1$ (Table 1b), no candidate has a quota after the election of a_{11} and

Table 1. STV election, $\mathcal{E}_1$, stating (a) the number of ballots cast with each listed above-the-line ranking over parties A to D, their equivalent below-the-line ranking over candidates a_{11} to d_{12}, and (b) the tallies after each round of election, and elimination.

Ranking ATL	Ranking BTL	Count
[A, B]	[$a_{11}, a_{12}, b_{11}, b_{12}$]	270
[B, A, D, C]	[$b_{11}, b_{12}, a_{11}, a_{12}, d_{11}, d_{12}, c_{11}, c_{12}$]	250
[C, D, A, B]	[$c_{11}, c_{12}, d_{11}, d_{12}, a_{11}, a_{12}, b_{11}, b_{12}$]	20
[D, C, A]	[$d_{11}, d_{12}, c_{11}, c_{12}, a_{11}, a_{12}$]	5

(a)

Seats: 3, Quota: 137

Candidate	Round 1	Rounds 2-3 a_{11}, b_{11} elected / 133 votes to a_{12} / 113 votes to b_{12}	Rounds 4-6 c_{12}, d_{12} eliminated / d_{11} eliminated / 50 votes to c_{11}	Rounds 7-8 c_{11} eliminated / 250 votes to a_{12} / a_{12} elected
a_{11}	270	–	–	–
a_{12}	0	0+133 = 133	133	133 +25 = 158
b_{11}	250	–	–	–
b_{12}	0	0+113 = 113	113	113
c_{11}	20	20	20 +5 = 25	–
c_{12}	0	0	–	–
d_{11}	5	5	–	–
d_{12}	0	0	–	–

(b)

Table 2. STV election, $\mathcal{E}_2$, stating (a) the number of ballots cast with each listed above-the-line ranking over parties A to D, their equivalent below-the-line ranking over candidates a_{21} to d_{22}, and (b) the tallies after each round of election, and elimination.

Ranking ATL	Ranking BTL	Count
[B, C, D, A]	$[b_{21}, b_{22}, c_{21}, c_{22}, d_{21}, d_{22}, a_{21}, a_{22}]$	2,000
[A, D, C, D]	$[a_{21}, a_{22}, d_{21}, d_{22}, c_{21}, c_{22}, d_{21}, d_{22}]$	2,100
[D, A, B, C]	$[d_{21}, d_{22}, a_{21}, a_{22}, b_{21}, b_{22}, c_{21}, c_{22}]$	1,700
[C, D, A, B]	$[c_{21}, c_{22}, d_{21}, d_{22}, a_{21}, a_{22}, b_{21}, b_{22}]$	1,700

(a)

Seats: 3, Quota: 188

Candidate	Round 1	Rounds 2-3 a_{21}, b_{21} elected / 22 votes to a_{22} / 12 votes to b_{22}	Rounds 4-6 d_{22}, c_{22} eliminated / b_{22} eliminated / 12 votes to c_{21}	Rounds 7-8 a_{22} eliminated / 22 votes to d_{21} / d_{21} elected
a_{21}	200	–	–	–
a_{22}	0	$0+22 = 22$	22	–
b_{21}	210	–	–	–
b_{22}	0	$0+12 = 12$	–	–
c_{21}	170	170	$170 + 12 = 182$	182
c_{22}	0	0	–	–
d_{21}	170	170	170	$170 + 22 = 192$
d_{22}	0	0	–	–

(b)

b_{11}. The candidates with the smallest tally, c_{12} and d_{12}, both with 0 votes, are eliminated in Rounds 4–5. In Round 6, d_{11}, with 5 votes, is eliminated. These 5 votes are transferred, at their current value, to c_{11}, as d_{12} is no longer standing. Candidate c_{11} now has 25 votes.

The STV counting process continues in rounds of electing candidates whose tallies have reached a quota, and elimination of candidates with the smallest tally. In $\mathcal{E}_1$, candidate c_{11} is eliminated in Round 7, with their votes distributed to a_{12}. In Round 8, a_{12} is elected to the final seat, with their tally having exceeded a quota's worth of votes.

Several STV variants exist, differing in the way that surpluses are distributed [7]. The method of reducing the value of transferred ballots described above is the Inclusive Gregory Method [5]. The precise rules used by the Australian Federal Senate for adjusting the values of transferred ballots are more complex, and outlined in legislation.

The approach we present in this paper searches for manipulations of the STV elections that form part of an Australian Federal Senate election that achieve a desired outcome. Given a favoured coalition of parties d, whose candidates have been awarded N_d seats in the un-manipulated election, we are interested in manipulations that award N_d+n candidates in d a seat. We define a manipulation of an STV election as follows.

Definition 3 (Manipulation $\mathcal{M}$). *A manipulation for an election $\mathcal{E} = (\mathcal{C}, \mathcal{P}, \mathcal{B}, Q, s)$ is a tuple $\mathcal{M} = (\mathcal{B}^+, \mathcal{B}^-)$, where: $\mathcal{B}^+$ denotes a multiset of ballots to add to $\mathcal{B}$; $\mathcal{B}^-$ a multiset of ballots to remove from $\mathcal{B}$; and $|\mathcal{B}^+| \equiv |\mathcal{B}^-|$. The result of applying $\mathcal{M}$ to an election $\mathcal{E}$ is a modified election profile $\mathcal{E}' = (\mathcal{C}, \mathcal{P}, \hat{\mathcal{B}}, Q, s)$, where $\hat{\mathcal{B}}$ is the result of removing each ballot in $\mathcal{B}^-$ from $\mathcal{B}$, and then adding each ballot in $\mathcal{B}^+$ to $\mathcal{B}$.*

To assess whether a given manipulation $\mathcal{M}$ awards n additional seats to our favoured coalition d, we simulate the STV counting process on the manipulated election profile $\mathcal{E}'$, and count the number of seats awarded to d in the outcome. We use a simulator, denoted SIM-STV, that captures the intricate rules specific to the Australian Federal Senate election, as defined in legislation. All the manipulations we generate in our experiments are validated on the full federal rules [4] using SIM-STV, and ballot data published by the AEC, standardized at https://vote.andrewconway.org/. An example manipulation for the election of Table 1 is shown in Example 1.

Example 1. Consider election $\mathcal{E}_1$ of Table 1. If we replace 111 ballots with the above the line ranking [A, B] with the above the line ranking [D], we no longer elect candidate a_{12} but elect d_{11} in their place. Candidates a_{11} and b_{11} are elected in the first two rounds, as before. Candidates d_{12}, c_{12}, and c_{11}, are then eliminated. The reduced flow of votes from a_{11} to a_{12} leaves a_{12} on only 22 votes, compared to d_{11}'s 136 and b_{12}'s 135 votes.

The rules used for Australian Federal Senate elections [6] are close to that described above, with some idiosyncrasies. For example, when ballots are distributed from one candidate's tally pile to another, the total value of those ballots is rounded down to the nearest integer. This practice causes a number of votes to be lost over the course of the tallying process. For further details of SIM-STV, we refer the reader to [1].

3 Finding n-Seat Senate Manipulations

We present an approach for computing a manipulation of one or more of the individual STV elections that form an Australian Federal Senate election, to shift the majority of seats away from an unfavoured coalition of parties to a favoured coalition. In the 2016 and 2019 Australian Federal Senate elections, a conservative coalition of parties had a 4 and 2 seat majority. Our approach looks for the best combination of manipulations to apply to the state and territory STV elections to realise a combined $n = 4$, and $n = 2$, seat shift to a progressive coalition. A shift of 2 seats could be realised by shifting 1 seat to our favoured coalition in Victoria, for example, and 1 seat in New South Wales.

Our approach consists of two stages. The first stage looks at each constituent s-seat STV election individually. We use a local search heuristic, described in Sect. 3.1, to find small manipulations that shift varying numbers of seats ($k = 1, \ldots, \min(s, n)$) away from the undesired coalition $u \in \mathbb{C}$ to candidates that belong to a desired coalition of parties $d \in \mathbb{C}$. The local search method is not optimal – it may not find the smallest possible manipulation that shifts k seats to our favoured candidates.

As a result of this first stage, we have a series of manipulations, for each state and territory election, that shift varying numbers of seats to our desired coalition. The second stage of our approach solves a simple integer program (IP) to select the combination of manipulations that realises our n-seat shift with the smallest number of required ballot changes. To achieve a shift of 4 seats, for example, we may shift 1 seat in each of four state elections, or 2 seats in one state and 2 seats in another.

Example 2. In Example 1, we manipulated $\mathcal{E}_1$ by 111 ballots (shifted from party A to D), giving 1 seat to D at the expense of A. In order to give 2 seats to a coalition of parties C and D, we need to shift ballots away from A and B to C and D. Consider a manipulation that removes 116 ballots with ranking [A, B], replacing them with the ranking [C], and 131 ballots with ranking [B,A,D,C], replacing them with [D]. This manipulation results in both c_{11} and d_{11} being elected at the expense of a_{12} and b_{11}.

3.1 Finding Manipulations with Local Search

Given an s-seat STV election $\mathcal{E}$, we present a local search heuristic for finding manipulations that award an additional k seats to a candidates in a desired coalition d. In the original outcome of $\mathcal{E}$, N_d seats have been awarded to candidates from d. We seek a manipulation of $\mathcal{E}$ in which $N_d + k$ seats are awarded to candidates from d. The heuristic is provided as input k candidate pairs of unfavoured original winner w, and favoured original loser l. We then search for smaller and smaller manipulations that aim to rob each w of a seat, and elect l. We repeatedly apply this heuristic to different sets of k candidate pairs, returning the smallest found successful manipulation as a result.

To identify sets of k winner-loser pairs to consider, we start with: a set of unfavoured original winners $\mathcal{W}$; and a set of favoured original losers $\mathcal{L}_d$.

1. Let $\overline{\mathcal{W}}$ denote the set of all k-candidate subsets of $\mathcal{W}$, and $\overline{\mathcal{L}_d}$ the set of all k-candidate subsets of $\mathcal{L}_d$.
2. The k-candidate subsets in $\overline{\mathcal{W}}$ are sorted in order of the total tally of candidates upon their election, from smallest to largest. This is the sum of each candidates tally in the round in which they were elected to a seat. The first subset in the sorted $\overline{\mathcal{W}}$ consists of candidates who were elected to a seat with the smallest tallies.
3. The k-candidate subsets in $\overline{\mathcal{L}_d}$ are sorted in order of the total tally of candidates upon their elimination, from largest to smallest. This is the sum of each candidates tally in the round in which they were eliminated. The first subset in the sorted $\overline{\mathcal{L}_d}$ consists of candidates who were eliminated with the largest tallies.
4. To limit the complexity of our approach, we restrict our attention to the first M subsets in $\overline{\mathcal{W}}$ and $\overline{\mathcal{L}_d}$. For each $W \in \overline{\mathcal{W}}$, we consider each $L \in \overline{\mathcal{L}_d}$. We apply our local search heuristic with k winner-loser pairs formed by pairing the first winner in W with the first loser in L, the second winner in W with the second loser in L, and so on. We return the best (smallest) successful manipulation found by applying our local search heuristic to each set of the $M \times M$ generated k winner-loser pairs.

Given a list of k unfavoured winner, favoured loser, pairs, our method aims to replace each unfavoured winner with its paired loser. However, any manipulation that elects $N_d + k$ candidates from d is considered to be successful. Each application of the local search heuristic involves two phases.

Phase 1. The first stage finds an initial, but potentially quite large, successful manipulation that, upon simulation of the manipulated election profile, elects at least $k + N_d$ candidates from our desired coalition $d \in \mathbb{C}$. This manipulation is denoted M_0.

Phase 2. We then repeatedly search for a good 'size reducing' move to apply to M_0. These moves reduce the number of ballots shifted between candidates, while still ensuring that the manipulation successfully elects $k + N_d$ candidates from d. In each iteration, we examine the set of possible changes (moves) we could make to the current 'best found' manipulation, selecting the move that results in the largest reduction in the number of ballot changes. When no 'size reducing' move can be found, search terminates and returns the best (smallest) manipulation it has found.

A manipulation defines k sets of ballot shifts between pairs of candidates from W and L. For each such (w, l) pair, our goal is to find a manipulation that replaces a certain number of ballots that favour w – ballots that form part of w's tally at the point of their election – with ballots that favour l. We consider three different approaches for specifying the ranking of these l-favouring ballots, denoted BTL, ATL, and IW. The latter, IW, uses the set of original winners from our desired coalition d, denoted $\mathcal{W}_d$.

BTL. A below the line vote that preferences l first, and each other loser in L subsequently, in the order they appear in L.

ATL. An above the line vote that preferences l's party first, and the parties of all other candidates in L subsequently, in the order they appear in L.

IW. A below the line vote that preferences l first, and each of the original winners from our desired coalition d, $\mathcal{W}_d$, subsequently.

Example 3. When seeking to elect $k = 2$ candidates from the coalition $d = \{C, D\}$ in $\mathcal{E}_1$, our list of original winners is $\mathcal{W} = \{a_{11}, a_{12}, b_{11}\}$ and favoured losers $\mathcal{L}_d = \{c_{11}, c_{12}, d_{11}, d_{12}\}$. Our winner subsets $\overline{\mathcal{W}}$, sorted in order of the total tally of the candidates, upon their election (smallest to largest), are $\overline{\mathcal{W}} = \{\{a_{12}, b_{11}\}, \{a_{12}, a_{11}\}, \{b_{11}, a_{11}\}\}$. Our subsets of favoured losers, sorted in order of the total tally of candidates, upon their elimination (largest to smallest), are $\overline{\mathcal{L}_d} = \{\{c_{11}, d_{11}\}, \{c_{11}, d_{12}\}, \{c_{11}, c_{12}\}, \{d_{11}, d_{12}\}, \{d_{11}, c_{12}\}, \{d_{12}, c_{12}\}\}$. Our approach will try to elect each pair of losers in $\overline{\mathcal{L}_d}$, at the expense of each pair of winners in $\overline{\mathcal{W}}$, starting with $\{c_{11}, d_{11}\}$ and $\{a_{12}, b_{11}\}$. For these winner-loser pairs, a_{12}-c_{11} and b_{11}-d_{11}, we find a M_0 that: replaces 226 ballots that sit in a_{12}'s tally upon their election, with a ranking that favours c_{11}; and 249 ballots that sit in b_{11}'s tally upon their election, with a ranking that favours d_{11}. The total size of this manipulation is 475. The IW method would replace 226 of a_{12}'s ballots with the ranking $[c_{11}]$. The ATL method would replace these ballots with the ranking $[C]$, where C is the party to which c_{11} belongs. The BTL method would form 226 ballots with ranking $[c_{11}, d_{11}, c_{12}, d_{12}]$, adding the remaining favoured losers after c_{11}.

Additional Notation. We use notation $\Delta_{i,j}$ to denote the number of ballots shifted between the ith of our k winner-loser pairs, (w, l), in a manipulation M_j. A 'shift' of $\Delta_{i,j}$ ballots between w and l replaces $\Delta_{i,j}$ ballots that sit in w's tally at the time they are elected with $\Delta_{i,j}$ ballots whose ranking has been specified according to one of the above methods (BTL, ATL, or IW). The notation $t[c]$ denotes the tally of candidate c upon their election (if they are an original winner) or elimination (if they lost).

Phase 1: Finding an Initial Manipulation. We define an initial manipulation M_0 by assigning a suitably high value to $\Delta_{i,0}$ for each winner-loser pair $i = 1, \ldots, k$ (see Fig. 1). We verify M_0 by simulating it with SIM-STV, and verifying that $k + N_d$ candidates from our coalition are elected in the manipulated election.

Phase 2: Reduce size of Manipulation. In the case where $k = 1$, we have one winner w that we want to replace with a loser l. Our initial manipulation

FINDINITIALMANIPULATION(k, N_d, W, L, t)

```
1    M_0 ← ∅
2    for i in 1..k do
3        w ← W[i]
4        l ← L[i]
5        Δ_{i,0} ← ⌈t[w] − t[l]⌉
6        verified ← Verify M_0 with SIM-STV.

7    if verified then
8        return M_0 as our initial manipulation
9    else
10       M'_0 ← M_0
11       while not verified do
12           M'_0 ← Increase each Δ_{i,0} by a factor of 2, capping each Δ_{i,0} by t[i].

13           verified ← Verify M'_0 with SIM-STV

14           if verified then
15               return M'_0 as our initial manipulation
16   return failure
```

Fig. 1. Phase 1: find initial manipulation to achieve the election of $k + N_d$ candidates from a desired coalition, where: W denotes original winners that are not in our desired coalition; and L are original losers who are in our desired coalition. Note that $t[c]$ denotes the tally of candidate c upon their election (if $c \in W$) or elimination (if $c \in L$).

MINIMISEMANIPULATION$_{k=1}$(M_0, k, N_d, α, γ)

```
1    M_best ← M_0
     ▷ Initialise step size δ based on size of initial manipulation
2    δ ← ⌈ Δ_{1,0}/γ ⌉
3    while true do
4        M_1 ← M_best
5        Δ_{1,1} ← Δ_{1,best} − δ
6        verified ← Verify M_1 with SIM-STV
7        if verified then
8            M_best ← M_1
9        else
10           if δ ≡ 1 then return M_best
11           δ ← ⌈ δ/α ⌉
```

Fig. 2. Phase 2 ($k = 1$): reduce size of an initial manipulation M_0 by reducing the number of shifted votes Δ by a step size δ. The step size δ is reduced each time the manipulation becomes too small (i.e., fails to realise the election of $k + N_d$ candidates from our desired coalition). In the above, $\alpha \geq 2$ and $\gamma \geq 2$ are predefined constants.

M_0 is iteratively reduced by only one type of move (as shown in Fig. 2). A 'step size', δ, controls how we reduce the size of our manipulation. We first reduce the number of ballots shifted between our winner and loser by the step size δ. If that reduction does not lead to a successful manipulation, we reduce δ, and keep trying (until we fail to find a better manipulation by shifting 1 less ballot). If a successful, smaller manipulation is found, we increase δ.

In the case where $k > 1$, our heuristic applies one of three types of moves in each iteration: reduce the shift of votes between one pair unfavoured winner and favoured loser (MOVE₁); reduce the shift of votes between each unfavoured winner and favoured loser pair (MOVE₂); and reduce the number of ballots shifted between one winner-loser pair while increasing the shift of votes between each other winner-loser pair (MOVE₃).

We maintain a step size δ_i^m for each move type m and winner-loser pair i. When we first use a particular move type $m \in \{1, 2, 3\}$ to reduce the size of a shift of ballots between the ith winner-loser pair, we reduce the number of ballots shifted by the step size δ_i^m. As in the $k = 1$ setting, if that reduction does not lead to a successful manipulation, we reduce δ. If a successful, smaller manipulation is found, we increase the step size for the next time this kind of move is applied. An interpretation of the steps sizes is that they are an estimate of how much we think we can reduce the size of a shift between two candidates, via each different move type, and achieve a successful manipulation.

We apply these moves iteratively, as follows. Pseudocode for each type of move is provided in Fig. 3. The predefined constants $\gamma \geq 2$ and $\alpha \geq 2$ are used when initialising, and updating, step sizes. The constant γ is used to initialise our step size δ – the amount by which we reduce the size of a manipulation as we look for smaller and smaller successful manipulations. Given an initial, quite large, manipulation that shifts $\Delta_{i,0}$ ballots between winner-loser pair i, our step size δ_i is initialised to $\lceil \frac{\Delta_{i,0}}{\gamma} \rceil$. The constant α is used to reduce our step size as the algorithm progresses (Step 11 in Fig. 2), allowing us to make more fine grained changes in the search for a minimal manipulation.

1. We maintain a running record of the best (smallest) manipulation found thus far, M_{best}, initialised to M_0.
2. Step sizes, δ_i^m, are first initialised to $\lceil \frac{\Delta_{i,0}}{\gamma} \rceil$ for $i = 1, \ldots, k$.
3. As per Fig. 3, we apply move type 1 (MOVE₁) to find a smaller manipulation than M_{best}, using the current set of step sizes δ_i^1. The result is a new manipulation M_1.
4. If $M_1 \neq \emptyset$, we have been able to reduce the vote shift between one winner-loser pair. We then apply move type 2 (MOVE₂ in Fig. 3) to M_{best} to find a smaller manipulation than M_1, denoted M_2, using the step sizes δ_i^2.
5. If either move type 1 or 2 were successful, we update M_{best} to the smallest of the two manipulations, M_1 or M_2, and return to Step 3.
6. If neither moves 1 and 2 were successful, we apply MOVE₃ to find a smaller manipulation than M_{best}, denoted M_3, using the current set of step sizes δ_i^3.
7. If $M_3 \equiv \emptyset$, we have failed to improve upon M_{best}, and return M_{best} as our best found manipulation. If $M_3 \neq \emptyset$, we replace M_{best} with M_3, reset our step sizes for move types 1 and 2 to their initial values, and return to Step 3.

Example 4. After finding an initial manipulation of 475 ballots to award candidates c_{11} and d_{11} a seat at the expense of a_{12} and b_{11}, we move to Phase 2

$\text{MOVE}_1(S, M_{current}, k, N_d, \alpha, \gamma)$
1   $M_{best} \leftarrow \emptyset, S_{best} \leftarrow S$
2   **for** i in $1..k$ **do**
3       $M_1 \leftarrow M_{current}$
4   **while** true **do**
5           $\Delta_{i,1} \leftarrow \Delta_{i,1} - \delta_i^1$
            ▷ Consider M_1 only if it is smaller than the size of the current best, S_{best}
6   **if** $|M_1| \geq S_{best}$ **then break**
7   **if** manipulation M_1 is verified by SIM-STV **then**
8               $M_{best} \leftarrow M_1, S_{best} \leftarrow |M_1|$
9               $\delta_i^1 \leftarrow \gamma \delta_i^1$
10   **break**
11   **else if** $\delta_i^1 \equiv 1$ **then break else** $\delta_i^1 \leftarrow \lceil \frac{\delta_i^1}{\alpha} \rceil$
12 **return** M_{best}

$\text{MOVE}_2(S, M_{current}, k, N_d, \alpha, \gamma)$
1   $M_{best} \leftarrow \emptyset, S_{best} \leftarrow S, M_2 \leftarrow M_{current}$
2   **while** true **do**
3   **if** $\sum_{i=1}^k \delta_i^2 \equiv 0$ **then break**
4       $\Delta_{i,2} \leftarrow \Delta_{i,2} - \delta_i^2$ for all $i \in \{1..k\}$
5   **if** $|M_2| \geq S_{best}$ **then break**
6   **if** manipulation M_2 is verified by SIM-STV **then**
7           $M_{best} \leftarrow M_2, S_{best} \leftarrow |M_2|$
8           $\delta_i^2 \leftarrow \gamma \delta_i^2$ for all $i \in \{1..k\}$
9   **break**
10   **else** Set all δ_i^2 that are smaller than γ to 0, and all remaining to $\lceil \frac{\delta_i^2}{\alpha} \rceil$
11 **return** M_{best}

$\text{MOVE}_3(S, M_{current}, k, N_d, \alpha, \gamma)$
1   $M_{best} \leftarrow \emptyset, S_{best} \leftarrow S$
2   **for** i in $1..k$ **do**
3       $M_3 \leftarrow M_{current}$
4   **while** true **do**
5           $\Delta_{i,3} \leftarrow \Delta_{i,3} - \delta_i^3$
            ▷ Distribute decrease of δ_i^3 across other pairwise shifts
6           $\Delta_{j,3} \leftarrow \Delta_{j,3} + \max\left(0, \lceil \frac{\delta_i^3}{k-1} \rceil - 1\right)$ for $j \in \{1..k\} \setminus \{i\}$
7   **if** manipulation M_3 is verified by SIM-STV **then**
8               $M_{best} \leftarrow M_3, S_{best} \leftarrow |M_3|$
9   **break**
10   **else**
11   **if** $\delta_i^3 \equiv 1$ **then break**
12              $\delta_i^3 \leftarrow \lceil \frac{\delta_i^3}{\alpha} \rceil$
13 **return** M_{best}

Fig. 3. Algorithms for move types one to three, where: S denotes the size of the best found manipulation in the current iteration of local search; $M_{current}$ is the best found manipulation at the start of the current iteration; k is the number of additional candidates we wish to elect from our desired coalition; N_d is the number of candidates from our desired coalition originally elected; and $\alpha \geq 2$, $\gamma \geq 2$ are predefined constants.

and try to find a smaller manipulation. In our initial manipulation M_0, we have $\Delta_{1,0} = 226$ and $\Delta_{2,0} = 249$, where winner-loser pair 1 is a_{12}-c_{11} and winner-loser pair 2 is b_{11}-d_{11}.

Using the parameters $\alpha = 5$ and $\gamma = 2$, we initialise our step sizes for each move and winner-loser pair combination as follows:

$$\delta_1^1 = \delta_1^2 = \delta_1^3 = \lceil 226/\gamma \rceil = 113 \qquad \delta_2^1 = \delta_2^2 = \delta_2^3 = \lceil 249/\gamma \rceil = 125$$

As per Fig. 3, we first apply MOVE$_1$ to reduce one of the shifts $\Delta_{1,0}$ and $\Delta_{2,0}$. We consider each $\Delta_{i,0}$ in turn. For pair 1, we can reduce $\Delta_{1,0}$ by the step size, from 226 to 113, and maintain a successful manipulation. Similarly, we can reduce $\Delta_{2,0}$ by its step size, from 249 to 124, leaving $\Delta_{1,0} = 226$, and successfully manipulate $\mathcal{E}_1$ to elect 2 candidates from C and D. We choose the downward shift that results in the largest reduction in ballot changes, and reduce $\Delta_{2,0}$ to 124. Our best found manipulation now shifts 350 ballots. We next consider MOVE$_2$ on our initial manipulation M_0. Here, we see if we can reduce both $\Delta_{i,0}$ by their step sizes δ_i^2, and still maintain a successful manipulation. We find we cannot, the resulting manipulation of 237 ballots is too small. After the first iteration of local search, we accept the best manipulation found across the three move types, MOVE$_1$ (of 350 ballots) in this case, and increase δ_2^1 by a factor of γ.[1] Note that we only consider MOVE$_3$ when neither MOVE$_1$ and MOVE$_2$ is successful.

In the next two iterations, MOVE$_2$ yields the largest reduction in manipulation size, resulting in a manipulation of 282 ballots ($\Delta_{1,best} = 193$ and $\Delta_{2,best} = 89$). In the fourth iteration, MOVE$_1$ and MOVE$_2$ are not successful, and we consider MOVE$_3$. We start by reducing $\Delta_{1,best}$ by δ_1^3, which is still 113 ballots, and increasing $\Delta_{2,best}$ by 112 ballots. The manipulation with $\Delta_{1,best} = 80$ and $\Delta_{2,best} = 201$ is successful, resulting in a new best manipulation size of 281. Reducing $\Delta_{2,best}$ and increasing $\Delta_{1,best}$ does not lead to a smaller manipulation, and we accept the shift of 80 and 201 ballots as our new 'best found manipulation'. After applying MOVE$_3$, the step sizes associated with move types 1 and 2 are reset to their initial values.

After 9 iterations, we have reduced our overall manipulation size to 247 ballots with a MOVE$_3$. In the next iteration, we cannot reduce the size of this manipulation further and local search terminates. This process is repeated for different combinations of subsets in $\overline{\mathcal{W}}$ and $\overline{\mathcal{L}_d}$, returning the smallest found manipulation as our result. In this example, the smallest successful manipulation we can discover is 247 ballots.

3.2   Choosing a Best Combination of Manipulations

Let $x_{i,k}$ denote a binary variable that takes on a value of 1 if we choose to apply a manipulation to election i that elects k additional candidates from our desired coalition d, and 0 otherwise. Let $|M_{i,k}|$ denote the size of the manipulation required to elect k additional candidates from d in election i. We formulate

---

[1] Where $\delta_i^m > \Delta_{i,j}$, we reset δ_i^m to $\lceil \Delta_{i,j}/\gamma \rceil$.

an integer program (IP), modelled as a knapsack problem, to select the best combination of manipulations that, when applied to their respective elections, realise a combined n-seat shift toward our coalition. Our objective is to minimise the total number of ballot changes required across all selected manipulations. We use s to denote the number of seats available in election i.

$$minimise \sum_i \sum_{k=1}^{min(s,n)} |M_{i,k}|\, x_{i,k} \tag{3}$$

subject to:

$$\sum_i \sum_{k=1}^{min(s,n)} k\, x_{i,k} = n \tag{4}$$

The constraint in Eq. 4 restricts the total number of seats shifted to our coalition, across the set of individual STV elections i, to n. Where our local search method was unable to find a manipulation that elects k additional favoured candidates to an election i, we fix $x_{i,k} = 0$. As we shall see in Sect. 4, there are a number of situations in which a k-seat shifting manipulation is not possible in a given election.

Example 5. For $\mathcal{E}_1$, the best found manipulation to award $k = 1$ extra seats to our coalition $d = \{$C, D$\}$ is 111 ballots in size. Awarding $k = 2$ extra seats to d requires 247 ballot changes, across all ballot replacement methods. For $\mathcal{E}_2$, 15 ballot changes are required to elect $k = 1$ more members from d (for IW, BTL, and ATL), and 121 ballots for $k = 2$ (using BTL). In the latter case, using IW and ATL result in a manipulation of 122 ballots. For our small 6-seat Senate, the best manipulation we can find to shift $n = 2$ seats to our coalition is to shift 2-seats in $\mathcal{E}_2$, with a cost of 121 ballots.

4 Case Studies

We use the 2016 and 2019 Australian Federal Senate elections as case studies. We have partitioned the set of parties taking part in these elections into two groups: conservative; and progressive. The conservative group includes parties such as the Liberal Party, the Nationals, and One Nation. The progressive group contains parties such as the Australian Labor Party and the Greens. The conservative coalition attained a 4-seat majority in 2016, and a 2-seat majority in 2019. Consequently, we use the progressive group as our desired coalition d in our experiments, and seek to find as small as possible a manipulation to award 4, and 2 respectively, additional seats to candidates in d in the 2016 and 2019 elections. All experiments have been run with parameters $\gamma = 2$ and $\alpha = 4$.

Table 3 reports the number of candidates standing, seats available, and formal (valid) votes cast in each of the individual STV elections forming part of these two Senate elections. In addition, we report the quota and number of candidates elected from d.

Table 3. For each of the individual STV elections forming part of the 2016 and 2019 Australian Federal Senate elections, we report the number of: seats available; candidates standing; and formal votes cast. We additionally state the quota, and number of candidates elected from our desired 'progressive' coalition d, for each election.

Region	2016 Senate election					2019 Senate election				
	Seats	$\|C\|$	Formal votes cast	Quota	Elected from d	Seats	$\|C\|$	Formal votes cast	Quota	Elected from d
ACT	2	22	254,767	84,923	1	2	17	270,231	90,078	1
NT	2	19	102,027	34,010	1	2	18	105,027	35,010	1
SA	12	64	1,061,165	81,629	7	6	42	1,094,823	156,404	3
VIC	12	116	3,500,237	269,250	6	6	82	3,739,443	534,207	3
QLD	12	122	2,723,166	209,475	5	6	83	2,901,464	414,495	2
NSW	12	151	4,492,197	345,554	5	6	105	4,695,326	670,761	3
WA	12	79	1,366,182	105,091	4	6	67	1,446,623	206,661	3
TAS	12	58	339,159	26,090	7	6	44	351,988	50,285	3

We report in Table 4 the sizes of the smallest manipulations our local search approach was able to find to shift $k = 1, 2$ seats toward our favoured candidates in coalition d, in each state and territory STV election in 2019. A '–' indicates that no manipulation was found to achieve a given shift of seats. In the ACT and NT, for example, only 2 seats are available for election. In each case, 1 candidate from d has been elected to a seat in the original outcome. We can only award 1 additional seat to candidates in d. We report the number of ballot shifts required to shift 1, and 2, seats toward our favoured candidates when using the BTL, ATL, and IW ballot replacement methods. Overall, the IW method leads to smaller manipulations. Recall that the IW approach replaces ballots that favour an undesired winner with a below the line vote that preferences a favoured loser first, and each of the original winners from our desired coalition subsequently.

Table 5 states the sizes of the smallest manipulations our local search approach could find to shift $k = 1..4$ seats toward our favoured coalition d, in each state and territory STV election in 2016. We use the IW method of replacing ballots for each election. As in 2019, we can only award 1 additional seat to candidates in d in the ACT and NT. In SA and TAS, we were unable to find a manipulation that awarded 4 additional seats to candidates in d. Both Tables 4 and 5 show that the degree of manipulation required to shift k seats to desired candidates increases significantly as k increases.

We apply the IP of Sect. 3.2 to the available manipulations for 2019, listed in Table 4. The coefficients of our objective are obtained from reported manipulation sizes. We use the smallest manipulation discovered for each state and territory, across the different ballot replacement methods. For example, $|M_{ACT,1}| = 12,938$ and $|M_{SA,2}| = 177,504$. The least cost way to shift 2 seats to our desired coalition is to shift 1 seat in ACT, with 12,938 ballot manipulations (4.8% of cast formal votes), and 1 seat in the NT, with 14,697 ballot changes (14% of the cast formal votes). The nature of the elected Senate in 2019 could have sig-

Table 4. Smallest manipulations found to elect 1 to 2 additional members of a centre-left leaning coalition of parties, in each state/territory for the 2019 Australian Federal Sentate election. For each region, the election quota, and number of ballot changes required to realise the desired change, are stated for each method of forming new ballots. We additionally state the number of ballot changes as a percentage of formal votes cast.

1 additional seat to desired coalition								
Region	Quota	Ballot shifts required						
ACT	90,078	BTL	**12,938** (4.8%)	ATL	**12,938** (4.8%)	IW	**12,938** (4.8%)
NT	35,010	BTL	**14,697** (14%)	ATL	14,922 (14.2%)	IW	**14,697** (14%)
SA	156,404	BTL	**50,535** (4.6%)	ATL	50,695 (4.6%)	IW	**50,535** (4.6%)
VIC	534,207	BTL	**126,906** (3.4%)	ATL	127,068 (3.4%)	IW	**126,906** (3.4%)
QLD	414,495	BTL	**56,913** (2%)	ATL	**56,913** (2%)	IW	58,605 (2%)
NSW	670,761	BTL	**296,472** (6.3%)	ATL	297,389 (6.3%)	IW	**296,472** (6.3%)
WA	206,661	BTL	**108,915** (7.5%)	ATL	**108,915** (7.5%)	IW	**108,915** (7.5%)
TAS	50,285	BTL	**19,824** (5.6%)	ATL	20,399 (5.8%)	IW	**19,824** (5.6%)
2 additional seats to desired coalition								
Region	Quota	Ballot shifts required						
ACT	90,078	BTL	–	ATL	–	IW	–
NT	35,010	BTL	–	ATL	–	IW	–
SA	156,404	BTL	177,554 (16.2%)	ATL	177,730 (16.2%)	IW	**177,504** (16.2%)
VIC	534,207	BTL	559,035 (14.9%)	ATL	558,734 (14.9%)	IW	**558,521** (14.9%)
QLD	414,495	BTL	370,091 (12.8%)	ATL	370,046 (12.8%)	IW	**353,692** (12.8%)
NSW	670,761	BTL	835,217 (17.8%)	ATL	835,180 (17.8%)	IW	**832,314** (17.8%)
WA	206,661	BTL	**294,005** (20.3%)	ATL	**294,005** (20.3%)	IW	**294,005** (20.3%)
TAS	50,285	BTL	**53,617** (15.2%)	ATL	55,275 (15.7%)	IW	54,295 (15.4%)

Table 5. Smallest manipulations found to elect 1 to 4 additional members of a centre-left leaning coalition of parties, in each state/territory for the 2016 Australian Federal Senate election. For each region, the election quota, and number of ballot changes required to realise the desired change (using the IW method of forming new ballots) are stated. We additionally state the number of ballot changes as a percentage of formal votes cast.

Region	Quota	Ballot shifts required			
		1 seat	2 seats	3 seats	4 seats
ACT	84,923	18,836 (7.4%)	–	–	–
NT	34,010	11,245 (11%)	–	–	–
SA	81,629	1,772 (0.17%)	57,607 (5.4%)	132,576 (12.5%)	–
VIC	269,250	45,046 (1.3%)	181,770 (5.2%)	420,880 (12%)	682,348 (19.5%)
QLD	209,475	49,829 (1.8%)	139,196 (5.1%)	354,475 (13%)	573,357 (21.1%)
NSW	345,554	12,313 (0.27%)	149,046 (3.3%)	386336 (8.6%)	731,280 (16.3%)
WA	105,091	14,678 (1.1%)	79,308 (5.8%)	161,963 (11.9%)	280,426 (20.5%)
TAS	26,090	21,692 (6.4%)	43,383 (12.8%)	65,698 (19.4%)	–

nificantly changed with a change in 27,635 votes. If we chose to minimise the percentage of formal ballots cast in any manipulated election, in place of the total number of ballots changed, we would instead shift 1 seat in QLD (56,913 manipulations, 2% of formal votes) and 1 seat in VIC (126,906, 3.4% of formal votes). The total manipulation size is significantly larger, at 183,819 ballots, yet it involves a smaller percentage of changes (a maximum of 3.4%).

In 2016, the least cost combination of manipulations to shift 4 seats to our coalition d are: a 1 seat shift in SA, with 1,772 manipulations (0.17%); a 1 seat shift in the NT, with 11,245 manipulations (11%); a 1 seat shift in NSW, with 12,313 manipulations (0.27%); and a 1 seat shift in WA, with 14,678 manipulations (1.1%). The nature of the elected Senate in 2016 could have significantly changed with a change in 40,008 votes.

5   Conclusion

We have presented a local search heuristic that, in combination with an integer program, finds an upper bound on the number of ballot changes required to change the nature of the majority in an elected Senate. We have found that in two case study elections, a relatively small, but not insignificant, number of cast ballots need to be changed to shift the majority from a conservative coalition of parties to one that is more progressive. This number is a lot larger, however, than the number of ballot changes required to realise any change in outcome. For example, the 2016 results in Tasmania were very close, requiring only 71 ballot changes to change the result [1].

References

1. Blom, M., Conway, A., Stuckey, P.J., Teague, V.J.: Did that lost ballot box cost me a seat? Computing manipulations of STV elections. In: IAAI (2020)
2. Blom, M., Stuckey, P.J., Teague, V.J.: Computing the margin of victory in preferential parliamentary elections. In: Krimmer, R., Volkamer, M., Cortier, V., Goré, R., Hapsara, M., Serdült, U., Duenas-Cid, D. (eds.) E-Vote-ID 2018. LNCS, vol. 11143, pp. 1–16. Springer, Cham (2018). https://doi.org/10.1007/978-3-030-00419-4_1
3. Blom, M., Stuckey, P.J., Teague, V.: Towards computing the margin of victory in STV elections. Inf. J. Comput. **31**(4), 636–653 (2019)
4. Conway, A.: Australian federal senate simulator. https://github.com/SiliconEconometrics/PublicService (2019). Accessed Aug 2019
5. Miragliotta, N.L.: Little differences, big effects: An example of the importance of choice of method for transferring surplus votes in PR-STV voting systems. Representation **41**, 15–24 (2004)
6. Australian federal senate election rules (2019). www.austlii.edu.au/au/legis/cth/consol_act/cea1918233/s273.html. Accessed Aug 2019
7. Weeks, L.: Tolerable chance or undesirable arbitrariness? Distributing surplus votes under PR-STV. Parliamentary Aff. **64**, 530–551 (2011)
8. Xia, L.: Computing the margin of victory for various voting rules. In: Proceedings of the 13th ACM Conference on Electronic Commerce, EC 2012, pp. 982–999. ACM, New York (2012)

Random Errors Are Not Necessarily Politically Neutral

Michelle Blom[1] , Andrew Conway[7] , Peter J. Stuckey[2] ,
Vanessa J. Teague[3,4(✉)] , and Damjan Vukcevic[5,6]

[1] School of Computing and Information Systems, University of Melbourne,
Parkville, Australia
[2] Faculty of Information Technology, Monash University, Clayton, Australia
[3] Thinking Cybersecurity Pty. Ltd., Melbourne, Australia
Vanessa@thinkingcybersecurity.com
[4] College of Engineering and Computer Science, Australian National University,
Canberra, Australia
[5] School of Mathematics and Statistics, University of Melbourne,
Parkville, Australia
[6] Melbourne Integrative Genomics, University of Melbourne, Parkville, Australia
[7] Silicon Econometrics Pty. Ltd, Melbourne, Australia
andrewelections@greatcactus.org

Abstract. Errors are inevitable in the implementation of any complex
process. Here we examine the effect of random errors on Single Transferable Vote (STV) elections, a common approach to deciding multi-seat
elections. It is usually expected that random errors should have nearly
equal effects on all candidates, and thus be fair. We find to the contrary
that random errors can introduce systematic bias into election results.
This is because, even if the errors are random, votes for different candidates occur in different patterns that are affected differently by random
errors. In the STV context, the most important effect of random errors
is to invalidate the ballot. This removes far more votes for those candidates whose supporters tend to list a lot of preferences, because their
ballots are much more likely to be invalidated by random error. Different
validity rules for different voting styles mean that errors are much more
likely to penalise some types of votes than others. For close elections this
systematic bias can change the result of the election.

1 Introduction

We investigate the effects of random errors on election outcomes, in the context
of preferential elections counted using the Single Transferable Vote (STV). It is
often assumed that random errors (whether from human or manual counting) are
unimportant because they are likely to have nearly equal effects on all candidates.
In this paper we show that this is not the case, using simulated random errors
introduced into real STV voting data. In some cases, this introduces a systematic
bias against some candidates.

Random errors have a non-random effect because real votes are not random.
Voters not only express different preferences, but express them in a different
way, according to whom they choose to support.

© Springer Nature Switzerland AG 2020
R. Krimmer et al. (Eds.): E-Vote-ID 2020, LNCS 12455, pp. 19–35, 2020.
https://doi.org/10.1007/978-3-030-60347-2_2

In STV, some candidates are elected mainly on the strength of their party listing; others rely on gathering preference flows from other parties, or on their individual popularity relative to their party's other candidates. So when we look at the votes that contributed to the election of different candidates, we find that the types of votes chosen by their supporters may be very different. Hence a random error that affects different types of votes differently introduces a systemic change in the election result.

One obvious kind of error is to misrecord a number. Usually, this either invalidates the ballot completely, or invalidates preferences below the error. The more preferences there are on a ballot, the more likely that at least one of them is misrecorded. So as a general rule, candidates that are more dependent on later preferences or long preference lists are more severely disadvantaged by random errors.

Although these results are significant, and need to be taken into account for close contests, we find that reasonable error rates produce changes in only very few elections, which (so far) correspond only to those that are obviously very close. It is possible for STV elections to have hidden small margins, but this seems to be uncommon—in almost all the elections we simulated, no plausible error rate produced a change in outcome. Typical random error rates will affect election results when the election is close, but are not expected to do so when the election is not close.

We do not consider the errors necessary to alter the election result in a targeted way by altering specific carefully chosen votes—they would obviously be much smaller. Hence the results of this paper apply to random errors, but not deliberate electoral fraud.

The remainder of the paper is organized as follows. In the next section we explain STV elections, in particular in the case of Australian Senate elections, and discuss how the votes are digitised and counted. In Sect. 3 we describe our experiment design and introduce the three error models we explore. In Sect. 4 we provide a number of different approaches to estimate the likely error rate that occurs for Australian Senate elections. In Sect. 5 we examine the result of applying simulated errors to Australian Senate elections and discuss how these errors can change the result of the election. Finally in Sect. 6 we conclude.

2   Background on STV Counting

2.1   The Single Transferable Vote (STV) Counting Algorithm

STV is a multi-winner preferential voting system. Candidates compete for s available seats. A candidate is awarded a seat when their tally reaches or exceeds the quota, Q, defined as a function of the number of ballots cast in the election, $|\mathcal{B}|$, and the number of seats, s. One popular definition is the Droop quota,

$$Q = \left\lfloor \frac{|\mathcal{B}|}{s+1} \right\rfloor + 1.$$

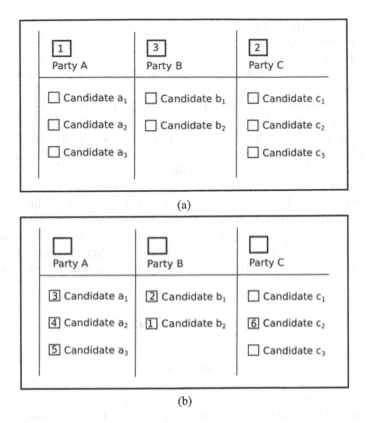

Fig. 1. **An example of two simple ballots for a 3-party STV election.** In (a), the voter has chosen to vote above the line, and in (b) they have voted below the line.

When a voter casts a ballot in one of these STV elections, they have the option of voting 'above the line' or 'below the line'. Figure 1 shows an example of a ballot for a simple STV election in which candidates from three parties are competing for s seats. Each party or group of independents fielding candidates in the election have a box sitting 'above the line' (ATL). A voter may rank these parties and groups by placing a number in their corresponding box (Fig. 1a). Alternatively, a voter may rank individual candidates by placing a number in their box, below the line (BTL) (Fig. 1b).

Tabulation starts by giving each candidate all the below-the-line ballots in which they have been ranked first. ATL ballots are awarded to the first candidate listed under the party that has been ranked first. For example, a ballot in which Party A has been ranked first sits in the first preference pile of candidate a_1. A BTL ballot in which candidate b_2 is ranked first sits in that candidate's first preference pile. Each ballot is assigned a weight, starting at 1, that changes as counting proceeds. The tally of a candidate is the sum of the weights of ballots sitting in their tally pile, possibly with some rounding.

Counting proceeds by awarding a seat to all candidates whose tallies have reached or exceeded Q. Their *surplus*—their tally after subtracting Q—is distributed to remaining eligible candidates. A candidate is eligible if they have not been eliminated, and their tally has not reached a quota's worth of votes. The ballots sitting in an elected candidate's tally pile are re-weighted so that their combined weight is equal to the candidate's surplus. These ballots are then given to the next most-preferred eligible candidate on their ranking. The ATL ballot in Fig. 1a is given to candidate a_2 if a_1 is elected to a seat. If neither a_2 or a_3 are eligible, the ballot then moves to candidate c_1. The BTL ballot in Fig. 1b is given to candidate b_1 if b_2 is elected or eliminated.

If no candidate has reached a quota, the candidate with the smallest tally is eliminated. The ballots in their tally pile are distributed to the next most-preferred eligible candidate in their rankings at their current weight.

Counting proceeds in rounds of election and elimination until all s seats are filled, or until the number of candidates that remain eligible equals the number of remaining seats. In this setting, each of the remaining candidates is awarded a seat.

2.2   Australian Vote Digitisation in Practice

Australians cast their votes on paper ballots. The Australian Electoral Commission (AEC) digitises the preferences in a hybrid manual and automated process. Precise details about this process are unavailable, but most ballots seem to receive both automated digitisation and secondary human data entry. (Ballots that are judged blank are not re-examined.) It is possible that manual data entry is performed on ballot papers.[1] Other pamphlets suggest that only the images, not the paper ballots, are used.[2]

An automated system then checks, for each ballot, whether the automated digitisation matches the human interpretation. Obviously this does not defend against software errors or deliberate manipulation, particularly downstream of the process, but it probably does produce reasonably low random error rates, assuming that the human errors are not highly correlated with the errors of the automated system.

Ballots are required to have a minimum number of preferences before they are considered valid; such ballots are referred to as *formal* ballots. In the 2016 and 2019 elections, a BTL formal vote must have every preference from 1 to 6 inclusive present exactly once; an ATL formal vote requires the preference 1 to be present exactly once and a formal BTL vote not to be present. According to the information about the digitisation processes mentioned above, non-blank informal ballots seem to get a second human inspection automatically.

The AEC publishes on their website the complete digitised preferences for all Senate votes, excluding blanks and votes judged to be informal.

---

[1] https://www.aec.gov.au/Voting/counting/files/css-integrity.pdf.
[2] https://www.aec.gov.au/Voting/counting/files/senate-count.pdf.

In summary, the published data could differ from the actual ballots for many reasons:

- random errors that match in both the automated and human digitisation process,
- random errors that occur in either the automated or human digitisation process, and are endorsed rather than corrected by the reconciliation process,
- erroneous exclusion of ballot papers judged to be informal,
- accidental alterations, duplicates or omissions caused by software bugs,
- deliberate manipulation by malicious actors, either of the images (before digitisation) or of the preference data (from digitisation to publication).

Our investigation does not apply to the last two kinds of errors, which could be introduced in a non-random way that worked for or against a particular candidate. It does apply to the errors that are random. In particular, we show that digitisation errors that randomly cause some ballots to be judged informal can impact candidates differently.

3 Experimental Design

Our analysis is performed on the AEC's published data for the 2016 and 2019 Australian federal elections for the Senate, i.e. the output of the process described in Sect. 2.2. Ideally our analysis would be based upon the actual marks that voters made on their ballots, or even what they intended to make, and the comparison with the AEC's output. However, these data are not available. Instead, we use the AEC's output as the 'actual' ballot data, and add simulated errors.

3.1 Analysis Code

For logistical reasons, and to make it easy for anyone to replicate this experiment, we extract those preferences that are actually considered valid in the election. If a number is absent or repeated in the preference marks, then it and all subsequent preferences are disregarded. We have made available a standardised ".stv" file format based on the data published by the AEC[3]. This common format does unfortunately mean that we lose some (invalid) marks that could conceivably have become valid when we added new random errors, or which could, through errors, invalidate earlier preferences.

We used the Java pseudo-random number generator `java.util.Random` to generate random numbers, and ensured that different executions used different seeds. Our code is available for download[4].

---

[3] See the downloads section for each election at: https://vote.andrewconway.org.
[4] https://github.com/SiliconEconometrics/PublicService.

3.2   Error Models

We simulate the effect of errors by making random changes to the votes. We are not certain exactly what "random" failures in the scanning process would be, so we have devised three different models for simulated errors, in increasing order of complexity and plausibility. The first models an error where, somewhere in the list, something goes wrong that invalidates the rest of the preference list. The second models an error in which a digit is randomly misread as another digit, chosen uniformly. The final model recognises that some misreadings are much more likely than others—for example, a 3 is more likely to be confused with an 8 than a 1—so we use a model that includes a specific error probability for each digit and each potential misreading.

Each model applies to a valid list of preferences and treats either each number or each digit separately with random errors chosen independently.

1. For each preference, with probability ϵ, truncate the list at that preference.
2. For each digit, with probability ϵ, replace that digit with a digit uniformly chosen from $\{0,1,2,3,4,5,6,7,8,9\}$, which may be the original digit.
3. Start with a table of pairwise error ratios for digits such as Table 1 (that is, the probability that a certain digit is mistranscribed into a certain other digit). For each digit, change it into a different digit with the probability given in the table.

Note that in all three models, the probability of at least one error on the ballot increases with the number of preferences listed on the ballot. We are primarily motivated by machine errors, so per-digit or per-number random errors seem plausible, but it is worth noting that other errors might be important too, such as models that considered that some voters (those with bad handwriting) were much more likely to have their vote misinterpreted than others.

After applying errors, formality rules are checked again, reducing the number of ballots considered for the election.

4   What Is a Realistic Error Rate?

As far as we know, there are no publicly available results from any rigorous estimate of Senate scanning random errors in Australia. However, there are several independent estimates, which give us a per-digit error rate ranging from 0.01% to 0.38%. We define an error to be a discrepancy between the paper ballot and the electronic preference list output at the end of the process.

4.1   Using Data from the Australian Electoral Commission

As far as we know, the AEC does not conduct, nor allow anyone else to conduct, a large random sample of Senate ballots for comparison between electronic and paper records. However, an Australian National Audit Office report[5] describes a process for gaining an estimate from a small sample. This process was conducted by AEC officials.

- A batch of 50 ballot papers was randomly selected and then six ballot papers from that batch were reviewed;
- Compliance inspectors recorded the first six preferences from the physical ballot paper on a checklist;
- Verification officers compared the preferences recorded on the checklist against those on the scanned image of the ballot paper and those in the related XML file;
- The IT security team compiled, investigated and reported on the findings.

The compliance inspection report outlined that a total of 1,510 ballot papers were inspected and 4 processing errors were identified. This seems to indicate an error rate of less than 0.3% per ballot. Although it wasn't recorded how many preferences were on each ballot, it seems to indicate a very small per-digit error rate. However, a careful reading of that experimental description shows that the officials verified only the numbers from 1 to 6. Errors in later preferences were ignored. So this estimate may substantially underestimate the overall rate of error.

To estimate the per-digit error rate implied by these data, we assumed that all of the 1,510 ballot papers that were inspected had six preferences marked on them, giving a total of 9,060 digits. We also assumed that the 4 'processing errors' were each a single-digit error. This gave a per-digit error rate of 0.04%, with a 95% confidence interval of (0.01%, 0.11%).

In reality, some proportion of these ballot papers were likely to be informal and have fewer than six preferences marked. Adjusting the above assumptions based on reported rates of informality by the AEC[6] had negligible impact on these estimates.

4.2 Informal Experiment

For the 2019 federal election, we conducted an informal experiment amongst 15 of our colleagues to get a rough estimate of the 'end to end' accuracy of the Senate vote digitisation process. Each of our colleagues decided on their Senate vote ahead of the election and made a private record of it for later comparison. On polling day, they each carefully completed their Senate ballot paper in accordance with their planned vote. After the election, it was possible to compare these against the electronic file of ballots published by the AEC. Each of our colleagues searched for a vote that matched their own vote either exactly or very closely.

All of our colleagues voted below the line in Victoria. Due to the very large number of possible ways to vote below the line, each of their votes was extremely

---

[5] https://www.anao.gov.au/work/performance-audit/aec-procurement-services-conduct-2016-federal-election.

[6] For example, https://www.aec.gov.au/Voting/Informal_Voting/senate/.

likely to be unique. In addition, the electronic file from the AEC also recorded the polling booth for each ballot. These two facts together allowed each of our colleagues to easily identify their own ballot paper in the file and be confident that it was indeed their own. This was true even if the match were not exact, since the next 'closest' matching ballot would typically vary substantially from each person's private record.

Of our 15 colleagues, 12 found ballots in the file that exactly matched their own records. This indicates perfectly accurate digitisation. The remaining 3 found a mismatch: each of them had a single one of their preferences recorded differently in the file than in their private record. These mismatches could be due to an error in the AEC digitisation process or to a transcription error on the part of our colleagues. However, they do give us at least a rough estimate of accuracy.

What per-digit error rate does this imply? We use the following assumptions: a) Each ballot had votes below the line; b) All boxes below the line were numbered; c) All of the reported errors were for a single digit. These assumptions maximise the number of possible digits and minimise the number of errors, and thus will give the lowest possible error rate estimate. There were 82 candidates for Victoria. This gives $9 + 73 \times 2 = 155$ digits per ballot, which is $155 \times 15 = 2,325$ digits in total. Out of these, we have 3 single-digit errors. These give a per-digit error rate of 0.13%, and a 95% confidence interval of (0.03%, 0.38%). The error rate here captures any errors either by a voter or by the digitisation process, so it provides a rough upper bound on the latter's error rate.

4.3   What Is the State of the Art in Digit Recognition Error Rate?

Accurately recognizing handwritten digits by computer is an important consideration for many applications where data crosses from the physical world into the digital. The MNIST (Modified National Institute of Standards and Technology) database is a large database of handwritten digits that is commonly used for training image processing systems. The database consists of digits written by high school students and American Census Bureau employees, and normalised to be represented as grayscale images of size 28×28 pixels. The current state of the art approach [1] to this dataset has an error rate of 0.18%.[7] Care must be taken with this result, which is on a well studied and well curated data set. While Australian ballot papers have boxes marked where each number should be filled in, not all digits written in practice fall completely within the box. Nevertheless, this gives an accurate lower bound on pure computer-based digit recognition accuracy. The AEC process involves human inspection which means that it may be able to achieve better overall digit recognition accuracy.

The errors in digit recognition are not uniform: some digits are easier to confuse, for example 1 and 7. Most work on digit recognition does not publish the cross-digit confusion rates. Table 1 gives a confusion table showing the percentage

---

[7] There is unpublished work claiming 0.17%.

Table 1. Pairwise error digit rates. The entry for row x and column y gives the percentage chance of (mis)recognizing a digit y as a digit x. A dash '−' indicates less than 0.01% chance of misrecognition.

	Digit	Actual									
		0	1	2	3	4	5	6	7	8	9
Predicted	0	99.22	−	0.08	0.02	0.10	0.04	0.14	−	0.06	0.20
	1	−	98.75	0.14	−	−	−	−	0.40	0.04	0.08
	2	0.12	0.28	99.56	0.24	−	−	−	0.18	0.02	0.10
	3	−	−	0.22	99.50	−	−	−	0.24	0.14	0.22
	4	0.16	0.16	−	−	98.65	0.08	0.10	−	0.12	0.30
	5	−	0.02	−	−	−	99.52	0.22	0.10	0.18	0.12
	6	0.10	0.12	−	−	0.06	0.08	99.48	−	0.14	−
	7	0.08	0.42	−	0.16	−	0.02	−	98.90	−	0.38
	8	0.10	0.06	−	−	0.48	−	−	−	99.16	0.26
	9	0.22	0.20	−	0.08	0.72	0.26	0.06	0.18	0.14	98.34

of each actual digit versus its predicted value from experiments reported by Toghi and Grover [3]. The overall digit recognition error in this work is 0.89%, which is substantially greater than the best results reported above.

4.4 Analysing the Election Data (NOT Simulations) to Infer the Error rate

We only have the reported ballots, not the ones that were ruled informal. (Except of course we cannot distinguish human mistakes from scanning errors.) Errors that make the vote informal are hidden.

Recall that the formality rules require at least 6 unambiguous preferences below the line, and that informal votes are not reported. We can estimate the number of hidden informal votes by observing the erroneous but formal ones. We use the number of repeated or missing numbers greater than 6 to approximate the number of repeated or missing numbers less than or equal to 6.

Table 2 shows the data, for BTL votes cast in Tasmania for the 2016 Senate election. The first column is the preference p on the ballot. The second column is the number of ballot papers that contain p more than once. The final column shows the number of ballots missing that preference, showing preference $p - 1$ and $p + 1$ but not p. A 0 is not required for $p = 1$. Note that there is a sudden drop at 12 because voters were instructed to list at least 12 preferences, so many people listed exactly 12. If the 12th preference was miswritten or misrecorded, then it did not count in our table (there being no 13).

There would be no informal BTL ballots at all, and perfect zeros in the first 6 rows of Table 2, except for one special formality rule: if there is *also* a valid ATL vote present on the same ballot paper, then it is counted instead, and both the valid ATL vote and the invalid BTL markings are reported in the final database. Hence we expect that the numbers in the first 6 rows are only a small fraction

Table 2. Counts of ballot papers with repeated and missed preferences.
Tasmanian ballots with BTL marks, 2016.

Preference	1	2	3	4	5	6	7	8	9	10	11	12	13
Ballots with preference repeated	573	385	303	231	212	211	492	494	542	372	256	250	122
Ballots with preference skipped	240	43	54	49	45	37	130	133	134	193	203	45	44

of the ballots rendered informal by either human or scanning errors. There is a sudden increase at the 7th preference, because BTL votes with a repeated or omitted 7th preference are still included in the tally, as long as their first 6 preferences are unambiguous.

There are 97,685 published votes with BTL markings. Most of these were valid BTL votes but some were only published because they had valid ATL votes as well. The most representative preferences are probably 7 to 9, being single digits whose count is not artificially suppressed due to repetitions in them causing the BTL vote to be informal and thus usually not published. For these preference numbers, the observed repetitions are on the order of 0.5%. This doesn't prove that the scanning process introduces errors at a rate of 0.5% per digit, because they could be caused by voter error. It could also underestimate the scanner error rate because it includes only those not rendered informal. Nevertheless this provides an estimate of voter plus process error.

5   Results

5.1   Results from Truncation and Digit Error Models

We simulated counts with errors using the ballot data for all 8 states and territories from both the 2016 and 2019 Senate elections. We used both the truncation and digit error models, across a wide range of error probabilities. For any given choice of model and error probability, we simulated 1,000 elections (each with their own random errors under that model).

For error rates between 0% and 1%, the only election for which we observed any change in the elected candidates was for Tasmania in 2016. This election was somewhat unusual in three ways. First, it was a very close election, with the difference in tallies between the final two remaining candidates, Nick McKim and Kate McCulloch, being only 141 votes. For comparison, 285 votes were lost due to rounding. Second, there was a popular labor candidate, Lisa Singh, who won a seat despite being placed fourth on the party ticket, and the candidate above her not winning a seat. This means she received many BTL votes specifically for her, rather than relying on ATL votes for the party. Finally, the 2016 election

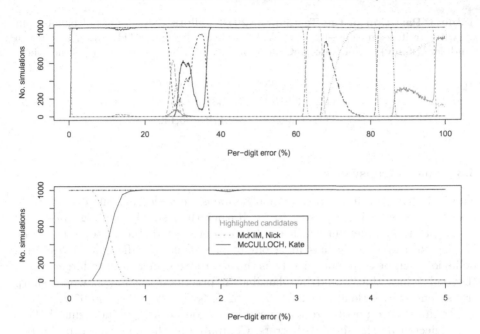

Fig. 2. Changing election outcomes as a function of error rate, Tasmanian Senate election 2016. The lower graph shows a complete reversal for a small error rate (about 0.5%), between the state in which McKim wins consistently (no error) and that in which McCulloch wins consistently (1% or greater error). The upper graph shows similar behaviour for larger error rates—with error rates of more than 20% there are sharp transitions between different election outcomes.

was a double dissolution, which means that twelve candidates were elected rather than the usual six.

In the real election, the 12th (final) candidate that was elected was Nick McKim. In our simulations, once we introduced a small amount of error we saw that a different candidate, Kate McCulloch, was sometimes elected instead. As we increased the per-digit error rate from 0% to 1%, we saw a complete shift from one candidate to the other, see Fig. 2. The truncation error model led to the same outcome (data not shown).

5.2   Pairwise Digit Error Model

We ran 1,000 simulations for Tasmania 2016 using the pairwise digit error model. Unlike the other models, we did not have a parameter to set but simply used the pairwise error rate matrix shown in Table 1. This model has an average per-digit error rate of 0.89%. Across the 1,000 simulations, we observed Kate McCulloch being elected 99.5% of the time, and Nick McKim for the remaining 0.5%. This is consistent with the simple per-digit error model, which also resulted in Nick McKim occasionally being elected when the per-digit error was comparable.

Table 3. Partition of the Tasmanian 2016 ballots. The number of ballots split by whether it is an above-the-line (ATL) or below-the-line (BTL) vote, and which candidate (if any) out of Kate McCulloch or Nick McKim is preferred over the other.

	McCulloch	McKim	Neither
ATL	73,975	97,331	72,468
BTL	17,066	42,170	36,149

5.3 Sharp Transitions

The fact that such a sharp transition happens from electing one candidate to another was initially surprising to us. Rather than simply 'adding noise' and leading to randomness in which candidates got elected, the noise seems to be leading to a systematic bias in favour of or against specific candidates. This behaviour can be seen more clearly as the error rate is increased to larger values (beyond values that would be plausible in practice), see Fig. 2, where sharp transitions are visible also at 28%, 36%, 62%, 68%, 82%, 86% and 97%.

To investigate possible reasons for this, we looked at how individual ballots were affected by the simulated errors. Compared to the no-error scenario, two broad types of outcome are possible:

- The ballot becomes informal and is not counted. This will happen when it does not meet the formality requirements, e.g., does not have at least a single first preference above the line or consecutive preferences numbered 1 to 6 below the line.
- The ballot ends up exhausting before reaching a candidate. This will happen if the preference order becomes disrupted due to an error, which has the effect of truncating the preferences and not enabling the ballot to be counted in favour of any candidates further down the preference list.

We investigated these effects in the context of the Tasmanian 2016 election; we report on this in the next few sections. We found that the first type of effect was the dominant factor in determining the election outcome.

5.4 Why Random Errors Affect Different Candidates Differently (Tasmania 2016)

We saw earlier that for small error rates, we have either Nick McKim (from the Australian Greens party) or Kate McCulloch (from the One Nation Party) elected as the final candidate. There were 339,159 formal ballots for this election. For each one, we looked at the preferences to see:

- whether it was an ATL or a BTL vote,
- which of the above two candidates (or their respective parties, if it was an ATL vote) was more highly preferred, or neither one.

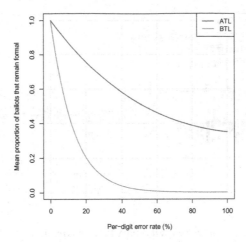

Fig. 3. Effect of the per-digit error rate on the formality of votes. The impact on above-the-line (ATL) and below-the-line (BTL) votes are shown separately.

Table 3 shows how the ballots split into these categories. The most important fact to note is the relative number of ATL and BTL votes in favour of each candidate: more than 80% of the ballots in favour of McCulloch were ATL votes, while for McKim it was less than 70%.

When errors are introduced, ballots that were BTL votes were much more likely to become informal. Figure 3 illustrates this: the larger the error rate, the greater the disparity in how many of the ATL or BTL ballots became informal. This on its own is enough to explain the systematic shift from McKim to McCulloch as error rates increase.

For more insight, we took a closer look at the simulations that used a per-digit error rate of 1%. For each ballot, we define the *formality rate* to be the proportion of simulations for which it remained formal. Figure 4 shows the distribution of the formality rate across different types of ballots. The left panel shows the clear disparity between ATL and BTL votes. This reiterates the difference we saw on average from Fig. 3, but in addition we see that this disparity is very consistent across individual ballots (from the very little overlap for the ATL and BTL ballots).

When we further divided the ballots based on where in the preference list the voters placed their preferred candidate out of McKim or McCulloch, the distribution of formality rates was relatively consistent (right panel of Fig. 4). This indicates that the major factor leading to McCulloch replacing McKim is simply the lower formality rate for BTL votes, after random errors were added, coupled with the fact that a larger proportion of ballots in favour of McKim were BTL votes.

For the less plausible larger errors, the sharp transitions came from new effects causing biases against major parties, who lost out as randomisation of preferences reduced their typical large first preference collection. This also caused

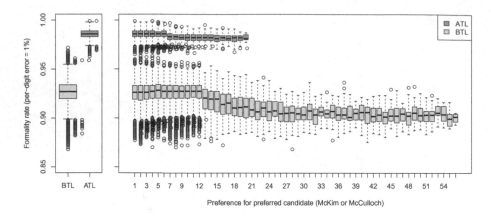

Fig. 4. Formality rates for votes with random errors injected. These are split by ATL/BTL (left panel) or by the position of the preferred candidate (right panel). Error rates vary greatly between ATL and BTL votes, but not much between preferences within those categories.

major parties to not get multiple candidates elected in the first counting round, which meant that major party candidates low down on the party ticket tended to get eliminated before they could get preferences passed on to them, as they were reliant on BTL votes to avoid being eliminated before the first candidates of minor parties who could get ATL votes.

5.5   Varying the Formality Requirements

The formality requirements differ for ATL and BTL votes. In particular, BTL votes require at least 6 consecutive preferences in order to be declared formal, whereas ATL votes only require a single preference. This is one reason why the formality rate for BTL is lower once errors are introduced.

We investigated whether changing the formality rules could ameliorate the systematic bias caused by the introduction of errors. Specifically, we varied the number of consecutive preferences required for a formal BTL vote, ranging from 1 (i.e. the same as ATL votes) to 9 (i.e. more stringent than the current rules).

Figure 5 shows the impact of these choices on how often McCulloch was elected instead of McKim. Making the formality requirement less stringent reduced the bias, and once the formality rules were aligned for ATL and BTL votes, the election result remained mostly unchanged even in the presence of errors.

5.6   Truncation of Preferences

Other than causing ballots to become informal, errors can result in votes not being counted for certain candidates if the error truncates the preference order.

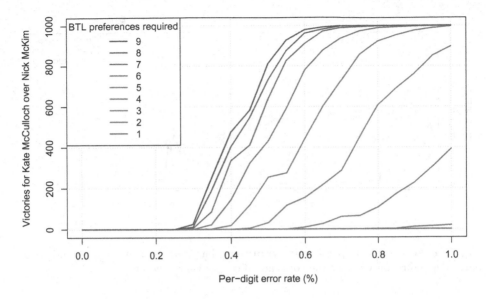

Fig. 5. The effect of formality rules on election outcomes. As the number of preferences required for a valid BTL vote increases, so does the rate at which BTL votes are excluded due to random errors. This produces a faster transition from one winning candidate to another as the error rate increases.

Candidates who obtain more of their votes from later (higher-numbered) preferences should be more affected by such truncation.

We investigated whether this might be occurring in our simulations. For each ballot, we compared the number of valid preferences before and after simulated errors. There was a clear signal of truncation: ballots that had around 60 valid preferences (which were all BTL) only had on average around 30 valid preferences remaining when the per-digit error was set to 1%. In contrast, ballots that had 10 valid preferences (irrespective of whether they were ATL or BTL) maintained almost 10 valid preferences on average.

While this extent of truncation is stark, it might not necessarily lead to any change in the election outcome because many of the later preferences might not actually be used during the election count.

In the case of the Tasmanian 2016 election, we looked at ballots in favour of each of McKim and McCulloch to see whether they tended to get their votes from earlier or later preferences. Figure 6 shows the distribution of these. Interestingly, we see that McCulloch relies more on later preferences than McKim. Therefore, it is McKim rather than McCulloch that should benefit from any truncation effect. This works in the reverse direction of the formality-induced bias described earlier, however the truncation did not act strongly enough to reverse that bias.

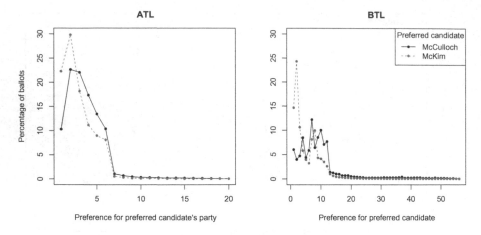

Fig. 6. Histograms of preference number. These are shown for a candidate or party depending on whether the votes are above or below the line.

6   Concluding Remarks

We are not aware of any previous study of the effects of random errors in digitization on election outcomes. While there is a considerable body of work on margin of error for polling, there is little study of the effect of errors on elections. Richey [2] examines how 'errors' in voting can effect elections, but here the error is that a voter votes for a party that does not represent their best interests.

The previous section clearly demonstrates that random errors during counting do not necessarily lead to 'random' changes to election outcomes. We were very surprised by the sharp transitions in election results as error rates changed, illustrated in Fig. 2. Systematic biases can arise due to interactions with the election rules.

For Australian Senate elections, a key factor is the formality requirements. BTL votes have more stringent requirements, which ends up creating a systematic bias against BTL votes in the presence of random errors. Candidates who rely on BTL votes (e.g. if they are relying on their individual popularity) will be more affected by random errors than those relying on ATL votes (e.g. via membership of their party). Changing the formality requirements to reduce the disparity between ATL and BTL votes also reduces this bias.

Candidates who rely on accumulating later preferences are more affected by random errors than candidates who rely primarily on their first-preference votes. However, this effect was much weaker than the bias induced by differences in formality requirements.

These results raise questions about how formality rules should be specified in order to be fair to candidates with different voting patterns. More relaxed formality rules could be applied which are less likely to have strong differences across different kinds of votes. For example, a BTL vote could be formal if the first 6 most preferred candidates are clear, even if they are not numbered from

1 to 6, e.g. a vote with preferences 1, 2, 4, 5, 6, 7 and no preference 3 still gives a clear ranking of the first 6 candidates.

In this paper we consider only Australian Senate elections with their particular ATL/BTL voting mechanism. Two lessons can be taken from this exercise to other forms of voting. First, if there are two or more forms of ballot and the rules for formality are different for these different forms of ballot, then random errors may affect the different forms differently, regardless of whether the voter can choose their form or different voters are assigned to different forms. This is applicable to any kind of election whether plurality voting or ranked voting. Second, considering elections where voters rank candidates with only one form of ballot, e.g. standard STV, Borda, or Condorcet elections, assuming the rules of formality are such that the ballot is truncated when the ranking becomes uninterpretable, then candidates relying on accumulating later preferences will be more affected by random errors than other candidates. But we do not have a real world case that illustrates that truncation errors alone lead to a change in a result.

Acknowledgements. We would like to thank our colleagues who participated in our informal experiment during the 2019 Australian federal election. Thanks also to Philip Stark for very valuable suggestions on improving the paper.

References

1. Dash, K.S., Puhan, N.B., Panda, G.: Unconstrained handwritten digit recognition using perceptual shape primitives. Pattern Anal. Appl. **21**(2), 413–436 (2016). https://doi.org/10.1007/s10044-016-0586-3
2. Richey, S.: Random and systematic error in voting in presidential elections. Polit. Res. Q. **66**(3), 645–657 (2013). http://www.jstor.org/stable/23563171
3. Toghi, B., Grover, D.: MNIST dataset classification utilizing k-NN classifier with modified sliding window metric. CoRR abs/1809.06846 (2018). http://arxiv.org/abs/1809.06846

Tripped at the Finishing Line: The Åland Islands Internet Voting Project

David Duenas-Cid[1,2](✉) , Iuliia Krivonosova[1], Radu Serrano[1] , Marlon Freire[3] ,
and Robert Krimmer[1,4]

[1] DigiGovLab, Ragnar Nurkse Department of Innovation and Governance, Tallinn University of Technology, Akadeemia tee 3, 12618 Tallinn, Estonia
{david.duenas,iuliia.krivonosova,radu.serrano,
robert.krimmer}@taltech.ee
[2] Management in Networked and Digital Societies, Kozminski University,
Jagiellonska 57/59, 03-301 Warsaw, Poland
dduenas@kozminski.edu.pl
[3] Faculty of Engineering, University of Porto, Porto, Portugal
marlonfreirephd@gmail.com
[4] Johan Skytte Institute of Political Studies, University of Tartu, Tartu, Estonia

Abstract. The Åland Islands spent years preparing an internet voting system, to be implemented for the first time in October 2019 for Parliamentary Elections. Despite this, the project was canceled the evening before the expected release date. In this paper, we explore the causes of this failure using a two-pronged approach including Information System failure perspectives and the approach to e-voting Mirabilis, focusing on organizational elements which provoked the decision not to use the system.

Keywords: Åland Islands · Internet voting · System failure · Organizations · Convenience voting

1 Introduction: Three Contextual Questions

The Åland Islands were expected to introduce an internet voting system (IVS) during their last Parliamentary elections (October 2019), for expatriate voters, with the expectation to extend use of the same system to Municipal elections too and to all possible voters on the next possible occasion. Unexpectedly, internet voting was cancelled the day before it should have started. This paper explores this case approaching it from an Information System (IS) failure framework [18, 20], describing how interactions between the different stakeholders involved are a central element for understanding the final decision, and the e-voting Mirabilis frame, focusing on the organizational elements which provoked the decision to not use the system.

1.1 What Are the Åland Islands and How Does Their Electoral System Operate?

The Åland Islands are a Swedish speaking autonomous region of Finland comprising around sixty inhabitable islands and around six thousand small rocky islands not suitable

© Springer Nature Switzerland AG 2020
R. Krimmer et al. (Eds.): E-Vote-ID 2020, LNCS 12455, pp. 36–49, 2020.
https://doi.org/10.1007/978-3-030-60347-2_3

for human habitation or settlement. The archipelago is situated in the opening to the Gulf of Bothnia, bordering south-western Finland and central-eastern Sweden and is inhabited by 29,789 citizens, 11,743 of them living in the capital, Mariehamn. The autonomy of the Åland Islands was affirmed in 1921 by the League of Nations, through which Finland would protect and guarantee the continuation of the culture, language and traditions of the archipelago, and the Ålandic Government would have a say in foreigners acquiring franchise and land in the isles [4]. Similarly, the autonomy of Åland was reaffirmed by the treaty for admitting Finland into the European Union. Amongst other elements of self-government, the Åland Islands have their own Parliament (Lagting) and Government (Landskapsregering), elected in their own independent elections.

The uniqueness of Åland's status translates to implementation of its elections, relating to both the archipelago and Finland. The Åland administration is in charge of organizing Parliamentary and Municipal elections, and uses the electoral system of proportional representation, in which voters cast votes for a particular candidate, instead of for a party. Votes are transferred into seats using the D'Hondt method. Participation in elections is determined by acquiring the Right of Domicile in Åland, or after having been an inhabitant of any Ålandic municipality for one year prior to Election Day (the latter only applies for municipal elections). Legislation regulating these elections is covered in the Election Act for Åland [1], adopted by their Parliament in January 2019, on the occasion of introducing internet voting.

1.2 Why Were the Åland Islands Attempting to Use Internet Voting?[1]

As the head of election administration, Casper Wrede describes [21], the idea to implement this voting channel in the Åland Islands was following the general worldwide trend and popularity of internet voting in the late 1990s, but the initial debate and research which produced the recommendation not to introduce the system until voter integrity and identification issues had been resolved. The idea of postponing introduction of a remote voting system in the islands was reinforced by the Finnish failure in their attempt to use electronic voting machines in 2008 local elections. Using internet voting was again introduced to political debating chambers after discussions on the reform of the electoral system in 2014 where, amongst other proposals, the suggestion was voiced to start introducing internet voting as an additional advance voting channel, only applicable for people living outside the Åland Islands. The introduction of internet voting was expected to be facilitated in two steps: 1) in 2019, only for expatriate, overseas voters in Parliamentary Elections; and 2) in 2023, based on the results of the 2019 experience, internet voting would become available for all voters [21]. Three main elements are mentioned as key factors triggering implementation of internet voting: convenience, turnout, and international projection.

Given the geographic location of the Åland Islands, it has been a long term goal of electoral authorities [19] to make voting more convenient for remote voters, as well as a traditional element considered as a driver for internet voting. The logic is based on two assumptions that 1) a general demand for convenience voting channels exists among the

---

[1] For a more detailed development of this point, see our previous work on the preparation of Åland's internet voting project [5].

population; and 2) trust has been established towards remote voting channels, implemented in an uncontrolled environment. The Åland Islands have a legacy of convenience and remote voting channels being available to the population, since even before 2019 they were already offering, a number of voting channels consisting of 1) early voting at general voting locations not linked to the voter's place of residence, meaning that a voter could vote at any early voting polling station across the Ålands during an 11-day period; 2) early voting at care institutions; 3) Election Day voting; and 4) Postal voting for those who "are out of the country or are ill/handicapped and unable to vote in any other way"[2].

Advance voting channels are quite popular for the population and currently are used by around 1/3 of all voters who cast a vote (35% in 2019 and 2014 EU Parliament Elections)[3]. Said differently, Postal voting was not able to gain popularity due to the cumbersome procedure. During 2015 elections to the Legislative Assembly, around 150 people voted by post, constituting only 0.7% of all eligible voters [3], with about 10% of postal ballots arriving too late to be counted for the elections. Besides Postal voting, no other voting channels are available to voters residing overseas, outside of the islands. Åland does not have any embassies, representative agencies, or consulates and, as a result, voters do not have the option to vote in foreign missions. It is no coincidence that expatriates – 'absentee, overseas' voters - constituted a target group for initial use of internet voting.

The introduction of internet voting was also connected to projecting Åland to the outside world. In recent years, the Government of Åland provided IT-services for the public sector and contributed to overall digitization of the islands in various ways, through the public company ÅDA[4]. Both the development of internet voting and digitization of the islands are elements for creating a digital narrative of Ålandic identity and creating a positive image to promote the islands as a place where innovation thrives, and to highlight the positive impacts of their self-government.

In contrast, the reduced costs and time required are not amongst primary reasons for introducing internet voting. Cost savings were highlighted as a potential advantage for the long term [2, 3], under the assumption that a realistic assessment of cost-efficiency would only be possible once the system had been consolidated and the number of users increased. Regarding time savings, another dimension which is often highlighted as a potential positive outcome of using internet voting, the small size of the electorate would limit the potential impact of using the system in this regards.

1.3 Why Are We Writing This Paper?

Discussions on the convenience of introducing internet voting to the Åland Islands were held for more than 20 years, intensifying during the last months of preparatory work. The first use of internet voting seemed to be ready for 'go live' on October 2019 but,

---

[2] As described in the leaflet produced by the government of Åland to explain how Elections function to citizens: "Election on Åland, 18 October 2015".

[3] Statistics and Research Åland, URL: https://www.asub.ax/sv/statistik/valet-europaparlamentet-2019.

[4] Åland Digital Agenda, see: www.ada.ax/.

at the very last minute and after the system had been set up, the use of internet voting was cancelled hours before elections opened. Our initial goal with this research was to approach the Ålandic case in order to observe their initial use of internet voting and conduct a cost-efficiency calculation of multichannel elections as we had already done for the case in Estonia [9, 10]. The fact that elections were cancelled when our team was already in-place and on site and we had already conducted extensive preparatory work (analysis of electoral law, preliminary interviews, initial study visit) made us direct our gaze towards analyzing the reasons for failure. We had the rare and unexpected opportunity to directly observe management of an electoral crisis and to interview the relevant actors. Our aim is to pinpoint the different elements which may have contributed to this final decision and try to extract lessons to be applied by other electoral managers and for implementing voting technologies. Failures help unveil processes which would remain hidden when assertions are made for systems that are successful [14], in this particular case, the complexity of electoral management and technological innovation and the interaction of different stakeholders.

To do this, we will propose and use a framework describing the Information System (IS) failure and interactions between the different stakeholders involved, relying on interviews conducted during our study visits to the islands.

2 Stakeholders and Models of Failure

Several studies targeted the issue of Information Systems (IS) failures [5, 6, 8, 12, 16, 22] over the last few years, and some proposed explanatory frameworks described the concept of IS failure and tackling the determinants for successful implementation [18, 20]. Definitions of an IS failure are generally in line with the two categories Ewusi-Mensah described [8]: either the system fails due to inability to perform to users' levels of expectations or due to the inability of producers to produce a fully-functional, working system for users. Sauer [18] considers the definition of an IS system failure as a system abandonment due to stakeholder dissatisfaction.

Sauer [18] developed an explanatory framework describing IS failure based on three key elements: 1) Supporters, 2) Project Organization and 3) IS. In it, he creates a triangle of dependencies between these three elements and there must be interaction between them to prevent eventual failure occurring. In his analysis, failure is presented as the outcome of the interplay between context, innovation process and support. Flaws occur if the context is inadequately addressed in the innovation process, and, if flaws should accumulate, the system loses support and faces risk of failure. Sauer also highlights the importance of system supporters and their perceptions regarding the system itself, rather than solely focusing on technological characteristics of the IS. In his interactive frame-work, the IS serves the supporters, while they in turn support the project's organization, and this last component innovates the system. According to Sauer's way of thinking, failure is seen as total abandonment of a system, which occurs when this triangle of dependencies breaks down. The role of Project Organization is seen as a middleman between stakeholders and the IS. What is more, the role of project organization is not limited to this: it also serves as "a mediator" between context, system and stakeholders.

Toots [20] iterated and adapted Sauer's model in order to develop an analytical framework for contextualizing and explaining factors which influence system failure for e-participation. The framework proposed by Toots consists of four key elements, focusing on: a) Innovation Process; b) Contextual Factors; c) Processes with contextual factors interacting with innovation process and stakeholders and; d) Project Organization, where they have the power to change influential contextual factors or if it can, to align the system to the context. The sub-elements of context include technology, organizational variables, and politics. In both frameworks mentioned above from Sauer and Toots, the elements complement one another, creating an interactive triangle of dependencies which allows us to understand the reasons for failure in exchanges occurring between different elements.

The Supporters in Sauer's model can be also viewed as stakeholders in Toots' model, but Toots includes a differentiation between "Project Organization" and "Stakeholders", based on the following logic: *stakeholders need the project organization to develop IS according to their interests* (p. 548). Therefore, Project Organization is viewed as a middleman between stakeholders and the IS, but the role is not limited solely to this, serving also as "a mediator" between context, system and stakeholders.

Even if Toots' efforts bring the causes for e-participation IS failure closer to the case we are analyzing, her model does not apply in full for understanding reasons for the Åland Islands' failure. Of the four key assumptions presented, only two of them are indicative for our case:

1. *"Implementation of an e-participation system may be regarded as an innovation process characterized by uncertainty and susceptibility to changes in the context;*
2. *While contextual factors and changes are not the immediate cause of failure, context may constitute an important trigger for failure."*

However, even these assumptions do not apply fully in our case, because Toots, following Macintosh's [13] definition of e-participation, explicitly distinguishes *e-participation from other e-democracy instruments such as e-voting* (p. 546). Ålands' IVS is a type of e-voting and thus could not fully benefit from applying a framework designed for e-participation, even if it is an excellent fulcrum for developing a new iteration of the model.

Some of the arrangements proposed for Toots' model relate to the role stakeholders play and the fact that the technology was never used. One of Toots' arguments is that if using an e-government system is not satisfactory for those who must use it, they will abandon its use and condemn the system to failure. In the case under analysis, the IVS was never used by stakeholders, so their impact is minor. On the contrary, the role of Project Organization and the Context in which the IVS is framed play a more relevant role, since the unequal discourses collected from Election Managers and Vendors highlight the existence of a difference in criteria towards the system. Also, some of the difficulties highlighted for developing IVS relate to adapting to the context, either legal or technological, of the Ålandic environment.

Taking one step forward, for iteration and for adapting Toots' framework to the case of the Åland Islands, we can detect different elements proposed in the framework mentioned: 1) Project Organization existed and managed creation, development and implementation of the system (here, also, a difference to Toots' model, since the role of Project Organization was not to innovate an IS which already existed, but to implement a brand new one); 2) the IS was in-place but never used; 3) the Supporters never accessed the system, but they could track developments through the media and further discard the system; 4) external contextual factors might have facilitated failure of implementation, such as the Data Protection Authority arriving late or integration of the IVS in the Finnish e-Government environment. Failure, in our case is transposed to being the decision to not proceed with internet voting, even with the system in-place, giving more relevance to the interaction between the different elements than to the IS itself.

Since some of the elements included in the frameworks proposed by Toots and by Sauer cannot be included in the same manner as has just been described, their models need to be iterated and adapted to the conditions of the case study. For this reason, we refer to the conceptual model analyzing e-voting implementation – the E-voting Mirabilis [11]. Including this allows enlarging the context in which the IVS is implemented. It focuses on four macro dimensions influencing application of ICT in elections:

- technological dimension;
- legal dimension;
- political dimension;
- social dimension.

For the technological dimension, we consider what supporting infrastructure for internet voting was already in place (in particular, voter register and voter identification). For the legal dimension, we trace how the legal framework has been amended to adjust for internet voting, and whether it covers such aspects as secure processing of voters' personal data. For the political dimension, we analyze what groups of voters' internet voting was supposed to enfranchise, how the IVS was evaluated, and what was the overall political discussion on its introduction. The social dimension focuses on citizens' understanding and level of trust in IVS.

The E-voting Mirabilis is also helpful for stakeholder categorization, distinguishing between Voters, Politicians, Election managers, Vendors, and Media representatives and election monitors or observers. Combined with Toots' model, distinguishing between stakeholders and project organization, categorization should look like this:

- Stakeholders: Voters; Politicians; Media representatives and election observers;
- Project organization: Vendors; Election managers, Project managers.

Therefore, our theoretical framework builds on the conceptual model of the 'E-voting Mirabilis' [11] and an adaptation of the information system failure framework by Toots [20]. Based on these, we propose and use the "Mirabilis of internet voting System (IVS) failure". Toots' 'e-Participation System' was replaced by the IVS, and inside it we find Krimmer's e-voting components. All around, the 'contextual factors' (Toots) or 'four main macro dimensions' (Krimmer) *that explain the areas that influence e-voting deployment* [11]. Afterwards, Krimmer's five stakeholder groups which help to apply ICT to the electoral process, are grouped as either a 'Stakeholder' or 'Project Organization', according to Toots' framework and to their direct involvement in implementation of internet voting. Relationships between IVS, Project Organization and Stakeholders have remained similar (with some minor changes) to Toots' original diagram (Fig. 1).

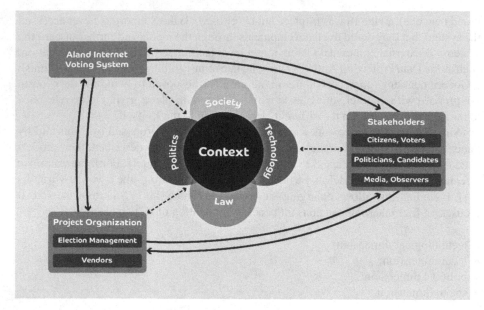

Fig. 1. Mirabilis of IVS failure.

In the context of the Åland Islands, project organization will be represented by the vendor (Scytl) and the organization responsible for the IVS procurement (ADA) and project management (Electoral Management Body). The rest of the actors will fit into the category Stakeholders: voters, government, election administration, parties, Data Protection Authority, and others. Stakeholders send requirements of IVS to project organization and provide them with the resources to fulfill those requirements. The IVS produced should satisfy stakeholders, otherwise, they will not use it. In other words, the IVS produced should meet the expectations of key stakeholders. In the context of the Åland Islands, this first and foremost concerns the stakeholders responsible for the decision on whether to start using internet voting. Already at the stage of modelling, we can observe that there is a possible mismatch between stakeholders' requirements formulated to project organization at the start of IVS development, and expectations which the final IVS should satisfy.

In this conceptual model, the context plays the key role: it shapes the demands of stakeholders, thus affecting the requirements they will send to project organization; it constrains or defines what is possible for project organization to fulfil the requirements; and the final IVS should serve the context.

3 Methodology

Data collection for developing this case study took place between March and December 2019. During this period, we conducted two visits to Mariehamn in teams of two researchers: 9–16 June and 14–22 October. Most of the interviews and observations included in this research were carried out during these visits to Åland, although we had completed some preparatory interviews with the Ålandic Electoral Management Body (EMB) before the first visit, and arranged some digitally mediated interviews after the second visit. A total of 20 semi-structured interviews were conducted with EMB, ADA, Scytl, Central Committee for Elections, Data Protection Authority, local politicians, and voters. Many interviews had more than one respondent and some interviewees were contacted at different times. In all, a total of 20 people were finally interviewed, and the interviews were anonymized (see Table 1). Data was analyzed using NVIVO qualitative data analysis software following a multi-stage inductive approach consisting of identifying a set of core themes during transcription (including, amongst others, 1) the electoral process, 2) government, 3) introduction of internet voting, 4) cancellation of internet voting and 5) voting organization) and the further coding of interviews based on the above themes. This inductive method was aligned with re-focusing of the research plan described below, allowing us to include the information collected in a context of crisis and relate our conclusions to the literature on Information Systems failure.

Table 1. List of interviewees, anonymized[a].

Occupation	Date
Head of election administration	March, 2019
Head of IT-unit at Ålands Landskapsregering	June, 2019
System administrator at Ålands Landskapsregering	June, 2019
Legal Director, Government Offices, Unit for Legal and International Affairs	June, 2019
CEO of Åda Ab	June, 2019
Project Manager at Åda Ab	June, 2019
Data Inspector	June, 2019
Minister	June, 2019
Minister	June, 2019
Head of election administration (II)	June, 2019
Voter	October, 2019
Voter	October, 2019
Head of election administration (III)	October, 2019
Data Inspector (II)	October, 2019
Head of IT-unit at Ålands landskapsregering (II)	October, 2019
CEO at Åda Ab (II)	November, 2019
Worker at Åda Ab	November, 2019
Worker at Scytl	November, 2019
Worker at Scytl	November, 2019
Worker at Scytl	November, 2019
Worker at Scytl	November, 2019

[a]The numbers in brackets refer to the number of times the person was interviewed.

The case of the Åland Islands was selected due to the fact that they intended to implement internet voting for the first time and it represented a good comparison to research already conducted by the research team. The size of the country and administration allowed swift, effective communication and privileged access to data. Also, it would have covered a relatively unexplored dimension of electoral analysis, the costs of initial implementation of voting channels and their evolution over time.

We must point out here that the methodological plan was reframed during the research, due to cancellation of the IVS. Whilst applying the methodology for calculating costs, the initial plan followed on from previous research [3, 4] and research mentioned in a previous publication on the same case [5]. Cancelling implementation of internet voting took place during the research team's second visit to the Åland Islands, at a time at which the analysis of electoral law and modelling of the electoral processes had already been completed, as well as several interviews for understanding and describing the electoral system, its management and the costs involved. The fact that the research team was on-site during the cancellation, allowed them to observe and conduct interviews about management of the crisis, which were followed by a second round of interviews with the key stakeholders. Hence, this publication is the result of refocusing our research goals, given the opportunity to gather information on a critical case study relating to management of an electoral crisis due to cancellation of a voting channel. As a result of this, the interview design was modified (*the contents of the questionnaire*) in the course of the data collection process, paying special attention to integrating the different steps of data collection in the final analysis of the data.

The value of the data collected is derived from the opportunity and the uniqueness of the situation but, at the same time, it may involve some limitations given that it was not possible to plan such a methodological reconfiguration in advance. Amongst the strengths of our data collection process: 1) we developed a deep analysis of the electoral system prior to cancellation, and so were able to rapidly identify the key stakeholders to interview and the key processes to direct our attention to; 2) the presence of our research team on the ground allowed us to gather first impressions and reflections after cancellation and to experience the moment of cancellation on-site: direct observation of events provides us some interpretative clues which it would not be possible to gather through other data collection methods [7]. Amongst the limitations: we could not access some information on grounds of secrecy and confidentiality; the sources which, according to some discourses, could shed light on legitimacy of their claims.

4 Data Analysis

The context surrounding the Åland IVS looked promising for implementation of the new voting channel. At a socio-political level, no objections were raised against the system, the media did not pay much attention to implementation of the voting channel and no political party openly opposed it. There were more concerns about lowering the age of voters to 16 years of age for example, a reform discussed simultaneously to introduction of internet voting.

The overall political discussion on internet voting was fairly positive. Stakeholder evaluation varies from feeling *fairly optimistic* (I-1) to endorsements: *I always thought that this is a good thing, this is something we need to do* (I-13). The Parliament also has not seen much of the debate on internet voting, besides *some discussion on the security issues* (but) *in general, all parties in Åland responded positively to this voting channel* (I-13). Media outlets in the Åland Islands were not interested in internet voting, until almost right before voting started: *here is not big interest because everybody's focused on the transformation of the municipalities* (I-13), *I think, as a journalist, the interest in the elections will awaken in the end of August, when the campaign starts* (I-13).

This smooth political development crystalized in the decision that, during the first binding trial during the 2019 Parliamentary elections only expatriates (*overseas, absentee voters*) were eligible to vote via the Internet, *most of [the expats] are young people, they are studying or have been studying and stay for some years after studying* (I-3). This decision was considered as a clear improvement of voting conditions for expat voters (*a very strong urge from the younger generation to have a simplified voting procedure, possibly electronic* – I-5) since they could avoid the problems associated with using postal ballots to cast their votes (*last election 10% of our postal votes came back too late to count* – I-5).

As a result of which, *the whole new electoral act passed unanimously* (I-3). The legal dimension, in accordance with Krimmer [11], regulates how the electoral code can be changed in order to permit votes cast by electronic means and to provide the level of accountability required to the voter and should further: 1) provide the voter with the ability to see how personal data are processed; 2) include the principle of proportionality when handling personal data; and 3) serve as a guiding indicator. The Election Act for Åland, issued on May 2019, consists of 15 chapters and 122 individual sections (or articles), and defines all voting channels including postal voting, advance voting, Election Day voting and contains *new provisions on internet voting* (I-5). The legal dimension was further bolstered by the 'Registerbeskrivning'[5] or Privacy Policy (2019) which describes processing of personal data in connection with implementation of the Parliamentary and Municipal elections in Åland, including a description of the personal data required, its use during various stages of the election process, and the entities responsible which may interact with it, either directly or indirectly.

In order to specifically implement internet voting, the government *decided quite early [for] the procurement process*, that they *should buy a service, not the system* and that they *need[ed] someone else to run* it (I-10). To this end, the law and the procurement requirements were written in "parallel". As confirmed by an interviewee, this was *not ideal, perhaps theoretically. But in practice, it was quite good because we could adjust the wording and the law, according to what we experience, what is possible and how things should be* (I-10). This procurement process was run by ADA, resulting in a bicephalous organizational structure from the side of the government: ADA for managing the contract and the Electoral Management Body for management of elections, both interacting with the vendor.

The development of IVS was accompanied by audits and evaluations. The checks and balances are prescribed by law: *the government […] should check and to have a third party to check everything, all the processes. So, we will also have somebody to check*

---

[5] Available at: https://www.val.ax/sites/default/files/attachments/subject/behandling-av-person uppgifter.pdf. Last accessed 15 June 2020.

when the election takes place that everything is [OK] (I-4). However, in June 2019, the independent body which would check and review the i-voting system had not yet been defined. The notions of who this independent body could potentially be were still vague: *It could perhaps be some authority from the Finnish state government, but it must be independent from the vendor and from the government... (...) it could also be some representatives from the Finnish authorities. Could be representatives from Estonia, for example. I mean, experts on internet voting, would be possible. Or it could be some audit company like KPMG, or whatever* (I-9).

At some point during development of the IVS, the Data Protection Authority of Åland became interested in auditing the process [17], for the following reasons: *Well, the biggest reason is because this is a new project, that has not been done before. And also, since this is a democratically critical process, pertaining to a lot of sensitive personal information or other special categories of personal information as in political opinions... since that kind of data is being processed [...] That is the kind of processes that the data protection authorities should be auditing to make sure that they're safe (I-17)*. The arrival of the Data Protection Authority brought a new along with it player to the table; since it was not possible to conduct the audit on their own, it was necessary to outsource this to an external consultant for *auditing the security documentation sent by [the vendor]. And to see if they fulfilled the safety requirements* (I-17). The main findings of the audit, were that the Data Protection Impact Analysis (DPIA) has not been completed[6].

From a technological perspective, the IVS used the digital infrastructure provided by Finnish government – e-ID systems (e-ID Cards and Mobile-ID) – and private institutions (e-Banking), and consisted of main elements such as an e-ballot box, a list of voters and candidates, voter identification and authentication as well as vote verification.

During the development process of the IVS, a number of deficiencies were detected with the e-Identification system: in relation to integration *during the first pilot we found errors in the Suomi.fi implementation. So when I cast a vote, I was not successfully logged out from the authentication (...) And then they have corrected one mistake in Suomi.fi identification but there was still one loop, one error more.* (I-19); *In June already. And then in July again and in August, again* (I-15). Discovery of these problems was motivation for outsourcing a penetration test to an external vendor who dealt directly with the vendor in charge of IVS. The interaction between both vendors presented some problems in relation to accessibility to the source code of the voting system, since the vendor in charge of the penetration test was allowed access to the code but in the premises of the IVS provider, in a different country, and this option was not accepted and delayed the auditing process[7]: *The argument that they were unable to access the source code for me is not a valid argument (...) they were invited... but even if they decided to not to come, this particular issue has been tested* (I-20).

---

[6] For further details on the General Data Protection Regulation in the Alandic elections, see the work of Rodríguez-Pérez [17].

[7] In this regard, it is worth noting that it was not possible to interview the vendor in charge of the penetration test due to a disclosure agreement. The views collected in this research might be distorted due to this issue.

According to the vendor's position, the problems detected challenged the development of the system: *during such integration, [or] maybe during any sort of customization or development, when you test, you find things, with the objective to correct them, fix them (I-20); The main challenge here is that, since we are not (...) Finnish, we don't have Finnish ID, so we have few test credentials that we can use in our tests to automate them (...) the personnel both from ADA and the government (were) very helpful as well in providing (them) to us (I-20)*. Problems were resolved according to their position, and the system was in place and ready to run during the elections as expected: *this issue with the verification of the digital signature. It was corrected, and was said that was corrected (by the vendor)*.

The report from the vendor in charge of the penetration test was finished very late on (*we got the report from the security company very late, so it was not so much time to evaluate that and also to have a meeting with them and to discuss about – I-19*) and, even if the problems might have been solved, *we have not run the pilot from start to end (...), never ran it from beginning to end in a test environment (...), it doesn't feel right to do it (run the elections)* (I-19). The result was, cancellation of using internet voting at the very last moment.

5 Discussion and Conclusions

In the complex environment of electoral management, many factors can tip the scales towards failure if these are not perfectly aligned. In the case analyzed, even if there was a long process of preparation, training and a well-documented Electoral Management Body with members and experienced vendors, their joint efforts did not match up to initial expectations and the IVSs could not be implemented. It is not our role (nor our aim) to blame anyone for this outcome, but to understand the process in order to gain some useful knowledge and experience for others who aim to implement similar systems.

As we described, the context in which the IVS was to be implemented appeared to be quite friendly, accommodating, and welcoming: positive political discussions, lack of external agents discussing the suitability of the decision taken. The law was approved on time, as was the procurement process too. The problem, then, relied on the process of adjusting the IVS and the interaction between the members of the project organization, particularly with relation to timing. The accumulation of delays in some deliveries, responses and interactions, combined with organizing pilots during the summer period (in June and in August) reduced the time available for resolving problems detected (problems of integrating IVS into the Finnish e-ID system). Developing two Penetration Tests in a relatively short period of time and the presumed problems of collecting data for the audits delayed the responses until a time when they were already redundant and no longer required. The Data Protection Authority's appearance late in June, and creating a new parallel legal and document audit probably superimposed a new layer of complexity onto implementing the system. Even if problems could have been resolved, as the vendor in charge of the IVS states, the authorities 'confidence in reliability of the system had already been damaged and the decision to cancel the elections could seem reasonable for those who were legally qualified to make it. Paraphrasing the idea expressed by Oostven and Van den Besselaar [15], *a voting system is only as good as the Administration* ("public" in the original version) *believes it to be.*

The key takeaway we can extract from this case is the relevant role which organization of the overall process plays in successful implementation. In the case under analysis, time management appears to be the main limiting factor for effective resolution of problems identified. We believe that with better time-management, four critical factors could have been managed more effectively: 1) the vendor could have resolved the problems detected in a timely manner, 2) project organizers would have had time to make sure these issues were resolved, 3) the final version of the system could have been tested, and hence, 4) the system could have been operated securely in real time. In addition to this, other factors, that without time constrictions could have had an irrelevant impact, in the case analyzed played an important role. Firstly, the bicephalous structure followed for project management divided the knowledge available on the side of project organizers, that is the technical knowledge separate from contract management and adding to the complexity of the process. Due to this fact, the process was slowed down at critical moments when a more directed management structure could have forced the vendor to react more swiftly in order to solve problems encountered. Secondly, the unexpected problems encountered related to the integration of the Finnish e-Identity system and their late resolution, damaged the trustability of the IVS. A faster detection and a smooth resolution of these problems could have walked the process to a different ending.

In contrast to the case proposed by Toots [20] in which the e-participation system failed due to a lack of a meaningful connection with stakeholders, in the case of the Åland Islands, failure originated on the side of interaction between project organization and the IVS itself, showing, in the end, the relevance of the organizational factor for creating, developing and implementing technological innovations.

Acknowledgements. This project has received funding from the European Union's Horizon 2020 research and innovation programme under grant agreement No 857622, and from the Estonian Research Council, under grant agreement PUT 1361.

References

1. Åland Culture Foundation: International Treaties and Documents Concerning Åland 1856–2009. http://www.kulturstiftelsen.ax/traktater/eng_fr/ram_right-enfr.htm
2. Arbetsgruppen för Internetröstning: Rösta per Internet? Mariehamn (2001)
3. Arbetsgruppen för översyn av vallagstiftningen: Slutrapport, Mariehamn (2015)
4. ÅSUB - Statistics and Research Åland: Åland in Figures, Mariehamn (2019)
5. Bartis, E., Mitev, N.: A multiple narrative approach to information systems failure: a successful system that failed. Eur. J. Inf. Syst. (2008). https://doi.org/10.1057/ejis.2008.3
6. Beynon-Davies, P.: Information systems 'failure': the case of the London ambulance service's computer aided despatch project. Eur. J. Inf. Syst. (1995). https://doi.org/10.1057/ejis.1995.20
7. DeWalt, K., DeWalt, B.: Participant Observation: A Guide for Fieldworkers. Altamira Press, Plymouth (2011)
8. Ewusi-Mensah, K.: Software Development Failures: Anatomy of Abandoned Projects. The MIT Press, Boston (2003)

9. Krimmer, R., Duenas-Cid, D., Krivonosova, I., Vinkel, P., Koitmae, A.: How much does an e-vote cost? Cost comparison per vote in multichannel elections in Estonia. In: Krimmer, R., Volkamer, M., Cortier, V., Goré, R., Hapsara, M., Serdült, U., Duenas-Cid, D. (eds.) E-Vote-ID 2018. LNCS, vol. 11143, pp. 117–131. Springer, Cham (2018). https://doi.org/10.1007/978-3-030-00419-4_8

10. Krimmer, R., Duenas-Cid, D., Krivonosova, I.: New methodology for calculating cost-efficiency of different ways of voting: is internet voting cheaper? Public Money Manag. 1–10 (2020). https://doi.org/10.1080/09540962.2020.1732027

11. Krimmer, R.: The Evolution of e-Voting: Why Voting Technology is Used and How it Affects Democracy. TUT Press, Tallinn (2012)

12. Lyytinen, K., Robey, D.: Learning failure in information systems development. Inf. Syst. J. (1999). https://doi.org/10.1046/j.1365-2575.1999.00051.x

13. Macintosh, A.: Characterizing e-participation in policy-making. In: Proceedings of the Hawaii International Conference on System Sciences (2004). https://doi.org/10.1109/hicss.2004.1265300

14. Mitev, N.: Are social constructivist approaches critical? The case of IS failure. In: Howcroft, D., Trauth, E. (eds.) Handbook of Critical Information Systems Research: Theory and Application, pp. 70–103. Edward Elgar Publishing, Cheltenham (2005)

15. Oostveen, A.-M., Van den Besselaar, P.: Security as belief User's perceptions on the security of electronic voting systems. Electron. Voting Eur. Technol. Law Polit. Soc. 47, 73–82 (2004)

16. Poulymenakou, A., Holmes, A.: A contingency framework for the investigation of information systems failure. Eur. J. Inf. Syst. (1996). https://doi.org/10.1057/ejis.1996.10

17. Rodríguez-Pérez, A.: My vote, my (personal) data: remote electronic voting and the General Data Protection Regulation. In: Krimmer, R. et al. (eds.) Fifth International Joint Conference on Electronic Voting, E-Vote-ID 2020. Springer, Cham (2020)

18. Sauer, C.: Why Information Systems Fail: A Case Study Approach. Alfred Waller Ltd. Publishers, Oxfordshire (1993)

19. Szwed, K.: Głosowanie elektroniczne na Wyspach Alandzkich – idea bez pokrycia czy realny scenariusz? PRZEGLĄD PRAWA Konst. 4(50), 13–32 (2019)

20. Toots, M.: Why E-participation systems fail: The case of Estonia's Osale.ee. Gov. Inf. Q. Preprint (2019). https://doi.org/10.1016/J.GIQ.2019.02.002

21. Wrede, C.: E-voting in a Small Scale – the Case of Åland. In: Krimmer, R. et al. (eds.) The International Conference on Electronic Voting. E-Vote-ID 2016, pp. 109–115. TUT Press, Bregenz (2016)

22. Yeo, K.T.: Critical failure factors in information system projects. Int. J. Proj. Manag. (2002). https://doi.org/10.1016/S0263-7863(01)00075-8

Revisiting Practical and Usable Coercion-Resistant Remote E-Voting

Ehsan Estaji[1], Thomas Haines[2], Kristian Gjøsteen[2], Peter B. Rønne[1(✉)], Peter Y. A. Ryan[1], and Najmeh Soroush[1]

[1] SnT & University of Luxembourg, Luxembourg City, Luxembourg
{ehsan.estaji,peter.ronne,peter.ryan,najmeh.soroush}@uni.lu
[2] Norwegian University of Science and Technology, Trondheim, Norway
{thomas.haines,kristian.gjosteen}@ntnu.no

Abstract. In this paper we revisit the seminal coercion-resistant e-voting protocol by Juels, Catalano and Jakobsson (JCJ) and in particular the attempts to make it usable and practical. In JCJ the user needs to handle cryptographic credentials and be able to fake these in case of coercion. In a series of three papers Neumann et al. analysed the usability of JCJ, and constructed and implemented a practical credential handling system using a smart card which unlock the true credential via a PIN code, respectively fake the credential via faking the PIN. We present several attacks and problems with the security of this protocol, especially an attack on coercion-resistance due to information leakage from the removal of duplicate ballots.

Another problem, already stressed but not solved by Neumann et al, is that PIN typos happen frequently and would invalidate the cast vote without the voter being able to detect this. We construct different protocols which repair these problems. Further, the smart card is a trusted component which can invalidate cast votes without detection and can be removed by a coercer to force abstention, i.e. presenting a single point of failure. Hence we choose to make the protocols hardware-flexible i.e. also allowing the credentials to be store by ordinary means, but still being PIN based and providing PIN error resilience. Finally, one of the protocols has a linear tally complexity to ensure an efficient scheme also with many voters .

Keywords: Electronic voting · Coercion-resistance · Usable security

1 Introduction

One of the main threats in remote electronic voting is that they are inherently susceptible coercion-attacks due to the lack of a voting booth. In their seminal paper, Juels, Catalano and Jakobsson [10] gave a formal definition of coercion-resistance and further devised a protocol (JCJ) satisfying this strong security

This research were supported by the Luxembourg National Research Fund (FNR).

R. Krimmer et al. (Eds.): E-Vote-ID 2020, LNCS 12455, pp. 50–66, 2020.
https://doi.org/10.1007/978-3-030-60347-2_4

property. To achieve this, JCJ assumes a coercion-free setup phase where the voter get a credential which is essentially a cryptographic key. To cast a valid ballot this key needs to be entered correctly together with the vote. In case of coercion, the voter can simply give a fake random credential to the coercer and even cast a vote together with the coercer using this fake credential – the corresponding vote will be removed in the tally process. The tally process of weeding out the ballots with fake credentials and duplicates, however, suffers from a quadratic complexity problem in the number of voters and cast ballots. Several paper are devoted to reduce the tally complexity in JCJ, see e.g. [2,6,18, 20], however, each with their drawbacks. JCJ and similar constructions however also suffer from usability deficits, see also [14]. Especially, the voter intrinsically cannot directly check if a cast ballot is valid and will be counted, see however [8].

Moreover the handling and storing of long credentials is a notorious usability problem, getting even harder with a coercer present. The usability was analysed by Neumann et. al. [5,15,16] and led to a protocol using smart cards for handling voter's credentials. The stored credential is combined with a PIN code to produce the full credential which will be compared with the credential stored by the authorities on the bulletin board. In this paper we revisit this protocol and present several attacks on coercion-resistance and verifiability, but also possible repairs.

Whereas the smart card provides a solution to the usability problem, it also comes with strong trust assumptions and problems

- The smart card is generally needs to be trusted. A malicious card could e.g. use the wrong credential invalidating the cast ballot without detection, and we cannot let the voter check if the ballot is correct without introducing coercion threats.
- The coercer can take the smart card away from the voter to force abstention.
- It is more expensive, less flexible and harder to update than a purely software solution.
- One of the attacks that we found is that a coercer can use the smart card to cast ballots on his own. This not only endangers coerced voter's real vote, but due to a leak of information in the weeding phase, the coercer can also detect, with non-negligible probability, whether the coerced voter has cast an independent ballot against his instructions.

In this paper we will present protocols that repair, or at least diminishes the attack probability of, the last point by constructing new duplicate removal methods in JCJ. Further, the protocols constructed in this paper are hardware-independent: they could use a smart card, or they can be implemented using combination of a digitally stored cryptographic length key and a PIN only known by the voter. The long credential could be stored in several places – or even hidden via steganography. At ballot casting time the software will take as input the digital key and the password to form the credential submitted with the vote. Depending on the level of coercion, the coerced voter can either fake the long credential or, for stronger levels of coercion, the voter can reveal the digitally stored credential to the coercer, but fake the PIN. Due to our improved tally, the coercer will not know if he got faked credentails or PINs.

Another major problem with the original construction, already discussed as an open problem in [16], is the high chance of users doing a PIN typo error which will invalidate the vote and remain undetected. Note that naively giving feedback on the correctness of the PIN is not possible for coercion-resistance as it would allow the coercer to check whether he got a fake PIN or not. Instead, we will define a set of allowed PIN errors (e.g. chosen by the election administrator), and we will consider a ballot as valid both if it has a correct PIN or an allowed PIN error, but invalid for other PINs. We construct protocols which at tally time secretly check whether a given PIN is in the set of allowed PINs and will sort out invalid ballots. The protocols can accommodate general PIN error policies, however Wiseman et al. [22] studied usual errors in PIN entries. Two frequent errors are transposition errors (i.e. entering "2134" instead of "1234") and wrong digit number errors (i.e. entering "1235" instead of "1234"). Correcting for both of these errors is however problematic, as we will see, since the set of independent PINs becomes small.

The outline of paper is as follows. In Sect. 2 we present attacks and problems of the orignal NV12 scheme. Our improved protocols are presented in Sect. 3. In Sect. 4 we make a preliminary analysis of how many independent PINs exist when allowing certain PIN errors. Finally we conclude in Sect. 5.

2   Analysis of NV12: Attacks and Problems

Neumann et al. [16] carried out a usability analysis of JCJ and proposed a new scheme (NV12) for handling the credentials and vote-casting. In [15] a few modification were made to prevent side-channel attacks and an efficiency analysis was done, and finally [5] presented a prototype implementation and its efficiency.

2.1   The Scheme:

In this subsection we give a brief overview of the NV12 scheme, we refer to [15] and the JCJ/Civitas papers [4,10] for more details. The entities participating in the NV12 protocol are: **A supervisor:** who is in charge of running election and declaring election authorities; **The voter:** who intends to cast her vote; **The voter's smart card, reader and computer:** which serves as interface between the voter and the JCJ/Civitas system. The smart card reader has a screen and PIN entry interface; **A registrar:** who administrates the electoral register; **A supervised registration authority and a set of registration tellers:** that provide the voter with her credential;

A set of tabulation tellers: that are in change of the tallying process; **A set of ballot boxes:** to which voters cast their votes; **A bulletin board, BB:** that is used to publish information. The ballot boxes will publish to BB.

The framework of the scheme is as follows

1. **Setup Phase.** This step is the same as JCJ/ Civitas; an election public key, pk, will be computed and published.
2. **Registration Phase.** After offline and online registration phases, the voter's credential divided by the chosen PIN is stored on the smart card alongside with a designated verifier proof.
3. **Voting Phase.** The voting procedure is split into two phases implementing Benaloh challenges to the vote encryption
   - **Challenge:** The smart card commits to an encryption of the vote by displaying $\text{hash}(\text{enc}(\text{vote}, \text{pk}, r))$. The voter notes down this hash, and if the encryption is challenged, the smart card releases the randomness r to the voter's computer, and the voter can verify the hash indeed was consistent with the vote choice via a third device. This challenge procedure can be reiterated.
   - **Cast:** When the voter chooses to cast, she then enters the PIN. Now, the ballot of the form $\langle \{\text{CRD}\}_{\text{pk}}, \{vote\}_{\text{pk}}, \sigma, \phi \rangle$ is generated where σ is a zero-knowledge proof (ZKP) of well-formedness of the vote and ϕ is a ZKP of knowledge of both the credential and vote. This is sent anonymously to a ballot box. $\text{hash}(\langle \{\text{CRD}\}_{\text{pk}}, \{vote\}_{\text{pk}}, \sigma, \phi \rangle)$ is displayed and written down by the voter, and can be checked with the stored ballot in the ballot box to ensure stored-as-cast verifiability.
4. **Tallying Phase.** This step is also the same as JCJ/ Civitas.

The important trust assumptions made in [15] are

- For privacy it was assumed:
  - Half of the remote registration tellers and the supervised registration authority are trustworthy.
  - Neither the smart cards nor smart card readers can be corrupted.
  - The adversary is not able to corrupt a threshold set of tabulation tellers.
- For coercion-resistance we further need:
  - There is a point in the voting phase, in which the adversary cannot control the voter.
  - The adversary cannot control the voter's computer.
  - The channel to the ballot boxes is anonymous
- For verifiability it was assumed:
  - The adversary is not able to corrupt smart cards. With the Benaloh challenges implemented this was reduced further to [16]: The adversary cannot control the voting environment and the verification environment at the same time.

2.2 Attacks

We will now present attacks and discuss how to repair these.

Benaloh Challenge Problem: The first attack is on individual verifiability. The Benaloh challenge is available for the user to challenge whether the encryption of the vote is done honestly. The smart card and reader commits to the hash of the encryption via the screen of the smart card reader. The problem is that this hash is not checked for the cast ballot. Instead, what is checked for the cast ballot is that the hash of the full ballot including the encryption of the credential and ZKPs matches what is received in the ballot box. This means that the smart card can at first encrypt all votes honestly and commit to these. However, when the PIN is entered to cast a ballot, it can encrypt its own vote choice and include this in the ballot without being detected even if the verification environment is honest – this violates the trust assumption above.

Repair: Both the hash of the vote encryption and the full ballot needs to be compared with the values that can be calculated from the ballot received by the ballot box. This however reduces usability as now two hashes needs to be checked by the voter, a task which is not trivial. Particularly, the adversary can precompute hashes that are hard to distinguish for the voter - e.g. matching on the leading part. Another choice is to commit to the full ballot in the Benaloh challenge, however this requires the voter to enter the PIN for each challenge. Since it is a general problem in e-voting that verification checks are too infrequent among real voters, having to enter a PIN for each challenge further undermines the Benaloh challenge security. It might also happen that a voter would then maximally challenge once, and hence an efficient strategy for the adversary would be to cheat after the first challenge.

Brute Force Attack: The second attack in on coercion-resistance for a coercer demanding access to the smart card, alternatively on verifiability for a local adversary who manages to get access to the smart card undetected. The adversary could here simply try to guess the PIN and cast a vote. This is not detectable by the voter due to anonymity of the vote casting. Unfortunately, the PIN space cannot be scaled since it is upper bounded by the ability of the voter to remember and enter PINs correctly. Hence, the probability of guessing the PIN is not negligible. Further, the probability can be boosted by casting multiple votes. Note also, whereas we can assume that it is in the interest of the voter to use a correct smart card reader, the adversary can use a maliciously constructed reader. Thus the ballot casting can be automated and the PIN space can be covered to get a probability of a valid cast vote to be 1. This is not impossible, e.g. according to [5] vote casting took about 13 s including network time. The theoretical value with network was around 8 s, and the value of modern smart cards should be much lower. However, even with the 2014 timings, the creation of the ballots (without sending) could be done in 22 h. Note that whether the ballot is counted in the end will depend on the vote update policy, and when the voter is casting her own vote, however, here the adversary is free to optimise his strategy, e.g. try to cast last.

Repair: The smart card could demand that a certain time has to pass between each ballot cast. This time can however not be too long, otherwise a coercer might detect it or utilise it for a forced abstention. Thus this repair can only lower the probability for casting a ballot with correct PIN.

Leaky Duplicate Removal: This is an attack on coercion-resistance, but can also be an attack on verifiability to boost the attack above. In the simplest form the coercer uses the smart card to cast a vote with some trial PIN. The coercer wants to determine if this trial PIN is a correct PIN. According to the protocol the voter will cast her true vote using the correct PIN at some secret point during the voting phase. However, in the tally phase credentials are weeded using plaintext equivalence tests (PETs) of the encrypted credentials directly on the submitted ballots.[1] If the coercer now sees an equivalence with his submitted trial ballot, he can guess that it was the voter casting the other ballot, and probably with the correct PIN. Thus he has determined the correct PIN and that the voter defied his instructions in one go. To boost the attack he can simply try several PINs.[2] In standard JCJ such an attack would not work since the submitted trial credential would have the same probability of being identical to the coerced voter's credential as for it to be identical to any other voter's credential, and further the probability would be negligible.

A local adversary getting access to the smart card could also follow this strategy to try to know the PIN and cast valid votes. This might actually be detected by the voter if he checks the weeding on *BB* and sees a duplicate of his own vote (note this was also mentioned in [17]), but in the protocol the voter is not instructed to do this. Thus the PIN is not really protecting against unauthorized use of the smart card.

Repair: It is actually surprisingly hard to make a tally protocol which does not leak information to prevent this attack. The original JCJ protocol relies on the fact that guessing the real full credential can only happen with negligible chance. A first repair could be to mix the ballots before doing weeding, but after verifying the ZKPs. This makes it difficult to implement certain policies, like the last valid vote counts; however, it fits nicely with the policy that a random selection from the valid votes count. Unfortunately, this does not prevent the attack. The coercer could mark his ballot by casting it a certain number of times which is likely to be unique. He then checks if he sees this number of duplicates or

---

[1] In general this is not good for coercion-resistance since a coercer might detect a voter not following instructions across elections, see [8].

[2] Note that the coercer does not have to let the voter know that he follows this strategy. The voter only knows that the coercer has access to the card for some short time. Based on this, she could also decide not to cast her true vote at all, but then the protocol could not really be called coercion-resistant since the coercer has a very efficient strategy to force abstention.

one more. Even if mix between each duplicate removal, which would be horrible for an efficiency perspective, we do not get a leak-free tally. The distribution of time until a PET reveals a duplicate will depend on whether the PIN was correct or not. Especially the coercer could cast a lot of votes with the same trial PIN which would make detecting this more visible. There are other methods to limit the information leak in the tally which we will present below. Further, we will present a protocol that does not leak information about the number of duplicates per voter, and does have linear tally complexity (compared to the quadratic in JCJ), but which has an obfuscated form of participation privacy.

Fake Election Identifier: This is an attack on verifiability. As mentioned in the original JCJ paper, the zero-knowledge proofs need to include a unique election identifier. This identifier is announced by the election administrator and prevents that ballots are copied from one election to another, i.e. the proofs would not verify when the wrong identifier is used. However, the smart card needs to be updated with this identifier before vote casting. However, we cannot trust this is done correctly, i.e. an adversary e.g. controlling the voter's computer could try to provide a wrong credential.

Repair: The voter could enter the election identifier herself, but this is error prone. The simplest solution is that the voter checks that the submitted ballot has a zero-knowledge proof that verifies according to the real election identifier. This could be done when the hash of the full ballot is checked, but will mean that the voter has to wait a bit longer before being able to do this check.

Smart Card Removal: An obvious forced abstention attack is that the coercer simply demand to hold the smart card during the election period.

Repair: This problem seems quite inherent to the smart card approach. We could let the voter hold several smart cards. However, holding several cards would be physical evidence which a voter with a local coercer probably would not want to risk. Further, the number of cards allowed per voter could necessarily not be bounded. If each voter were allowed to hold e.g. 5 cards, the coercer would simply ask for five cards. If this is troublesome it seems better to leave the smartcard only approach and allow the voter to also hold the credential as a piece of data as in standard JCJ. This can more easily be hidden (steganography could be an option here) even though theoretically this also has problems [19]. Our protocols below can be implemented with or without smart cards.

2.3   Security Problems

In this section we discuss some problems with the protocol, that do not fall under the category of attacks.

The main usability and verifiability problem with the protocol is that PIN entry is error prone, as was already stressed in the papers by Neumann et al. An obvious solution is to have a PIN check, e.g. a checksum check. However, this would mean that only certain PINs are valid PINs, and in order for a voter to present a fake PIN to a coercer, she would first have to prepare a valid fake PIN, which is less usable.

An option with higher usability is to have a policy of allowed PIN errors and accept full credentials that corresponds to the PIN being entered with allowed errors. This is the approach we will essentially follow in this paper, however our solutions will also work for checksum checks.

If JCJ had a method of verifying the cast votes, we would also be able to at least detect such PIN errors. Such a verification mechanism was suggested in [8] using the Selene approach. However, this check can only be made after vote casting has ended, thus too late to update a PIN typo.

Another problem is the assumption that the smart card is trustworthy. This does not seem like a valid assumption, at least for important election. The smart card could simply use a wrong credential in a ballot, which would invalidate the vote. Further, this cannot be detected since the smart card is the only holder of the credential. At least the encryption of the PIN could be Benaloh tested, but not the credential. Further, the smart card reader is also trusted. However, this might not be enough in practice. As an example, if the middleware on the reader allows the voter's computer or the network to display messages on the screen, e.g. to say it is waiting for a connection, then it could e.g. try to display fake hash values. A corrupted smart card could also easily break privacy by using the encryption choice as a subliminal channel for the vote choice. In light of this the smartcard can also be seen as *a single point of failure*. We will thus focus on hardware-independent protocols.

3   Protocol Description

In this section we will present two protocols which tolerate PIN errors and prevents leak of information in the deduplication phase.

In our voting scenario the voter has two keys: a long key which is stored on her device (smart card or another device) and a short PIN, which is memorized.

To efficiently evaluate whether a PIN is allowed we will use polynomial evaluation. To this end, given a user's PIN a, we generate an $\mathsf{ErrorList}_a = \{a_1 = a, a_2, \ldots, a_k\}$ of allowed PINs. Note the number of PINs here is constant for every voter and might contain duplicates. From this, we generate a polynomial, $\mathsf{poly}_{\mathrm{PIN}}(x) = \prod_{i=1}^{k}(x - a_i) = \sum_{i=0}^{k} p_i x^i$ which has all $\mathsf{ErrorList}_a$ members as its root. In order to check the validity of the PIN, typed by the voter, it is then sufficient check whether the polynomial value on this PIN is equal to zero or not.[3] It is obvious that this polynomial should kept secret otherwise an adversary can recover the PIN by factorizing the polynomial. Therefore we have to

---

[3] Note there is a small problem here since we are in composite order groups and the polynomials might have more roots than the allowed PINs. However, the probability in general is negligible.

work with encrypted polynomials and a main challenge is the polynomial evaluation under this encryption. Assume we have $\mathsf{Enc}(\mathsf{poly}_{\mathrm{PIN}}(x)) = \sum_{i=0}^{k} \mathsf{cp}_i x^i$ and $\mathsf{CT}_{\mathrm{PIN}} = \mathsf{Enc}(\hat{a})$, we need to find a way to efficiently compute $\mathsf{Enc}(\mathsf{poly}_{\mathrm{PIN}}(\hat{a}))$.

The next challenge is to find a way to prove publicly that the individual voter's polynomial are correctly evaluated without endangering the coercion-resistance. This would e.g. rule out voters evaluating the polynomials on voter side only.

Further, while solving this problem, we will also focus on efficient protocols to obtain a practical JCJ scheme with (almost) linear tally time in the number of voters. To obtain this we need to sacrifice perfect privacy. In the first scheme we only have participation privacy by obfuscation inspired by [6,11]. Here ballots are submitted with an ID and homomorphic Paillier encryption can then be used to evaluate the polynomial. Everybody, e.g. also a separate authority, can cast votes labelled with ID which will later be discarded as invalid. Thus the actual participation of the voter is obfuscated and the voter can deny having participated in the election. Optionally, we could also follow the JCJ alternative method in [6] to achieve perfect privacy, however the cost will be that the voters twice have to defy the coercer and interact with the voting system. In the second scheme using BGN encryption, the information leak from duplicate removal will not be negligible, but bounded, and this scheme does not satisfy linear tally efficiency.

Due to space limitations, we will just explain the basic building blocks and their algorithm and suppress some details about ballot integrity and non-malleability from the zero-knowledge proofs, e.g. the inclusion of election identifiers and the correct form of the Fiat-Shamir transformations. Also, for simplicity, we describe the protocol with a single trusted party, but it is possible to distributively run this protocol. We will also not specify all parts of the distributed registration phase and the Benaloh challenges, this can be implemented as in the NV12 scheme with some obvious modifications and with the repairs mentioned above.

3.1 Paillier Instantiation

The first instantiation relies on the Paillier public-key cryptosystem which is a partially homomorphic and its security is based on the hardness of the decisional composite residuosity assumption. A ciphertext on message $m \in \mathbb{Z}_n$ has the form $\mathsf{CT} = (g^m \cdot r^n \mod n^2)$ which $n = pq$ and p, q are two same-length prime numbers, and g is a proper member of group $\mathbb{Z}_{n^2}^*$. Its homomorphic property allows us to evaluate the polynomial without decrypting the coefficients of the polynomials. Further it allows an efficient multi-party computation protocol to compare and (and hence sort) ciphertexts by plaintext values without decryption [13]. This algorithm is linear in the bit length, i.e. logarithmic in the security parameter, and can be made public verifiable [12]. Using this technique allows us to do the weeding process secure and efficient, but at the cost of all ballots being submitted with a voter identifier. To achieve participation privacy, obfuscating votes needs to be cast too.

eVoting Protocol with Paillier Instantiation: In Set-Up phase, CA generates the pair of keys, for Paillier cryptosystem: $\mathsf{pk} = (n = pq, \mathbb{G}, g)$, $\mathsf{sk} = (p, q)$

1. **Registration Phase:** For voter V_{id} the registrar, does the following steps:
   - Long credential: Pick $\mathsf{crd} \leftarrow \mathbb{Z}_n$, store crd on voter's device.
   - Short credential: Pick random PIN $a \in$ PIN-Set and send it to voter V_{id}.
   - Compute the error list for a based on the election policy: $\mathsf{ErrorList}_a = \{a_1 = a, a_2, \dots, a_k\}$ and set $\mathsf{poly}_{id} = \prod_{i=1}^{k}(x - \mathsf{crd} - a_i) = \sum_{i=0}^{k} p_i x^i$
   - Encrypt polynomial coefficients: For $i = 0, \dots k$: $\mathsf{cp}_i = \mathsf{Enc}(p_i)$
   - Provide a designated proof of validity for the ciphertexts, cp_i, $i = 0, \dots k$.
   - Publish $V_{id} : \big(\mathsf{CP} = (\mathsf{cp}_0, \dots, \mathsf{cp}_k), \mathsf{Enc}(\mathsf{crd})\big)$ on bulletin board.
2. **Casting ballot:** Voter chooses her candidate m, and enter her choice of PIN, $\hat{a}$. The voting algorithm runs the following steps:
   - Encrypt m and long credential, $\mathsf{CT}_{vote} = \mathsf{Enc}(m)$, $\mathsf{CT}_{crd} = \mathsf{Enc}(\mathsf{crd})$
   - For $i = 1, \dots, k$ compute $\mathsf{cp}_i^* = \mathsf{cp}_i^{(\hat{a}+\mathsf{crd})^i} \cdot r_i^{*n}$ and $\mathsf{CT}_i = \mathsf{Enc}((\hat{a}+\mathsf{crd})^i)$ for random number r_i, r_i^*. Provide a proof, π_{ballot}, (also proof of knowledge) for the following relation:

$$R_{ballot} = \Big\{ (x, w), x = (\mathsf{CT}_{vote}, \mathsf{CT}_{crd}, \mathsf{CT}_i, \mathsf{CP} = (\mathsf{cp}_i)_{i \in [k]}, \mathsf{CP}^* = (\mathsf{cp}_i^*)_{i \in [k]})$$
$$w = (\mathsf{vote}, r_{vote}, \hat{a}, \mathsf{crd}, r_{crd}, \{r_i, r_i^*\}_{i \in [k]}) :$$
$$\mathsf{CT}_{vote} = g^{\mathsf{vote}} \cdot h^{r_{vote}}, , \mathsf{vote} \in \text{List of candidats}, \mathsf{CT} = g^{\mathsf{crd}} \cdot h^{r_{crd}},$$
$$i = 1, \dots, k : \mathsf{CT}_i = g^{(\mathsf{crd}+\hat{a})^i} \cdot h^{r_i}, \mathsf{cp}_i^* = \mathsf{cp}^{(\mathsf{crd}+\hat{a})^i} \cdot h^{r_i^*} \Big\}$$

This proof can be implemented efficiently using Sigma protocols and will rely on the DDH assumption, and will be given in a long version of the paper. They can be made non-interactive using the strong Fiat-Shamir heuristic. Note that the hash should contain all parts of the ballot.
   - Cast $\mathsf{ballot}_V = (\mathsf{CT}_{crd}, \mathsf{CT}_{vote}, \{\mathsf{cp}_1^*, \dots, \mathsf{cp}_k^*\}, \pi_{ballot})$ with her ID.
   - Obfuscate: Everybody can cast (invalid) votes with any voter ID. This will obfuscate whether voter ID participated in the election as in [6,11]
3. **Tally Phase:** Using the Paillier encryption scheme, allows us to efficiently sort ciphertexts based on plaintext values without decrypting them, see [13]. This techniques can be done in a multi-party computation which provide privacy for the e-voting protocol. MPC_{min} the algorithm that takes as input the ciphertexts $\mathsf{ct}_1 = \mathsf{Enc}(m_1), \mathsf{ct}_2 = \mathsf{Enc}(m_2), \dots, \mathsf{ct}_t = \mathsf{Enc}(m_t)$ and outputs the index i^* such that $\mathsf{ct}_{i^*} = \mathsf{Enc}(m_{i^*}) : m_{i^*} = \min\{m_1, \dots, m_t\}$. We use this algorithm in the Tally phase:
   - **Ballot Validity check:** In the first step, we remove exact ballot copies and all ballots with invalid proof π_{ballot}. In the next step we need to remove extra ballots for each voter, making sure a valid ballot is kept, if existing.
   - **Weeding:** Since each voter will be associated with possibly more than one ballot, we need to weed them. We make sure a valid ballot is chosen - if existing. Assume there are q ballots with the same ID, $\mathsf{ballot}_1, \dots, \mathsf{ballot}_q$, We now homomorphically combine the public ciphertext cp_0 with the

submitted encryptions to obtain an encrypted polynomial evaluation for each ballot: $\mathsf{Enc}(\mathsf{poly}_{\mathsf{id}}(\mathsf{crd}_i + \hat{a}_i)) = \mathsf{cp}_0 \cdot \prod_{j=1}^{k} \mathsf{cp}_j^*, i = 1, \ldots q$. Denote by $t_i = \mathsf{poly}_{\mathsf{id}}(\mathsf{crd}_i + \hat{a}_i)$ and note this is zero if the ballot has a valid credential and pin. We now verifiably mix the pairs $\mathsf{Enc}(t_i), \mathsf{Enc}(\mathsf{vote}_i)$ and run the $\mathsf{MPC}_{\min}$ algorithm on the first ciphertexts to determine the one with the minimal t_i. We only keep this ciphertext and the corresponding encrypted vote and discard the rest. Note that this will select valid ballots having $t_i = 0$ if they exist.[4]

- **Ballot anonymization:** We delete the ID, run all the remaing pairs $\mathsf{Enc}(t), \mathsf{Enc}(\mathsf{vote})$ through a verifiable parallel mixnet for re-encryption and permutation.
- **Final PIN and Credential validity check:** Finally, for each ballot, we decrypt the polynomial evaluation. All ballots with non-zero polynomial evaluation will be discarded. We need to do this step without revealing any information about t_i for non-zero evaluation. Thus the tally tellers first jointly and verifiably multiply some random number onto t_i and then decrypt. We accept ballots with output zero and discard the rest.
- **Vote decryption:** Decrypt the remaining vote ciphertexts and compute the voting result.

Error Tolerance Property of the Scheme: Note the following computation:

$$\mathsf{cp}_i = g^{p_i} \cdot r_i^n \, , \ \mathsf{cp}_i^* = \mathsf{cp}_i^{(\hat{a}+\mathsf{crd})^i} \cdot r_i^{*n} \Rightarrow \mathsf{cp}_i^* = g^{(\hat{a}+\mathsf{crd})^i p_i} \cdot r_i'^{n}$$

$$\Rightarrow \mathsf{cp}_0 \cdot \prod_{i=1}^{k} \mathsf{cp}_i^* = g^{\sum_{i=0}^{n}(\hat{a}+\mathsf{crd})^i p_i} \cdot r^n = g^{\mathsf{Poly}_{\mathsf{id}}(\mathsf{crd}+\hat{a})} \cdot r^n$$

Decrypting this gives us the polynomial evaluation. Note that this evaluation will only check if $\hat{a} + \mathsf{crd}$ is valid. This should be sufficient for security. However, to check that both the credential is corrected and the PIN is in the allowed space, we can use a distributed plaintext equivalence test [21] between the submitted credential and the registrered credential and add the outcome under encryption to the polynomial evaluation.

Security Analysis: The main advantage of this instantiation is sorting the ciphertexts without decrypting them. Note that $\mathsf{poly}_{\mathsf{id,PIN}}$ has the range in nonnegative integers. Therefore if there is any ballot with valid credential and PIN, the output of $\mathsf{MPC}_{\min}$ will be a valid ballot. On the other hand, it does not reveal whether any ballot has a valid pin or not, thus sidestepping the attack on the standard duplicate removal.

3.2 BGN Instantiation

The second instantiation is based on composite order groups introduced by [3] and the Groth-Sahai NIWI-proof system [7] with security are based on the Subgroup decision assumption.

---

[4] This will give a random correct vote. The policy "Last valid vote counts" can be implemented by adding the received order to t_i.

The main point of using those in this instantiation are, BGN is a homomorphic encryption scheme which can be efficiently implemented in a bilinear group. Having bilinear map allows us to do the polynomial evaluation in an efficient and secure way and also having the efficient NIWI-proof system.

Definition 1. *BGN Cryptosystem works as follows. Its Key-Generation algorithm,* KGen *outputs a pair of keys:* $\left(\mathsf{pk} = (n, \mathbb{G}, \mathbb{G}_T, \mathsf{e}, g, h = g'^q), \mathsf{sk} = (p, q)\right)$ *which* $\mathbb{G} = \langle g \rangle$ *and* $\mathbb{G}_T$ *are two groups of order* n *and the secret key consists of two primes* p, q *such that* $n = pq$. $\mathsf{e} : \mathbb{G} \times \mathbb{G} \to \mathbb{G}_T$ *is bilinear* $(\forall a, b \in \mathbb{Z}, g \in \mathbb{G} : \mathsf{e}(g^a, g^b) = \mathsf{e}(g, g)^{ab})$, *non-degenerate* $(\mathbb{G} = \langle g \rangle \Rightarrow \mathsf{e}(g, g) \neq 1_{\mathbb{G}_T})$ *and commutable map. A ciphertext on message* $m \in [T]$, *for* $T < q$ *has the form* $\mathsf{CT} = g^m h^r \in \mathbb{G}$ *for some random number* r. *Decryption: raise the ciphertext to power* p *and compute the discrete log.*

BGN E-voting Protocol:

1. **SetUp Phase:** The central authority runs the BGN key-generation algorithm to generate $(\mathsf{sk}_{\mathsf{BGN}} = p, q, \mathsf{pk}_{\mathsf{BGN}} = (n, \mathbb{G}, \mathbb{G}_T, \mathsf{e}, g, h)$. Then chooses four random group elements $f_1, f_2, f_3, f_4 \in \mathbb{G}$. Note that $\mathbb{G} = \langle g \rangle$ is a cyclic group so there exists a unique integers $z_i, i \in [4]$ such that $f_i = g^{z_i}$. Set the secret key of election as $\mathsf{SK}_{\mathsf{election}} = (p, f_1, f_2, f_3, f_4)$ and public key of election as $\mathsf{PK}_{\mathsf{election}} = (n, \mathbb{G}, \mathbb{G}_T, \mathsf{e}, g, h)$. Publish $\mathsf{PK}_{\mathsf{election}}$ on the bulletin board.

2. **Registration Phase:** Registrar, $\mathcal{R}$, for voter V does the following steps:
   - Generate credential and pin: crd, a as in the Paillier instantiation.
   - Generate the list of errors, $\mathsf{ErrorList}_a = \{a_1 = a, a_2, \ldots, a_k\}$. Then compute $\mathsf{poly}_a = \prod_{i=1}^{k}(x - a_i) = \sum_{i=0}^{k} p_i x^i$ and the following ciphertexts: $i \in [k] : \mathsf{cp}_i = \mathsf{Enc}(p_i) = g^{p_i} h^{r_i}, \mathsf{cp}_0 = g^{p_0} \cdot f_1^{\mathsf{crd}} h^r = \mathsf{Enc}(p_0 + \mathsf{crd} \times z_1)$. Note that, technically cp_0 is the encryption of $p_0 + \mathsf{crd} \times z_1$. Although z_1 is not a known value to any parties, the registrar can compute cp_0 without knowing its value.
   - Generates a designated proof of validity of the polynomial poly_a and all cp_i, for $i = 0, \ldots k$.
   - Store $\mathsf{CP} = (\mathsf{cp}_0, \mathsf{cp}_1, \ldots, \mathsf{cp}_k), \mathsf{CRD} = g^{\mathsf{crd}}$ in the user device and publish $\mathsf{Enc}(\mathsf{crd}) = g^{\mathsf{crd}} \cdot h^r, \mathsf{CP}$ on bulletin board.

3. **Casting ballot:** Voter V chooses her candidate vote, and enter her choice of PIN, $\hat{a}$. The voting algorithm runs the following steps:
   - Compute, $\mathsf{CT}_{\mathsf{vote}} = \mathsf{Enc}(\mathsf{vote})$ and $\mathsf{CT}_{\mathsf{crd}} = \mathsf{Enc}(\mathsf{crd}) = \mathsf{CRD} \cdot h^r$.
   - PIN encryption: For $i = 1, \ldots, k$ compute $\mathsf{CA}_i = \mathsf{Enc}(\hat{a}^i)$.
   - Re-randomize cp_i for $i = 0, \ldots, k$ by multiplying in a random $h^{r_i^*}$ to generate cp_i^*.
   - Set $\mathsf{CA} = (\mathsf{CA}_1, \ldots, \mathsf{CA}_k), \mathsf{CP}^* = (\mathsf{cp}_0^*, \ldots, \mathsf{cp}_k^*)$ and provide a proof (Proof of knowledge), π_{ballot} for the following relation, including a joint proof of plaintext-knowledge for all the other ciphertexts in the ballot and include the rest of the ballot in the hash for non-malleability. This proof can be generated using the Groth-Sahai technique.

$$R_{\text{ballot}} = \Big\{ (x, w), x = (\mathsf{CT}_{\text{vote}}, \mathsf{CT}_{\text{crd}}, \mathsf{CA}), w = (\mathsf{vote}, r_{\text{vote}}, \mathsf{CRD}, r_{\text{crd}}, \hat{a}, \{r_i\}_{i \in [k]}) :$$
$$\mathsf{CT}_{\text{vote}} = g^{\text{vote}} \cdot h^{r_{\text{vote}}}, \mathsf{vote} \in \texttt{List of candidats},$$
$$\mathsf{CT}_{\text{crd}} = \mathsf{CRD} \cdot h^{r_{\text{crd}}}, \{\mathsf{CA}_i = g^{(\hat{a})^i} \cdot h^{r_i}\}_{i=1,\dots,k} \Big\}$$

- Cast ballot $= (\mathsf{CT}_{\text{vote}}, \mathsf{CT}_{\mathsf{CRD}}, \mathsf{CA}, \mathsf{CP}^*, \pi_{\text{ballot}})$

Polynomial Evaluation: The following computation shows how to evaluate the polynomial on the input value $\hat{a}$, the PIN that was used by the voter:

$$\mathbf{e}(\mathsf{CT}_{\text{crd}}, f_1)^{-1} \cdot \mathbf{e}(\mathsf{cp}_0^*, g) \cdot \mathbf{e}(\mathsf{cp}_1^*, CA_1) \cdots \mathbf{e}(\mathsf{cp}_k^*, CA_k) =$$
$$\mathbf{e}(\mathsf{CRD} \cdot h^r, f_1)^{-1} \cdot \mathbf{e}(g^{p_0}(f_1)^{\text{crd}} h^{r_0}, g) \cdot \mathbf{e}(g^{p_1} h^{r_1}, g^{\alpha_i} h^{\gamma_i}) \cdot \dots \mathbf{e}(g^{p_k} h^{r_k}, g^{\alpha_k} h^{\gamma_k}) =$$
$$\mathbf{e}(\mathsf{CRD}, f_1)^{-1} \cdot \mathbf{e}(h, f_1)^{-r} \mathbf{e}(g^{p_0} f_1^{\text{crd}} h^{r_0}, g) \cdot \mathbf{e}(g^{p_1} h^{r_1}, g^{a^i} h^{\gamma_i}) \cdot \dots \mathbf{e}(g^{p_k} h^{r_k}, g^{a^k} h^{\gamma_k}) =$$
$$\mathbf{e}(\mathsf{CRD}, f_1)^{-1} \mathbf{e}(f_1, h^r) \mathbf{e}(f_1, \mathsf{CRD}) \mathbf{e}(g^{p_0} h^{r_0}, g) \cdot \mathbf{e}(g^{p_1} h^{r_1}, g^{a^i} h^{\gamma_i}) \cdot \dots \mathbf{e}(g^{p_k} h^{r_k}, g^{a^k} h^{\gamma_k}) =$$
$$\cdot \mathbf{e}(h^r, f_1) \Big(\prod_{i=0}^{k} \mathbf{e}(g^{p_i}, g^{\alpha_i})\Big) \cdot \Big(\prod_{i=0}^{k} \mathbf{e}(g^{p_i}, h^{\gamma_i})\Big) \cdot \Big(\prod_{i=0}^{k} \mathbf{e}(g^{\alpha_i}, h^{r_i})\Big) \Big(\prod_{i=0}^{k} \mathbf{e}(h^{\gamma_i}, h^{r_i})\Big)$$
$$\mathbf{e}(g, g^{\sum_{i=0}^{k} p_i \alpha_i})\big) \cdot \mathbf{e}(g, h^r) = \mathbf{e}(g, g^{\text{poly}_a(\hat{a})}) \cdot \mathbf{e}(g, h^r)$$

Hence, if we raise above term to power p, if $\text{poly}_a(\hat{a}) = 0$ the result is equal to 1 and otherwise not. Due to the secret f_1 and zero-knowledge proofs, malicious voters cannot construct a zero-evaluation dishonestly.

- **Tally Phase:** First, we check the validity of the proofs, π_{ballot}. In case any of any failure, the ballot will be discarded.

- Step 1: Compute the encrypted polynomial evaluation as above and provide a proof of its validity (efficient using the Groth-Sahai technique). Call this $\mathsf{Enc}_T(t)$ with t being the polynomial evaluation which can be seen as an encryption in the target space. Note that this is computed from the ballot alone. Now verifiably mix the tuples $(\mathsf{CT}_{\text{crd}}, \mathsf{CT}_{\text{vote}}, \mathsf{Enc}_T(t))$. For each ballot we now create $\mathsf{Enc}_T(\mathsf{crd} + t)$ and remove duplicates ballot having the same $\mathsf{crd} + t$ which basically means same credential and same error-equivalent PIN for honest ballots. We will do this via PETs. If we have a small number of voters, we can mix between each duplicate removal. For a larger number we suggest to split the board in two, remove duplicates separately, then mix and do duplicate removal again. This will decrease the information from the distribution of confirmed duplicates to a coercer carrying out the "leaky duplicate removal attack" mentioned in Sect. 2.
- Step 2: We now want to select eligible valid votes. We mix the above list and the list of registered encrypted credential. Then we perform PETs between each registered credential and the submitted credential and homomorphically add the polynomial value to this before decrypting the result. This will be

one if the credential is correct and the polynomial evaluation is correct. When we get a positive test result we do a further PET against the credentials. This will reveal malicous authorities creating valid polynomial evaluations on their own. If this is positive too, we decrypt the vote and continue to the next registered credential.

4 PIN Space Coverings

Our voting protocol ensures that the voter's credential is validated even if they make certain typos in their PIN. This could e.g. be a transposition error or a single wrong digit.

The interesting question from a security viewpoint is now how much this reduces the entropy of the PINs. To have a precise research question, we investigate how many PINs an attacker needs to try to cover the whole PIN space. This is related to the brute force attack of an attacker holding the real credential e.g. in the smart card. We will not solve this exactly in generality, but give some upper and lower bounds. Note also, that users generally are not good at choosing random PINs as revealed in PIN frequency analyses. We thus recommend that the PIN should be generated uniformly at random and not chosen by the voter.

We first focus on the case where we allow PIN swaps and an error in one digit. Let us denote the PIN by $p_1 p_2 \cdots p_k$. We first compute the number of PINs covered by a PIN try. Let us start with the case $k = 2$. By $[p_1 p_2]$, we mean the set of numbers covered by this PIN. Clearly $[p_1 p_2] = \{p_1 p_2, p_2 p_1, p_1*, *p_2\}$, where $* \in \{0, 1, 2, \ldots, 9\}$. After removing the repeated cases we will have $||[p_1 p_2]|| = 20$ for the case $p_1 \neq p_2$ and it will be 19 for the case $p_1 = p_2$. Actually, for $2r$ distinct digits $p_1, \ldots, p_{2r}$, one can verify that the r 2-digits numbers $p_1 p_2, p_3 p_4, \ldots, p_{2r-1} p_{2r}$ will cover a total of $20r - 2\binom{r}{2}$ PINs. The formula can also be used to give an upper bound of PINs cover by r PIN trys, and thus it shows that the attacker needs at least 8 PINs to cover the entire PIN space of all 2-digits numbers. Since the attacker is trying to cover the PIN space with the minimum number of attempts, a good strategy seems to be to add PINs with distinct digits as much as possible to the basis. In the case there is no possible new PIN with distinct digits, we will then add a PIN which increase the size of current basis the most, and so forth until the PIN space is covered. We have implemented an algorithm in Python following this idea, but using random sampling to find the next optimal element for efficiency. For the case of 2-digits PIN, a basis of size 9 was found which is close to the theoretical lower bound.

Let us now consider the case of 3-digit PINs. For any PIN $p_1 p_2 p_3$ the maximum size of all covered PIN, $||[p_1 p_2 p_3]||$ is 30. Therefore 34 will be an lower bound for the size of basis of PIN space in this case.

Assume that only swapping errors are tolerated. For 2-digit PINs, finding a basis is equivalent to finding a basis for upper triangular matrices. There the basis size is 55 which the Python code also finds. For $k \geq 3$, an upper estimate of the cover of a single PIN is k (including itself) thus $10^k / k$ is a lower bound.

We collect the lower theoretical bounds and the upper bounds resulting from our Python code for PIN lengths between 2 and 5 in Table 1. We ran the code 1000 times in the case of 2,3 and 4 and just one time for the case 5.

Table 1. S+W means the system accepts swapping errors and wrong digit errors, where S means a system that just tolerate swapping errors.

PIN length	2	3	4	5
S+W lower bound	8	34	250	2000
S+W upper bound	9	78	713	6490
S upper bound	55	465	4131	

5   Conclusions and Outlook

In this paper we have presented attacks and repairs on the NV12 scheme, especially, we have also presented protocols which are resilient to human errors in the form of PIN typos. It is interesting to notice that the digitally stored key could be combined or replaced with a key derived from biometric data. An important future direction is to make the error correction here so efficient that we can allow using noisy biometric data without fuzzy extraction.

For the Paillier-based system that we have presented it would be natural to add the tally system from Ordinos [12] since this is also based on Paillier encryption. Ordinos will only reveal the winner or the ranking of the candidates in the election, and will thus help for coercion-resistance in the case where there are candidates which expected to only get few or no votes. Another method that could used in both protocols is the risk-limiting tally method described in [9] which gives plausible deniability for the voter.

The PIN space analysis might be of general interest, and more precise results should be found. Interestingly, the one-digit error in k-digit PINs is related to Rook-polynomials, [1], in a k-dimensional chessboard.

Finally, some socio-tehcnical research questions are: 1) Which type of PIN errors do voters do when the are in a vote setting and do not get any feedback on the correctness of the PIN. 2) Related to this, what it the optimal PIN policy that corrects as many PIN typos while still keeping the entropy of the PIN space sufficiently high. 3) If we do not use a smart card, or use both a smart card and key storage: how well can voters be trained to handle, fake and hide secret keys.

Of course a main missing part is to provide proofs of security for our protocols.

Acknowledgments. This work was supported by the Luxembourg National Research Fund (FNR) and the Research Council of Norway for the joint project SURCVS and by the FNR CORE project FESS.

References

1. Allenby, R.B.J.T., Slomson, A.: How to Count: An Introduction to Combinatorics. Discrete Mathematics and Its Applications, 2nd edn. Taylor & Francis, New York (2011)
2. Araújo, R., Barki, A., Brunet, S., Traoré, J.: Remote electronic voting can be efficient, verifiable and coercion-resistant. In: Clark, J., Meiklejohn, S., Ryan, P.Y.A., Wallach, D., Brenner, M., Rohloff, K. (eds.) FC 2016. LNCS, vol. 9604, pp. 224–232. Springer, Heidelberg (2016). https://doi.org/10.1007/978-3-662-53357-4_15
3. Boneh, D., Goh, E., Nissim, K.: Evaluating 2-DNF formulas on ciphertexts. In: TCC, pp. 325–341 (2005)
4. Clarkson, M.R., Chong, S., Myers, A.C.: Civitas: toward a secure voting system. In: 2008 IEEE Symposium on Security and Privacy, 18–21 May 2008, Oakland, California, USA, pp. 354–368. IEEE Computer Society (2008)
5. Feier, C., Neumann, S., Volkamer, M.: Coercion-resistant internet voting in practice. In: Plödereder, E., Grunske, L., Schneider, E., Ull, D., (eds.) 44. Jahrestagung der Gesellschaft für Informatik, Informatik 2014, Big Data - Komplexität meistern, 2014, vol. P-232 of LNI, pp. 1401–1414. GI (2014)
6. Grontas, P., Pagourtzis, A., Zacharakis, A., Zhang, B.: Towards everlasting privacy and efficient coercion resistance in remote electronic voting. In: Zohar, A., et al. (eds.) FC 2018. LNCS, vol. 10958, pp. 210–231. Springer, Heidelberg (2019). https://doi.org/10.1007/978-3-662-58820-8_15
7. Groth, J., Sahai, A.: Efficient non-interactive proof systems for bilinear groups. In: Smart, N. (ed.) EUROCRYPT 2008. LNCS, vol. 4965, pp. 415–432. Springer, Heidelberg (2008). https://doi.org/10.1007/978-3-540-78967-3_24
8. Iovino, V., Rial, A., Rønne, P.B., Ryan, P.Y.A.: Using selene to verify your vote in JCJ. In: Brenner, M., et al. (eds.) FC 2017. LNCS, vol. 10323, pp. 385–403. Springer, Cham (2017). https://doi.org/10.1007/978-3-319-70278-0_24
9. Jamroga, W., Roenne, P.B., Ryan, P.Y.A., Stark, P.B.: Risk-limiting tallies. In: Krimmer, R., et al. (eds.) E-Vote-ID 2019. LNCS, vol. 11759, pp. 183–199. Springer, Cham (2019). https://doi.org/10.1007/978-3-030-30625-0_12
10. Juels, A., Catalano, D., Jakobsson, M.: Coercion-resistant electronic elections. In: Chaum, D., et al. (eds.) Towards Trustworthy Elections. LNCS, vol. 6000, pp. 37–63. Springer, Heidelberg (2010). https://doi.org/10.1007/978-3-642-12980-3_2
11. Kulyk, O., Teague, V., Volkamer, M.: Extending helios towards private eligibility verifiability. In: Haenni, R., Koenig, R.E., Wikström, D. (eds.) E-Voting and Identity, pp. 57–73. Springer International Publishing, Cham (2015)
12. Küsters, R., Liedtke, J., Mueller, J., Rausch, D., Vogt, A.: Ordinos: a verifiable tally-hiding e-voting system. IACR Cryptol. ePrint Arch. **2020**, 405 (2020)
13. Lipmaa, H., Toft, T.: Secure equality and greater-than tests with sublinear online complexity. In: Fomin, F.V., Freivalds, R., Kwiatkowska, M., Peleg, D. (eds.) ICALP 2013. LNCS, vol. 7966, pp. 645–656. Springer, Heidelberg (2013). https://doi.org/10.1007/978-3-642-39212-2_56
14. Silva Neto, A., Leite, M., Araújo, R., Pereira Mota, M., Sampaio Neto, N., Traoré, J.: Usability considerations for coercion-resistant election systems. In: Mota, M., Serique Meiguins, B., Prates, R., Candello, H., (eds.) Proceedings of the 17th Brazilian Symposium on Human Factors in Computing Systems, IHC 2018, Brazil, 2018, pp. 40:1–40:10. ACM (2018)
15. Neumann, S., Feier, C., Volkamer, M., Koenig, R.: Towards a practical JCJ/Civitas implementation. In: INFORMATIK 2013-Informatik angepasst an Mensch, Organisation und Umwelt (2013)

16. Neumann, S., Volkamer, M.: Civitas and the real world: problems and solutions from a practical point of view. In: Seventh International Conference on Availability, Reliability and Security, Prague, ARES 2012, Czech Republic, 20–24 August 2012, pp. 180–185. IEEE Computer Society (2012)
17. Roenne, P.B.: JCJ with improved verifiability guarantees. In: The International Conference on Electronic Voting E-Vote-ID 2016 (2016)
18. Rønne, P.B., Atashpendar, A., Gjøsteen, K., Ryan, P.Y.A.: Coercion-resistant voting in linear time via fully homomorphic encryption: towards a quantum-safe scheme. arXiv preprint arXiv:1901.02560 (2019)
19. Shamir, A., van Someren, N.: Playing 'Hide and Seek' with Stored Keys. In: Franklin, M. (ed.) FC 1999. LNCS, vol. 1648, pp. 118–124. Springer, Heidelberg (1999). https://doi.org/10.1007/3-540-48390-X_9
20. Spycher, O., Koenig, R., Haenni, R., Schläpfer, M.: A new approach towards coercion-resistant remote e-voting in linear time. In: Danezis, G. (ed.) FC 2011. LNCS, vol. 7035, pp. 182–189. Springer, Heidelberg (2012). https://doi.org/10.1007/978-3-642-27576-0_15
21. Ting, P.-Y., Huang, X.-W.: Distributed paillier plaintext equivalence test. Int. J. Netw. Secur. 6(3), 258–264 (2008)
22. Wiseman, S., Cairns, P., Cox, A.: A taxonomy of number entry error. In: Proceedings of the 25th BCS Conference on Human-Computer Interaction, pp. 187–196. British Computer Society (2011)

Privacy-Preserving Dispute Resolution in the Improved Bingo Voting

Rosario Giustolisi$^{(\boxtimes)}$ and Alessandro Bruni

IT University of Copenhagen, Copenhagen, Denmark
{rosg,brun}@itu.dk

Abstract. Dispute resolution mechanisms are important components of voting schemes, deterring a voting authority to change the election outcome as any alteration can be *proved* by such mechanisms. However, these mechanisms are useless if not triggered by voters, who should not have to choose to either raise a dispute or keep their vote private. Hence, voting schemes should include privacy-preserving dispute resolution.

In this work, we advance the formal analysis in the symbolic model of an improved version of the Bingo Voting scheme, whose enhancements include privacy-preserving dispute resolution mechanisms. Most of our analysis of several verification, dispute resolution, and privacy properties is done automatically using ProVerif, which we complement with manual induction proofs as necessary. We find that the scheme meets some properties only if one makes additional trust assumptions to those stated in [6]. For example, we find that dispute resolution is met assuming an honest voting authority. Moreover, our work provides an understanding of privacy-preserving dispute resolution in general, which can be beneficial to similar analyses of other voting schemes.

1 Introduction

Consensus on the election outcome and vote privacy are two main pillars of voting schemes. On the one hand, voting schemes that fail in achieving consensus are worthless, hence a voting scheme should provide high confidence in the result of the election despite voters do not necessarily trust the voting authority. On the other hand, failing to provide vote privacy opens to effective manipulation of voters and to control the outcome of the election. Intuitively, consensus on the election outcome and vote privacy seem to be two contrasting properties: more evidence would increase confidence in the election outcome at the risk of fewer privacy guarantees. Recent work [12] has shown that vote privacy implies individual verifiability. However, individual verifiability only enables a voter to *check* that her ballot has been counted, but not to publicly *prove* it. This means that a dishonest voting authority may still change the election outcome and there is no public evidence that could prove so.

One can deter a voting authority from changing the election outcome by introducing dispute resolution mechanisms that enable a voter to prove to any observer that her vote was not included in the tally. This should be possible

© Springer Nature Switzerland AG 2020
R. Krimmer et al. (Eds.): E-Vote-ID 2020, LNCS 12455, pp. 67–83, 2020.
https://doi.org/10.1007/978-3-030-60347-2_5

for the voter without giving up vote privacy, hence dispute resolution should be privacy-preserving.

In this paper, we provide a formal analysis of an improved version of the Bingo Voting scheme [6,18], which aims at ensuring privacy-preserving dispute resolution mechanisms among other features. We check automatically several verification, dispute resolution, and privacy properties in ProVerif, and identify the additional trust assumptions required by the scheme respect to the ones stated in [18]. To the best of our knowledge, this work represents the first formal treatment of the improved version of Bingo Voting. We provide the precise algorithm that enables an observer to dispute the outcome of an election and details the aftermath of a privacy-preserving dispute resolution at the voting phase, considering different mitigation scenarios. The outcome of our analysis pinpoints the difficulties in designing privacy-preserving dispute resolution mechanisms and can be useful for other voting schemes.

Outline. This paper is organised as follows. Section 2 details the improved Bingo Voting scheme as well as its properties and trust assumptions. Section 3 presents the formal analysis of verification, dispute resolution, and privacy properties in the improved Bingo Voting. Then, it discusses the outcome of the analysis. Section 4 presents some related work. Finally, Sect. 5 concludes the paper.

2   Background

Bingo Voting was originally proposed by Bohli, Müller-Quade and Röhrich in 2007 [7]. The underlying idea of Bingo Voting is that each voter receipt assigns to each candidate either a *dummy* random number or a *fresh* random number. The voting authority generates the dummy random numbers before the voting phase starts. A trusted random generator (TRNG) creates the fresh random numbers during the voting phase. The voting machine then assigns the fresh random number to the candidate chosen by the voter and a different dummy random number to each of the remaining candidates.

In Bohli et al. [6] and later in Henrich [18], several improvements are proposed to the original Bingo Voting system, including extensions to use Bingo Voting for more complex elections and ways to address usability limitations. In this paper, we consider two key improvements, hence we will refer to the resulting system as the *improved Bingo Voting*. The first improvement that we consider consists of two privacy-preserving dispute resolution procedures, one at the voting and the other at tallying. The other improvement regards the optimisation of the proof of correct distribution of dummy votes, which in the improved version is done after the voting phase. Figure 1 presents a message sequence chart of the scheme. The details of the scheme are outlined below.

Before the voting phase, the voting authority generates and publishes a set of *dummy votes*. A dummy vote consists of a pair of Pedersen commitments that hide both the dummy random number and the assigned candidate. Each candidate receives the same number of dummy votes, that is, the number of

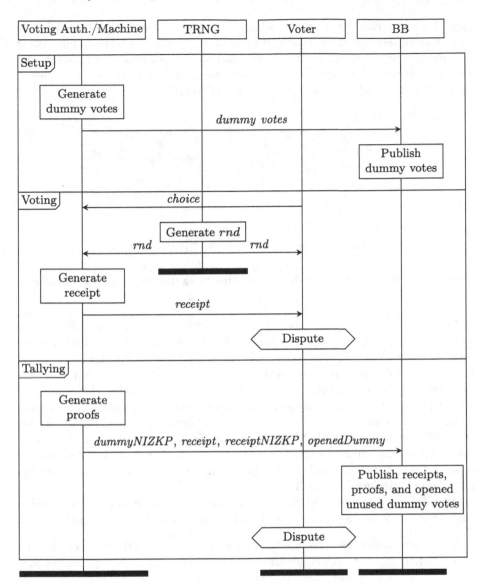

Fig. 1. Message sequence chart of the improved Bingo Voting

registered voters. Thus, the total number of generated dummy votes is equal to the product of the number of voters and the number of candidates.

Inside the voting booth, a display shows the fresh random number generated by the TRNG. The voter records her choice on a paper ballot and feeds it into the voting machine, which is equipped with a scanner-based interface. The voting machine scans the paper ballot and generates a receipt such that the fresh random number is printed next to the name of the candidate chosen by the voter.

Unused dummy random numbers, which the voting authority generated before the voting phase, are instead printed next to any other candidates. The voting machine also prints an identical barcode onto both paper ballot and receipt, and keeps the paper ballot inside a special compartment unless the voter decides to raise a dispute should she receive an incorrect receipt.

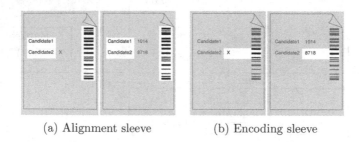

(a) Alignment sleeve   (b) Encoding sleeve

Fig. 2. The privacy sleeves for the privacy-preserving dispute resolution at voting

In the case of a dispute, the voter can use two different pairs of privacy sleeves to prove that the printed receipt is incorrect, without revealing the way she voted. Each pair of privacy sleeves is to be used with both paper ballot and receipt. The first type of privacy sleeve leaves uncovered candidate names and the barcodes (see Fig. 2a) and enables a third party to check whether the candidates are not placed identically in respect to the barcode on the paper ballot and the receipt. The second type of privacy sleeve leaves uncovered the marking area for one candidate on the paper ballot and one row of random numbers on the receipt (see Fig. 2b). This enables a third party to check whether there is a discrepancy between the voter choice and the receipt as the printed random number differs from the one displayed on the TRNG.

At tallying, the voting authority publishes the final result of the election along with the following sets of data on an append-only bulletin board

- A non-interactive zero-knowledge proof of correct distribution of dummy votes showing that each candidate gets the same number of dummy votes.
- A non-interactive zero-knowledge proof for each receipt showing that it contains the correct amount of dummy random numbers and that each dummy random number is assigned to the right candidate.
- The list of all printed receipts.
- The list of opened unused dummy votes, which determines how many votes each candidate has received.

Since all the receipts are published, every voter can verify whether their vote is correctly counted. If not, they can raise a privacy-preserving dispute resolution at tallying proving that their receipt has not been published. Morever, any observer can check the correctness of the election outcome by verifying that the tally is indeed the sum of all votes cast.

Properties. The improved Bingo Voting aims at the following properties:

- *Individual verifiability*: a voter can check that the receipt encodes her vote.
- *Privacy-preserving dispute resolution at voting*[1]: a voter can prove that the receipt incorrectly encodes her vote, without revealing her vote.
- *Privacy-preserving dispute resolution at tallying*[2]: a voter can prove that her receipt is not in the bulletin board, without revealing her vote.
- *Global verification*: anyone can prove that the tally is incorrectly computed.
- *Vote privacy*: No one knows how the voter votes.
- *Receipt freeness*: The voter has no evidence proving how she voted.
- *Coercion resistance*: A voter deviating from the intended voting process receives no evidence that may be used to prove how she voted.

The improved Bingo Voting requires a number of trust assumptions to meet the security properties outlined above. The most important are that only eligible voters get access to a voting machine and that each voter casts a single ballot. Also, it is assumed that voters are unobserved as they cast their ballot, which is known as the *voting booth assumption*. Bulletin board (BB) and TRNG are always considered uncorrupted. For vote privacy, it can be assumed that both voting authority and the voting machine can be dishonest as soon as they do not communicate. For receipt freeness and coercion resistance, the voting authority should be uncorrupted, and the voting machine should not be able to communicate with an attacker. In the next section, we analyse the improved Bingo Voting in ProVerif to determine any necessary additional assumptions.

3   Formal Analysis

ProVerif [5] allows one to analyse reachability and equivalence-based properties in the symbolic attacker model. We chose ProVerif mainly because its input language fits well with our approach in modelling the verification and dispute resolution mechanisms. It is also one of the few tools that enable the automated analysis of privacy properties using observational equivalence. The input language of ProVerif is the applied π-calculus [1], which the tool automatically translates to Horn clauses. Cryptographic primitives can be modelled by means of equational theories. An equational theory E describes the equations that hold on terms built from the signature. Terms are related by an equivalence relation $=$ induced by E. For instance, the equation $dec(enc(m, pk(k)), k) = m$ models an asymmetric encryption scheme. The term m is the message, the term k is the secret key, the function $pk(k)$ models the public key, the term enc models the encryption function, and the term dec models the decryption function.

---

[1] In our formal analysis we separate this property into *dispute resolution at voting*, which checks the correctness of the test as a reachability property, and *vote privacy after a dispute*, which checks vote privacy in terms of observational equivalence.

[2] Since all the receipts are eventually published, vote privacy implies that dispute resolution at tallying is privacy-preserving.

The equational theory for the improved Bingo Voting is described in Table 1. It includes the equations for digital signature (in our case *checksign* returns the signed message only if one uses the correct verification key, and it fails otherwise), Pedersen commitment, dummy vote, and non-interactive zero-knowledge proofs (NIZKP) that prove the correctness of dummy votes and published receipts. To prove the correctness of the dummy votes, the voting authority uses the function *zkp1* showing that the content of the second commitment of each dummy vote is equal to the list of the two candidates cA and cB. The function *zkp2* allows the voting authority to prove that the content of a receipt $(cA, cB, Rtrg, rX)$ is identical to the content of the used dummy vote pair $dvp(com(rX, r1), com(cB, cr1))$ and to random number displayed on the TRNG ($Rtrg$), which is hidden into the fresh dummy vote pair $dvp(com(Rtrg, tr), com(cA, cr0))$. An auditor can check both proofs against the dummy vote pairs and the receipts published on the BB.

We specify the processes modelling voting authority, voter, TRNG, and bulletin board into a ProVerif library and reuse it to check each property. This guarantees that all the properties are checked against the same model of the improved Bingo Voting.

Table 1. Equational theory modelling the improved Bingo Voting

Primitive	Equation
Digital signature	$checksign(sign(m, ssk), spk(ssk)) = m$
Commitment & Dummy vote	$openCommit(com(val, r)) = (val, r)$ $openDummyVote(dvp(com0, com1)) = (com0, com1)$
NIZKP dummy vote	$checkzkp1(cA, cB, dvp(com0A, com(cA, cr0)),$ $dvp(com0B, com(cB, cr1)),$ $zkp1(cA, cB, cr0, cr1, com(cA, cr0), com(cB, cr1)) = OK$
NIZKP receipt (candidate A)	$checkzkp2(cA, cB, Rtrg, rX, dvp(com(Rtrg, tr), com(cA, cr0)),$ $dvp(com(rY, r0), com(cA, cr0)), dvp(com(rX, r1), com(cB, cr1)),$ $zkp2(cA, cB, rX, dvp(com(Rtrg, tr), com(cA, cr0)),$ $dvp(com(rX, r1), com(cB, cr1)),$ $cr1, cr0, r1, tr)) = OK$
NIZKP receipt (candidate B)	$checkzkp2(cA, cB, rY, Rtrg, dvp(com(Rtrg, tr), com(cB, cr1)),$ $dvp(com(rY, r1), com(cA, cr0)), dvp(com(rX, r1), com(cB, cr1)),$ $zkp2(cA, cB, rX, dvp(com(Rtrg, tr), com(cB, cr1)),$ $dvp(com(rY, r1), com(cA, cr0)),$ $cr0, cr1, r1, tr)) = OK$

3.1 Verification and Dispute Resolution

All the verification and dispute resolution properties of the improved Bingo Voting can be modelled as reachability properties. In line with the verification approach defined in [8,24], we identify the *tests* that decide whether a goal of the improved Bingo Voting fails. We then check that each of the tests meets soundness, completeness, and sufficiency conditions, as outlined in Table 2.

Table 2. $\mathcal{A}(\cdot)$: external attacker; $\mathcal{A}(VA)$: attacker controlling the voting authority; V: voter instances; V_{test}: voter instance running the test; τ: a trace representing a run of the improved Bingo Voting; $\mathcal{T}$: the set of all traces. BB and TRNG are always honest according to the improved Bingo Voting assumptions.

	Strategy			Condition
	Individual verification	Dispute resolution	Global verification	
(Soundness)	$\mathcal{A}(\cdot)$	$\mathcal{A}(V)$	$\mathcal{A}(V)$	$\forall \tau \in \mathcal{T} \mid goal$ holds in $\tau \implies test(\tau)$: true
(Completeness)	$\mathcal{A}(VA, V \setminus V_{test})$	$\mathcal{A}(VA, V \setminus V_{test})$	$\mathcal{A}(VA, V)$	$\forall \tau \in \mathcal{T} \mid test(\tau)$: true $\implies goal$ holds in τ
(Sufficiency)	$\mathcal{A}(VA, V \setminus V_{test})$	$\mathcal{A}(VA, V \setminus V_{test})$	$\mathcal{A}(VA, V)$	$\exists \tau \in \mathcal{T} \mid test(\tau)$: false

Soundness guarantees that if the goal holds, then the test always succeeds. For dispute resolution and global verification, it means that an honest voting authority should never be blamed by any test. Note that individual verification requires a different verification strategy than dispute resolution, as the former considers no inside attacker since the verification is based on (the honest) voter's knowledge of the way she voted. In fact, individual verification does not give the voter a way to prove that the voting authority misbehaved. Conversely, in case of dispute resolution or global verification, in which tests are decided upon public information, we consider no honest voters, who may try to feed the tests with incorrect information. We prove that an honest voting authority cannot be unfairly blamed.

Completeness guarantees that whenever a test does not blame the voting authority, then the goal holds. Note that this is logically equivalent to saying that whenever a goal does not hold, then the test blames the voting authority. Thus, we check that a dishonest voting authority cannot feed the tests with incorrect information so that the test succeeds but the goal fails. The verification strategy for completenessregarding global verification is different from the one regarding individual verification and dispute resolution: in principle, global verification should hold even if all voters are dishonest as any election observer can run the test. However, as we shall see later, global verification can provide only guarantees up to dishonest voters.

While soundnessand completenessare conforming to [8], we introduce a third condition, *sufficiency*, which formalises that the misbehaviour of selected parties alone is sufficient to make the test fail. Without this condition, a protocol that does not permit any violation might still fulfil criteria to blame a party [23].

The conditions described in Table 2 show that the main difference between individual verification and dispute resolution boils down to be the verification strategy for checking soundness. Thus, a protocol that is dispute free for a specific goal is also individually verifiable for that goal. This is the case for individual verification and dispute resolution at voting for the improved Bingo Voting.

Due to space limitations, we only discuss the details of the dispute arising due to the global verification test in the improved Bingo Voting. The ProVerif code for all properties is available in [16]. Global verification enables any observers, including those who have not participated in the election at all, to verify the correctness of the election outcome. Global verification ensures that all candidates have received the same number of dummy votes and that for each receipt all but one candidate lose one dummy vote. This is the most complex test in improved Bingo Voting and requires the voting authority to release some information. The original paper presenting the improved Bingo Voting does not detail a specific algorithm for the test, thus we propose the test as defined in Algorithm 1. Our test considers two candidates, cA and cB. The input data of the test is published by the voting authority on the bulletin board.

We can define the goal for global verification $goal_{gv}$ as follows. Let us consider the set of all voters V of type $\mathcal{V}$, the set of voters' choices C of type $\mathcal{C}$, the set of candidates K of type $\mathcal{K}$, the set of honest voters $V_h \subseteq V$, and the set of choices of honest voters $C_h \subseteq C$. Let us now consider the relation Choice as the votes accepted by the bulletin board according to the published receipts, linking voters to their choices such that Choice $\subseteq V \times C$. Similarly, consider the relation Choice_h that links honest voters to their choices such that Choice$_h \subseteq V_h \times C_h$. Let Count: $(\mathcal{V} \times \mathcal{C}) \rightarrow (\mathcal{K} \times \mathbb{N})$ be an ideal counting function that returns the number of votes for each candidate. We can say that the $goal_{gv}$ holds in τ if Choice$_h \subseteq$ Choice and the election result is equal to Count(Choice).

All our proofs consider an unbounded number of voters. While ProVerif can automatically prove sufficiency for global verification, it is not possible to prove soundnessand completenesssince, according to Algorithm 1, we need to iterate over all receipts, but ProVerif does not support loops. We thus prove the base case in ProVerif, in which we consider only one published receipt. Then, we provide a manual induction proof that generalises the ProVerif results to the general case with an arbitrary number of published receipts.

ProVerif proves soundnessand completenesswhen only one published receipt is considered. To prove the general case that considers an unbounded number of published receipt, it is necessary to show that

$$test(\tau) : \textbf{true} \Leftrightarrow \text{Choice}_h \subseteq \text{Choice} \wedge \text{ the election results is equal to}$$
$$\text{Count}(\text{Choice})$$

It can be assumed that the number of published receipts is equal to the number of the published dummy votes and of the opened dummies. Any observer can check that these numbers coincide by looking at the bulleting board.

Theorem 1. *Let $test_k(\cdot)$ be the test applied to an execution that considers k receipts; let $test_k(\cdot) \rightarrow^* \textbf{true}$ denote the test that outputs $\textbf{true}$ after some steps; let τ be a trace that has n receipts; let τ_j be a version of τ that only considers the jth receipt that is associated with a honest voter i_j and corresponding choice c_j. For soundness, we prove that*

$$\forall 1 \leqslant i \leqslant n : test_1(\tau_j) \rightarrow^* \textbf{true} \Rightarrow (i_j, c_j) \in \text{Choice} \wedge \text{ the election results is}$$
$$\text{equal to } \text{Count}(\text{Choice})$$

For completeness, we prove that

$$\forall 1 \leqslant i \leqslant n : (i_j, c_j) \in \mathsf{Choice} \wedge \text{ the election results is equal to}$$
$$\mathsf{Count}(\mathsf{Choice}) \Rightarrow test_1(\tau_j) \rightarrow^* \mathbf{true}$$

Proof. $test_n(\tau)$ checks all the receipts, dummy votes, and proofs published in the bulletin board as defined in Algorithm 1. Similarly, the test $\forall 1 \leqslant j \leqslant n : test_1(\tau_j)$ does the same check for the jth entry in the bulletin board. It follows that

$$test_n(\tau) \rightarrow^* \mathbf{true}$$
$$\Downarrow$$
$$\forall 1 \leqslant j \leqslant n : test_1(\tau_j) \rightarrow^* \mathbf{true}$$
$$\Downarrow_{(by\ ProVerif)}$$
$$\forall 1 \leqslant j \leqslant n : (i_j, c_j) \in \mathsf{Choice} \wedge \text{ the election results is equal to } \mathsf{Count}(\mathsf{Choice})$$
$$\Downarrow$$
$$\mathsf{Choice}_h \subseteq \mathsf{Choice} \wedge \text{ the election results is equal to } \mathsf{Count}(\mathsf{Choice})$$

which proves soundnessalso for the general case.

$$\mathsf{Choice}_h \subseteq \mathsf{Choice} \wedge \text{ the election results is equal to } \mathsf{Count}(\mathsf{Choice})$$
$$\Downarrow$$
$$\forall 1 \leqslant j \leqslant n : (i_j, c_j) \in \mathsf{Choice} \wedge \text{ the election results is equal to } \mathsf{Count}(\mathsf{Choice})$$
$$\Downarrow_{(by\ ProVerif)}$$
$$\forall 1 \leqslant j \leqslant n : test_1(\tau_j) \rightarrow^* \mathbf{true}$$
$$\Downarrow$$
$$test_n(\tau) \rightarrow^* \mathbf{true}$$

which proves completeness also for the general case.

3.2 Privacy

Like in the verification of the verifiability and dispute resolution properties, we prove privacy by encoding the protocol into one ProVerif library – with a few modifications compared to the previous one – and then check privacy of different setups. The main practical change required for proving privacy is to remove the channel that voter, voting authority, and bulletin board use to feed the test with the evidence, and let the attacker read all public data and impersonate misbehaving parties, including an unbounded number of dishonest voters. As the improved Bingo Voting requires that voters are unobserved as they cast their vote, all communications between honest voters, the voting machine, and the TRNG are done over private channels.

Algorithm 1: Global Verification

Data: $cA, cB, receipt : (cx, cy, rx, ry, barcode), zkp1, dummy\_vote, zkp2,$
$new\_dummy, opened\_dummy : (ca, ra)$

foreach *receipt* in BB **do**

    if checkzkp1$(cA, cB, dummy\_vote, zkp1) =$ OK **then**

        if $cx = cA \wedge cy = cB \wedge$

        checkzkp2$(cA, cB, rx, ry, new\_dummy, dummy\_vote, zkp2) =$ OK $\wedge$

        $rx \neq ry \wedge rx \neq cx \wedge rx \neq cy \wedge ry \neq cx \wedge ry \neq cy \wedge$ **then**

            if dummy$(ca, ra) \in dummy\_vote \wedge ra \neq rx \wedge ra \neq ry$ **then**

            | **return true**

        else

            | **return false**

        else

        | **return false**

    else

    | **return false**

In the privacy setting, we observe two voters in particular, hence the bulletin board needs to shuffle the votes specifically to avoid trivial attacks to privacy. We check vote privacy, receipt freeness, and coercion resistance considering an honest voting authority. We also check vote privacy, and vote privacy of disputed receipt at the voting phase consider a dishonest voting authority. First, we check whether vote privacy holds in the improved Bingo Voting. Specifically, we check that if two honest voters swap their votes in two different runs of the protocol then the attacker cannot distinguish the two resulting systems as in [22]:

$$S[V_A\{^a/_v\} \mid V_B\{^b/_v\}] \approx_l S[V_A\{^b/_v\} \mid V_B\{^a/_v\}]$$

Similarly, we check whether vote privacy holds after a dispute at the voting phase. We let the honest voters reveal the fresh random number obtained by the trusted random number generator and the dummy random number on the receipt that is revealed by the privacy sleeve.

To check receipt freeness, we additionally let the voters publish their receipts on the public channel, and verify that privacy still holds:

$$S[V_A\{^a/_v\} \mid V_B\{^b/_v\}] \approx_l S[V' \mid V_B\{^a/_v\}]$$

where V' is a process such that $V'^{\backslash \mathrm{out}(chc,\cdot)} \approx_l V_A\{^b/_v\}$, i.e. V' is the process that acts like V_A voting for candidate B, but pretends to cooperate with the attacker.

Finally, to check whether the scheme is coercion resistant, we set up the protocol so that one of the voters receives the instruction on how to vote from the attacker and then provides the receipt to the attacker. We check that

$$S[C[V_A\{^?/_v\}^{c_1,c_2}] \mid V_B\{^a/_v\}] \approx_l S[C[V'] \mid V_B\{^c/_v\}]$$

where $V_A\{^?/_v\}^{ch,a}$ is the coerced voter process that votes for candidate B, no matter their original intention, reveals all its private information to the attacker via channels c_1, c_2, while V_B is the other voter process intended to balance the resulting votes, that is, if V_A votes for candidate A, then V_B votes for candidate B and vice versa. Note that with the setup described here there is a trivial attack, which only appears in the model, as the bulletin board should not reveal whether the votes were swapped or not. In practice, this is done by shuffling. Thus, we let the bulletin board swap the order of published ballots if and only if the voters actually swap their choice following the attacker's instruction.

3.3 Findings

ProVerif proves individual verification and both dispute resolution at voting and at tallying automatically. It also proves global verification for one receipt, then we provide a manual inductive proof for the unbounded case. The outcome of our analysis shows that the improved Bingo Voting meets some properties only if one makes additional assumptions to the ones already defined in [6,18]. The additional assumptions are reported in Table 3. For dispute resolution at voting, we need to assume that the test does not blame the voting authority if the barcode printed on the paper ballot does not match with the one printed on the receipt. This avoids an attack due to a dishonest voter handing her receipt to another voter [8]. Without this assumption, the latter, isolated in the voting booth, may swap the receipt printed by the voting machine with the ones handed by the dishonest voter, leading to a successful blaming of the voting authority.

We also need to make additional assumptions for proving global verification. As already noted by in [24], it is only possible to have global verification up to the votes of dishonest voters since a dishonest voting authority can alter votes cast by such voters without being detected. Moreover, we found that honest voters should check that their receipts are well-formed at voting and at tallying, and raise disputes otherwise.

As regards privacy properties, we found that vote privacy, receipt freeness, and coercion resistance hold if the voting authority is honest and the voting machine cannot decide which dummy vote should be assigned to which receipt. This can be achieved by prearranging dummy votes in *clusters* [18], which limits the voting machine's choice on selecting the dummy votes. Considering two candidates, each cluster contains two dummy votes, one per candidate. The voting authority publishes the clusters in the same order in which the voting machine uses them for the receipts. The voting authority can prove in zero-knowledge that each receipt used the dummy votes from the expected cluster. However, the verification process of the correct order of clusters requires that the bulletin board publishes the receipts as they are issued. Revealing the order in which the receipts are issued may not be acceptable for many elections. In fact, ProVerif finds that if the bulletin board does not randomly shuffle the receipts before publishing them, the voting authority can easily break vote privacy by just looking at the order of voters, which is normally available in the voter registration record at the polling place. Thus, for vote privacy, it is not enough assuming that a dishonest voting authority does not communicate with a dishonest voting machine as suggested in [18]. We need to assume that at least either the voting authority or the voting machine is honest.

Table 3. The additional assumptions required in the improved Bingo Voting respect to the ones stated in [6,18], according to the outcome of our formal analysis

Property	Assumptions in [6,18]	Additional assumptions
Individual verification	Honest $TRNG$ and BB	–
Dispute resolution at voting	Honest $TRNG$ and BB	Do not blame the VA if barcodes are different
Dispute resolution at tallying	Honest $TRNG$ and BB	–
Global verification	Honest $TRNG$ and BB	Up to dishonest voters. Voters check and dispute incorrect receipts at voting and at tallying
Vote privacy if dispute at voting	Honest $TRNG$ and BB. VA has no access to the voting machine	Honest VA
Vote privacy	Honest $TRNG$ and BB. VA has no access to the voting machine	Honest VA or voting machine
Receipt freeness	Honest $TRNG$, BB, VA, and voting machine	–
Coercion resistance	Honest $TRNG$, BB, VA, and voting machine	–

ProVerif can prove that vote privacy holds after a dispute if the disputed receipt is not published on the bulletin board and the dummy vote corresponding to the dummy random numbers revealed by the privacy sleeve is not opened. In fact, if the receipt is published, vote privacy does not hold any more because the random number generated by the TRNG is revealed during the dispute. If the dummy vote is opened, vote privacy does not hold as well because this would reveal one of the candidates not chosen by the voter. However, we found that not revealing the receipt and not opening the dummy vote after a dispute might break vote privacy.

Privacy Attack Due to Dispute Resolution. Let us consider the scenario with two candidates in which a voter mistakenly disputes a valid receipt at voting. This vote should not be counted because the receipt is not published. Also, we require that a pair of dummy votes that are not in any receipts should not be opened

- The *disputed* dummy vote containing the disputed dummy random number associated with the candidate not chosen by the voter printed on the receipt.

– A dummy vote associated with the candidate chosen by the voter so that the disputed receipt is not counted at tallying.

Then, the voting authority should prove in zero-knowledge that the pair of dummy votes contain the list of the candidates. However, we observe that *any* pair of dummy votes containing the list of the candidates can serve for such proof since the corresponding receipt will not be published. Thus, a dishonest voting machine can signal a different dummy random number to the voting authority and print the disputed dummy random number again into another receipt, which will be published on the bulletin board. This would reveal how the disputing voter voted, breaking vote privacy. If one considers a dishonest voter, this attack is even more harmful. A dishonest voter can dispute a vote on purpose to learn how another voter voted since the dishonest voter knows the disputed dummy random number.

Note that the voting machine does not need to communicate with the dishonest voter to break vote privacy of another voter, and that this attack works even considering an honest voting authority. Of course, the attack is not possible if one considers an honest voting machine but there would not be need of dispute resolution at all in the first place if one makes such an assumption.

None of the papers presenting the improved Bingo Voting describes what happens after a dispute. Prearranging dummy votes may mitigate the attack at the cost of assuming an honest voting authority. Another possible mitigation to such an attack might be to allow voters who dispute their votes to revote. Revoting requires to generate additional dummy votes. The total amount of needed dummy votes should be the double of the original amount in order to avoid denial of voting attacks. However, this is a partial solution as it would not mitigate attacks due to dishonest voters.

4 Related Work

Several voting schemes have considered notions of dispute resolution or related properties. The FOO protocol [14] is one of the first voting schemes that enables voters to prove certain frauds due to a dishonest voting authority. Pret â Vòter [27] and vVote [13] provide some dispute resolution and accountability guarantees as a voter can use invalid proof and a ballot confirmation check as evidence. Remotegrity [31], Scantegrity II [9], and Scantegrity III [29] detail dispute resolution processes that allow voters to file disputes in case of incorrect designated ballots or *confirmation codes*, which are invisible random codes preprinted on the ballots. sElect [25] features a fully automated verification procedure that performs cryptographic checks without requiring any voter interaction. The procedure is capable to single out a specific misbehaving party and producing the necessary evidence of the misbehaviour. Schoenmarkers [28] and Kiayias and Yung [20] design dispute-free voting schemes, whose aim is to neutralise faults rather than providing mechanisms to address them. Some of the above protocols have been formally checked for accountability and/or privacy properties.

However, no formal analysis has been done to check whether disputes leak any information regarding how the voter voted.

Prior works on the formalisation of dispute resolution and related properties, such as accountability, include the seminal work by Küsters et al. [24], who advance accountability notions in the symbolic and computational models. Moreover, they provide an analysis of accountability and coercion resistance [26] of the original Bingo Voting scheme. Bruni et al. [8] propose formal definitions of accountability that are amenable to automated verification. One of their case studies is the improved Bingo Voting, which they analyse up to the voting phase, finding that it does not meet dispute resolution at voting. In contrast, we find that, if the dispute resolution test does not blame the voting authority when the barcodes are different between the paper ballot and the receipt, then the improved Bingo Voting achieves that property. Künneman et al. [23] give verification conditions that imply accountability based on *counterfactual relations*, capturing what actually happened to what could have happened. Basin et al. [2] proposed a definition of dispute resolution for voting requiring that voters get evidence that their ballot is incorrectly recorded before the end of the election.

The notions of individual verifiability and universal verifiability have been extensively studied in voting [3,4,10,11,19]. Kremer et al. [21] formalised both individual and universal verifiability in the applied pi-calculus, including the requirement of *eligibility verifiability*, which expresses that auditors can verify that each vote in the election result was cast by a registered voter, and there is at most one vote per voter. Smyth et al. [30] used ProVerif to check verifiability in three voting protocols expressing the requirements as reachability properties. Gallegos-Garcia et al. [15] studies how to achieve verifiability without any trust assumptions. Giustolisi et al. [17] observe that privacy-preserving verifiability can be achieved using non-interactive zero-knowledge proofs and functional encryption techniques. More recently, Cortier and Lallemand [12] have shown that a voting scheme that does not meet individual verifiability fails to achieve vote privacy, when one considers the same trust assumptions. This line of work opens up to interesting questions on how stronger properties such as dispute resolution and coercion resistance relate.

5   Conclusion

Dispute resolution mechanisms are essential components of a voting scheme, enabling the correctness of an election outcome. They can provably expose a misbehaving voting authority, hence deterring it by doing so. However, dispute resolution is useless if it is not triggered when it should be, and voters should not have to choose to either raise a dispute or keep their vote private. In this work, we have looked at the privacy-preserving dispute resolution mechanisms described in the improved Bingo Voting.

The formal analysis of the improved Bingo Voting allows us to identify precisely the necessary assumptions that enable the scheme to meet all the stated properties. It is found that global verification, which enables any observer to dispute the correctness on an election, cannot be achieved without dispute resolution both at voting and at tallying. To the best of our knowledge, it is an open question whether this is just for the improved Bingo Voting or it is a requirement for any voting scheme.

It is also found that assuming that the voting authority has not illegitimate access to the voting machine is not enough to guarantee vote privacy: either the voting authority or the voting machine must be honest at least. However, it is found that dispute resolution at voting can be achieved only assuming an honest voting authority as prearranging dummy votes would enable the voting authority to link votes to voters.

The results of this work also show that designing privacy-preserving dispute resolution mechanisms with minimal trust assumptions is not a trivial task in voting. The voting booth assumption should ideally be the sole assumption made in a voting scheme. Also, the details of the aftermath of a dispute resolution procedure in voting need to be described and thought with the same precision and care as are the *standard* voting procedures. For the improved Bingo Voting, we observe that, while cancelling an election due to a dispute is not an option, allowing voters who wrongly contest a receipt to revote mitigates an attack due to a dishonest voting machine. However, it does not help against a voting machine colluding with a dishonest voter.

Other voting schemes might achieve privacy-preserving dispute resolution with fewer assumptions than the improved Bingo Voting. With this work, we stress the importance of detailing the aftermath of disputes and aim at stimulating the voting community to make similar analyses to other voting schemes.

Acknowledgments. We are grateful to Rasmus Dilling Møller and Sean Wachs for helping out with the privacy analysis of an early model of Bingo Voting.

References

1. Abadi, M., Fournet, C.: Mobile values, new names, and secure communication. In: POPL, pp. 104–115. ACM, New York (2001)
2. Basin, D.A., Radomirovic, S., Schmid, L.: Dispute resolution in voting. CoRR abs/2005.03749 (2020). https://arxiv.org/abs/2005.03749
3. Benaloh, J.: verifiable secret-ballot elections. Ph.D. thesis, Yale University, December 1996
4. Benaloh, J., Tuinstra, D.: Receipt-free secret-ballot elections (extended abstract). In: STOC, pp. 544–553. ACM (1994)
5. Blanchet, B.: An efficient cryptographic protocol verifier based on prolog rules. In: CSFW, pp. 82–96. IEEE Computer Society (2001)
6. Bohli, J.M., Henrich, C., Kempka, C., Muller-Quade, J., Rohrich, S.: Enhancing electronic voting machines on the example of bingo voting. IEEE Trans. Inf. Forensics Secur. **4**, 745–750 (2009)
7. Bohli, J.-M., Müller-Quade, J., Röhrich, S.: Bingo voting: secure and coercion-free voting using a trusted random number generator. In: Alkassar, A., Volkamer, M. (eds.) Vote-ID 2007. LNCS, vol. 4896, pp. 111–124. Springer, Heidelberg (2007). https://doi.org/10.1007/978-3-540-77493-8_10

8. Bruni, A., Giustolisi, R., Schuermann, C.: Automated analysis of accountability. In: Nguyen, P., Zhou, J. (eds.) ISC 2017. LNCS, vol. 10599, pp. 417–434. Springer, Cham (2017). https://doi.org/10.1007/978-3-319-69659-1_23

9. Carback, R., et al.: Scantegrity II municipal election at Takoma park: the first E2E binding governmental election with ballot privacy. In: USENIX Conference on Security. USENIX (2010)

10. Cohen, J., Fischer, M.: A robust and verifiable cryptographically secure election scheme (extended abstract). In: FOCS, pp. 372–382. IEEE (1985)

11. Cortier, V., Galindo, D., Küsters, R., Müller, J., Truderung, T.: SoK: verifiability notions for e-voting protocols. In: IEEE Symposium on Security and Privacy, pp. 779–798 (2016)

12. Cortier, V., Lallemand, J.: Voting: you can't have privacy without individual verifiability. In: CCS, pp. 53–66. ACM (2018)

13. Culnane, C., Ryan, P.Y.A., Schneider, S., Teague, V.: vVote: a verifiable voting system (DRAFT). CoRR abs/1404.6822 (2014)

14. Fujioka, A., Okamoto, T., Ohta, K.: A practical secret voting scheme for large scale elections. In: Seberry, J., Zheng, Y. (eds.) AUSCRYPT. LNCS, pp. 244–251. Springer, Heidelberg (1992). https://doi.org/10.1007/3-540-57220-1_66

15. Gallegos-García, G., Iovino, V., Rial, A., Rønne, P.B., Ryan, P.Y.A.: (universal) unconditional verifiability in e-voting without trusted parties. CoRR abs/1610.06343 (2016). http://arxiv.org/abs/1610.06343

16. Giustolisi, R., Bruni, A.: The ProVerif code used to verify the Improved Bingo Voting. https://itu.dk/people/rosg/code/evoteid20code.tar.gz

17. Giustolisi, R., Iovino, V., Lenzini, G.: Privacy-preserving verifiability - a case for an electronic exam protocol. In: SECRYPT, pp. 139–150. SciTePress (2017)

18. Henrich, C.: Improving and analysing bingo voting. Ph.D. thesis (2012). https://doi.org/10.5445/IR/1000030270

19. Hirt, M., Sako, K.: Efficient receipt-free voting based on homomorphic encryption. In: Preneel, B. (ed.) EUROCRYPT. LNCS, vol. 1807, pp. 539–556. Springer, Heidelberg (2000). https://doi.org/10.1007/3-540-45539-6_38

20. Kiayias, A., Yung, M.: Self-tallying elections and perfect ballot secrecy. In: Naccache, D., Paillier, P. (eds.) PKC 2002. LNCS, vol. 2274, pp. 141–158. Springer, Heidelberg (2002). https://doi.org/10.1007/3-540-45664-3_10

21. Kremer, S., Ryan, M., Smyth, B.: Election verifiability in electronic voting protocols. In: Gritzalis, D., Preneel, B., Theoharidou, M. (eds.) ESORICS 2010. LNCS, vol. 6345, pp. 389–404. Springer, Heidelberg (2010). https://doi.org/10.1007/978-3-642-15497-3_24

22. Kremer, S., Ryan, M.: Analysis of an electronic voting protocol in the applied pi calculus. In: Gritzalis, D., Preneel, B., Theoharidou, M. (eds.) ESOP 2005. LNCS, vol. 3444, pp. 186–200. Springer, Heidelberg (2005). https://doi.org/10.1007/978-3-540-31987-0_14

23. Künnemann, R., Esiyok, I., Backes, M.: Automated verification of accountability in security protocols. In: CSF, pp. 397–413. IEEE (2019)

24. Küsters, R., Truderung, T., Vogt, A.: Accountability: definition and relationship to verifiability. In: CCS, pp. 526–535. ACM (2010)

25. Küsters, R., Müller, J., Scapin, E., Truderung, T.: sElect: a lightweight verifiable remote voting system. In: CSF, pp. 341–354. IEEE (2016)

26. Küsters, R., Truderung, T., Vogt, A.: A game-based definition of coercion-resistance and its applications. In: CSF, pp. 122–136. IEEE (2010)

27. Ryan, P.Y.A., Bismark, D., Heather, J., Schneider, S., Xia, Z.: PrÊVoter: a voter-verifiable voting system. IEEE Trans. Inf. Forensics Secur. 4, 662–673 (2009)

28. Schoenmakers, B.: A simple publicly verifiable secret sharing scheme and its application to electronic voting. In: Wiener, M. (ed.) CRYPTO 1999. LNCS, vol. 1666, pp. 148–164. Springer, Heidelberg (1999). https://doi.org/10.1007/3-540-48405-1_10

29. Sherman, A.T., Fink, R.A., Carback, R., Chaum, D.: Scantegrity III: automatic trustworthy receipts, highlighting over/under votes, and full voter verifiability. In: Shacham, H., Teague, V. (eds.) EVT/WOTE. USENIX (2011)

30. Smyth, B., Ryan, M., Kremer, S., Mounira, K.: Towards automatic analysis of election verifiability properties. In: Armando, A., Lowe, G. (eds.) ARSPA-WITS 2010. LNCS, vol. 6186, pp. 146–163. Springer, Heidelberg (2010). https://doi.org/10.1007/978-3-642-16074-5_11

31. Zagórski, F., Carback, R.T., Chaum, D., Clark, J., Essex, A., Vora, P.L.: Remotegrity: design and use of an end-to-end verifiable remote voting system. In: Jacobson, M., Locasto, M., Mohassel, P., Safavi-Naini, R. (eds.) ACNS 2013. LNCS, vol. 7954, pp. 441–457. Springer, Heidelberg (2013). https://doi.org/10.1007/978-3-642-38980-1_28

Bayesian Audits Are Average But Risk-Limiting Audits are Above Average

Amanda K. Glazer$^{(\boxtimes)}$, Jacob V. Spertus, and Philip B. Stark

Department of Statistics, University of California, Berkeley, CA, USA
{amandaglazer,jakespertus,pbstark}@berkeley.edu

Abstract. Post-election audits can provide convincing evidence that election outcomes are correct—that the reported winner(s) really won— by manually inspecting ballots selected at random from a trustworthy paper trail of votes. Risk-limiting audits (RLAs) control the probability that, if the reported outcome is wrong, it is not corrected before the outcome becomes official. RLAs keep this probability below the specified "risk limit." Bayesian audits (BAs) control the probability that the reported outcome is wrong, the "upset probability." The upset probability does not exist unless one invents a prior probability distribution for cast votes. RLAs ensure that if *this* election's reported outcome is wrong, the procedure has a large chance of correcting it. BAs control a *weighted average probability* of correcting wrong outcomes over a hypothetical collection of elections; the weights come from the prior. In general, BAs do not ensure a large chance of correcting the outcome of an election when the reported outcome is wrong. "Nonpartisan" priors, i.e., priors that are invariant under relabeling the candidates, lead to upset probabilities that can be far smaller than the chance of correcting wrong reported outcomes. We demonstrate the difference using simulations based on several real contests.

Keywords: Election integrity · Risk-limiting audits · Bayesian audits

1 Introduction

The 2016 U.S. Presidential election was attacked by Russian hackers, and U.S. intelligence agencies warn that several nation-states are already mounting attacks on the 2020 election [22, 29–31]. Almost every U.S. jurisdiction uses computers to count votes; many use computers to record votes. All computerized systems are vulnerable to bugs, misconfiguration, and hacking [26]. Voters, poll workers, and election officials are also bound to make mistakes [15]. Enough error from any source—innocent or malicious—could cause a losing candidate to appear to win.

The reported tallies will almost certainly be off by at least a little. Were the tallies accurate enough to ensure that the reported winner(s) really won—that the *reported outcome* is correct?

Authors listed alphabetically.

© Springer Nature Switzerland AG 2020
R. Krimmer et al. (Eds.): E-Vote-ID 2020, LNCS 12455, pp. 84–94, 2020.
https://doi.org/10.1007/978-3-030-60347-2_6

An election is *evidence-based* [26] if it provides convincing public evidence that the reported winners really won. The only federally certified technology that can provide such evidence is trustworthy paper ballots kept demonstrably secure throughout the election and canvass, then audited manually [2]. However:

- 14% of registered voters live in jurisdictions using Direct Recording Electronic (DRE) Systems for all voters. DREs do not retain a paper ballot [27].
- Some paper ballots are not trustworthy. For instance, touchscreen voting machines and ballot-marking devices are vulnerable to bugs, hacking, and misconfiguration that can cause them to print the wrong votes [3,4].
- Rules for securing cast ballots and for ensuring the paper trail remains trusworthy are uneven and generally inadequate.

Nonetheless, to focus on statistical issues, we assume here that elections produce a trustworthy collection of paper ballots containing voters' expressed preferences [2,3,11,26]. A trustworthy paper trail allows audits to check whether errors, bugs, or malfeasance altered the reported outcome. ("Outcome" means who won, not the exact vote tallies.) For instance, we could tabulate the votes on all the cast ballots by hand, as some recount laws require. But full manual recounts are expensive, contentious, and rare: according to Richie and Smith [19], only 27 statewide U.S. elections between 2000 and 2015 were manually recounted; three of the recounts overturned the original outcomes (11%).

Some states conduct tabulation audits that involve manually reading votes from some ballots. For instance, California law requires manually tabulating the votes on ballots in 1% of precincts selected at random.[1] Such audits typically do not ensure that outcome-changing errors will (probably) be detected, much less corrected. In contrast, risk-limiting audits (RLAs) [11,23] have a known minimum chance of correcting the reported outcome if the reported outcome is wrong (but never alter correct outcomes). RLAs stop without a full hand count only if there is sufficiently strong evidence that a full hand count would find the same winners, i.e., if the P-value of the hypothesis that the reported outcome is wrong is sufficiently small.

RLAs have been endorsed by the National Academies of Science, Engineering, and Medicine [15], the American Statistical Association [1], and many other organizations concerned with election integrity. There have been roughly 60 pilot RLAs in 15 U.S. states and Denmark. Currently 10 U.S. states require or specifically allow RLAs. There have been statewide RLAs or pilot RLAs in five U.S. states: Alaska[2], Colorado [8], Kansas[3], Rhode Island [7], and Wyoming (see Footnote 3), and a pilot RLA in Michigan in which 80 of 83 counties participated [13].

---

[1] The law is a bit more complicated, including provisions to ensure that every contest gets some scrutiny and options for sampling vote-by-mail ballots (including not sampling them if they arrive after election day).

[2] Organized by J. Morrell; one of us (PBS) provided software and support.

[3] J. Morrell, personal communication, 2020.

Bayesian audits (BAs, [20, 21]) have been proposed as an alternative to RLAs. BAs stop without a full hand count only if the "upset probability"—the posterior probability that the reported winner(s) actually lost, for a particular prior π, given the audit sample—is below a pre-specified threshold. They have been piloted in several states.

Bayesian and frequentist interpretations of probability are quite different. Frequentist probability is the long-run limiting relative frequency with which an event occurs in repeated trials. Bayesian probability quantifies the degree to which the subject believes an event will occur. A prior probability distribution quantifies beliefs before the data are collected; after the data are observed, Bayes' rule says how to update the prior using the data to obtain the posterior probability distribution.

Bayesian methods, including BAs, require stronger assumptions than frequentist methods, including RLAs. In particular, BAs require assuming that votes are random and follow a known "prior" probability distribution π.

Both RLAs and BAs rely on manually interpreting randomly selected ballots. In principle, both can use a wide range of sampling plans to accommodate differences in how jurisdictions handle and store ballots and variations in election laws and regulations. (To the best of our knowledge, BAs have been conducted only using "ballot polling" [9].) RLA methods have been developed to use individual ballots or groups of ballots as the sampling unit, to sample with or without replacement or to use Bernoulli sampling, to sample with and without stratification, and to sample uniformly or with unequal probabilities (see, e.g., Stark [11, 17, 18, 23–25]).

The manual interpretations can be used in two ways: *comparison audits* look at differences between the manual interpretation and the machine interpretation and tabulation, while *polling audits* just use the manual interpretation. (The two strategies can be combined in a single audit; see, e.g., Ottoboni et al. [18, 25].) Comparison audits require more of the voting system and require more preparation than polling audits, but for a given size sampling unit, they generally require smaller samples. (The sample size scales like the reciprocal of the margin for comparison audits, and like the square of the reciprocal of the margin for polling audits.) Below, we focus on polling audits that use individual ballots as the sampling unit: *ballot-polling audits*. These are the simplest conceptually and require the least of the voting system: just the reported winner(s), but no other data export.

Both RLAs and BAs lead to a full hand count if sampling does not provide sufficiently strong evidence that the reported outcome is correct. If they lead to a full hand count, that hand count replaces the reported results. Thus, they might confirm a wrong outcome, but they never overturn a correct outcome (Fig. 1). They make different assumptions, use different standards of evidence, and offer different assurances, as we shall explain.

```
while (!(full handcount) && !(strong evidence outcome is correct)) {
    audit more
}
if (strong evidence outcome is correct) {
    reported result is final
}
if (full handcount) {
    handcount result is final
}
```

Fig. 1. Pseudo code for sequential auditing procedures

2   Risk

The *risk* of an auditing procedure, given a trustworthy set of cast ballots and a reported outcome, is zero if the reported outcome is correct and is the chance that the procedure will not correct the reported outcome if the reported outcome is wrong. Formally, let θ denote a set of cast votes. For example, in a contest between (only) Alice and Bob in which n ballots were cast, all containing valid votes, θ is an element of $\{\text{Alice, Bob}\}^n$. (For sampling with replacement, we could also parametrize the cast votes as the fraction of votes for Alice; see Fig. 2.)

RLAs treat θ as fixed but unknown. The only probability in RLAs is the probability involved in sampling ballots at random—a probability that exists by fiat and is known to the auditor, because the auditor designs the sampling protocol.

In contrast, BAs treat θ—the cast votes—as random rather than simply unknown. The probability in BAs comes not only from the sampling but also from the assumption that votes are random and follow a probability distribution π known to (or believed by) the auditor.

Let $f(\cdot)$ be the social choice function that maps a set of cast votes to the contest winner(s). Then

$$\text{risk}(\theta) \equiv \begin{cases} \Pr(\text{audit confirms reported outcome}), & \text{reported winner} \neq f(\theta) \\ 0, & \text{reported winner} = f(\theta). \end{cases}$$

RLAs ensure that the risk does not exceed a pre-specified limit (denoted α), no matter what votes were actually cast. Because θ is fixed, probabilities in RLAs come only from the random sampling of ballots.

BAs control a weighted average of the risk rather than the maximum risk (whence the title of this paper). The weights come from the prior probability distribution on θ. In symbols:

$$\text{risk}_{\text{RLA}} = \max_{\theta} \text{risk}(\theta)$$

$$\text{risk}_{\text{BA}} = \frac{1}{c} \sum_{\theta} \text{risk}(\theta)\pi(\theta)$$

where $\pi(\theta)$ is the prior on θ and $c = \sum_{\theta:\text{reported winner} \neq f(\theta)} \pi(\theta)$ makes the weights sum to 1.

BAs can have a large chance of correcting some wrong outcomes and a small chance of correcting others, depending on the prior π. If π assigns much probability to wrong outcomes where it is easy to tell there was a problem (e.g., a reported loser really won by a wide margin) the average risk (the upset probability) can be much lower than the risk for the actual set of ballots cast in the election.

An RLA with risk limit α automatically limits the upset probability to α for any prior, but the converse is not true in general. (The average of a function cannot exceed the maximum of that function, but the maximum exceeds the average unless the function is constant.) Below, we demonstrate that the upset probability can be much smaller than the true risk using simulations based on close historical elections.

3   Choosing the Prior for a BA

In a BA, the prior quantifies beliefs about the cast votes and the correctness of the reported outcome before the audit commences. Beliefs differ across the electorate. To address this, Rivest and Shen [20] considered a "bring your own prior" BA: the audit continues until everyone's upset probability is sufficiently small (see Fig. 2A). Of course, if anyone's prior implies that a reported loser is virtually certain to have won, the audit won't stop without a full hand count.

Ultimately, Rivest and Shen [20] and Rivest [21] recommend using a single "nonpartisan" prior. A nonpartisan prior is one for which every candidate is equally likely to win, i.e., a prior that is invariant under permutations of the candidates' names (see Fig. 2B). We doubt this captures anyone's beliefs about any particular election. Beliefs about whether the reported winner really won may depend on many things, including pre-election polls and exit polls, the reported margin, reports of polling-place problems, news reports of election interference, etc.

For instance, it seems less plausible that the reported winner actually lost if the reported margin is 60% than if the reported margin is 0.6%: producing an erroneous 60% margin would require much more error or manipulation than producing an erroneous 0.6% margin if the reported winner really lost. On the other hand, when the *true* margin is small, it is easier for error or manipulation to cause the wrong candidate to appear to win. Moreover, a tight contest might be a more attractive target for manipulation.

If every audit is to be conducted using the same prior, that prior arguably should put more weight on narrow margins. Taken to the extreme, the prior would concentrate the probability of wrong outcomes at the wrong outcome with the narrowest margin: a tie or one-vote win for a reported loser.

Indeed, Vora [28] and Morin et al. [14] show that in a two-candidate plurality contest with no invalid votes, a ballot-polling BA using a prior that assigns probability 1/2 to a tie (or one-vote win for the reported loser) and probability

1/2 to correct outcomes is in fact an RLA (see Fig. 2C): the upset probability equals the risk.

Constructing priors that make BAs risk-limiting for more complicated elections (e.g., elections with more than two candidates, elections in which ballots may contain invalid votes, social choice functions other than plurality, and audit sampling designs other than simple random samples of individual ballots or random samples of individual ballots with replacement) is an open problem.[4]

4   Empirical Comparison

How are risk and upset probability related? The upset probability is never larger than the risk, but the risk is often much larger than the upset probability for BAs with non-partisan priors, as we show using data from three recent close U.S. elections: the 2017 House of Delegates contest in Virginia's 94th district, the 2018 Congressional contest in Maine's 2nd district, and the 2018 Georgia Governor contest. The simulations, summarized in Table 1, treat the reported vote shares as correct, but re-label the reported winner as the reported loser. "Simulated Risk" is the estimated probability that a BA with 5% upset probability corrects the reported outcome. The simulations use the nonpartisan prior recommended by Rivest [21], with initial "pseudo-counts" of 0.5. Each audit begins with a sample of 25 ballots. Each step of each audit simulates 1,000 draws from the posterior distribution to estimate the upset probability. If the upset probability is above 5%, then the sample is increased by 20%, and the upset probability is estimated again. Each audit stops when the upset probability falls below 5%, or all ballots have been audited. We simulate 10,000 ballot-polling BAs for each scenario. Code for the simulations is available at https://github.com/akglazer/BRLA-Comparison.

A recount of the 2017 Virginia 94th district contest gave a 1-vote win for Simonds over Yancey. (A three-judge panel later determined that a vote counted as an overvote should be attributed to Yancey; the winner was determined by drawing a name from a bowl [12].) The 2018 Maine Congressional election used ranked-choice voting (RCV/IRV). While there are methods for conducting RLAs of IRV contests [6, 25], we treat the contest as if it were a plurality contest between the last two standing candidates, Golden and Poliquin, a "final-round margin" of 3,509 votes.[5]

In these experiments, the actual risk of the BA is 4 to 9 times larger than the upset probability, 5%. For example, in the Virginia 94th District contest, the BA failed to correct the outcome 43% of the time, 8.6 times the upset probability.

---

[4] This is related to the problem of constructing *least-favorable priors* in statistical decision problems. There is a deep duality between Bayesian and frequentist procedures: under mild regularity conditions the Bayes risk for a *least-favorable prior* is equal to the *minimax risk* [5]. (Here, risk is a term of art, a measure of the performance of the procedure.) That is to say, for a particular choice of prior, the Bayesian procedure is in fact the frequentist procedure that does best in the worst case. The least-favorable prior is generally not "flat" or "uninformative."

[5] The final-round margin of an IRV contest is an upper bound on the true margin.

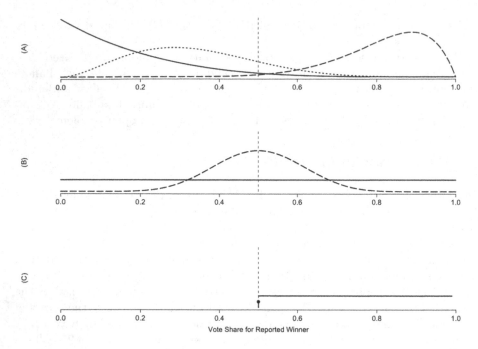

Fig. 2. Exemplar priors for the true vote share for the reported winner in a two-candidate election. Values to the right of the vertical dotted line (at $1/2$) correspond to correct reported outcomes: the winner got more than 50% of the valid votes. (A) plots three possible partisan priors. For BAs that allow observers to bring their own prior, a BA would stop only when all three posteriors give a sufficiently low probability to all outcomes where the reported winner actually lost: values less than or equal to $1/2$. (B) plots two nonpartisan priors (the priors are symmetric around $1/2$ and thus invariant under exchanging the candidates' names) including the flat prior recommended by Rivest and Shen [20]. The flat prior gives equal weight to all possible vote shares. (C) plots a least-favorable prior, a prior for which a BA is an RLA with risk limit equal to the upset probability. It assigns probability $1/2$ to a tie, the wrong outcome that is most difficult to detect. The rest of the probability is spread (arbitrarily) across vote shares for which the reported outcome is correct. In this illustration, that probability is uniform. That choice affects the efficiency but not the risk.

This results from the fact that the upset probability averages the risk over all possible losing margins (with equal weight), while the actual losing margin was small. Figure 3 shows the simulated risk of a BA with a nonpartisan prior and initial pseudo-counts of 0.5 for an election with 1,000,000 total votes cast. The risk is plotted as a function of the vote share for the winner. The empirical risk for a BA is very high for small margins, where auditing is especially important. As far as we know, there are situations where the risk can be an arbitrarily large multiple of the upset probability, depending on the actual cast votes, the social choice function, the prior, and details of the BA implementation (such as its rule for expanding the sample).

Table 1. Simulated risk of a Bayesian Audit using 5% upset probability with a "non-partisan" prior for the 2017 Virginia House of Delegates District 94 contest, the 2018 Maine 2nd Congressional District contest, and the 2018 Georgia gubernatorial contest. Column 2: the margin for each election in number of votes and percentage. Column 3: risk of the BA, i.e., the estimated probability that the BA audit will fail to correct the outcome.

	Number of Votes Cast	Margin	BA Risk (simulated)
Virginia 94th	23,215 votes	1 vote (0.004%)	43%
Maine 2nd	281,371 votes	3509 votes (1.25%)	23%
Georgia Governor	3,902,093 votes	54,723 votes (1.4%)	22%

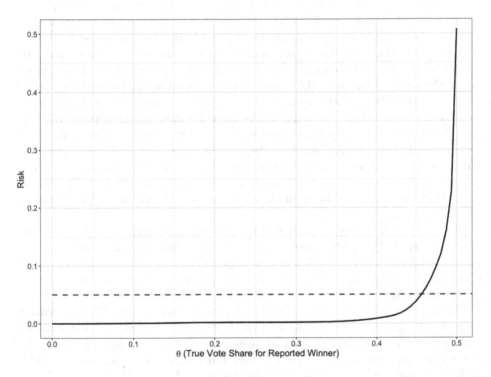

Fig. 3. Simulated risk (solid line) of a BA with nonpartisan prior for a two-candidate election with 1,000,000 total votes cast and no invalid votes. The x-axis is θ, the actual vote share for the reported winner. The reported winner really won if $\theta > 0.5$ and lost if $\theta < 0.5$. The y-axis is the actual risk, computed for $\theta < 0.5$ as the number of times the BA confirms the outcome over the total number of simulated audits. If $\theta > 0.5$ then the risk is 0. The dashed grey line at $Risk = 0.05$ is the upset probability threshold for the BA, and also the maximum risk for an RLA with risk limit 0.05.

5 Conclusion

Elections are audited in part to rule out the possibility that voter errors, poll-worker errors, procedural errors, reporting errors, misconfiguration, miscalibration, malfunction, bugs, hacking, or other errors or malfeasance made losing candidates appear to win. We believe that controlling the probability that the reported outcome will not be corrected when it is wrong—the risk—should be the minimal goal of a post-election audit. RLAs control that risk; BAs control the upset probability, which can be much smaller than the risk.

Both RLAs and BAs require a trustworthy paper trail of voter intent. RLAs use the paper trail to protect against the worst case: they control the chance of certifying the reported outcome if it is wrong, no matter why it is wrong.

BAs protect against an *average* over hypothetical sets of cast votes (rather than the worst case); the weights in the average come from the *prior*.

The priors that have been proposed for BAs do not seem to correspond to beliefs about voter preferences, nor do they take into account the chance of error or manipulation. Moreover, BAs do not condition on a number of things that bear on whether the reported outcome is likely to be wrong, such as the reported margin and the political consequences. As Vora [28] shows, some BAs are RLAs if the prior is chosen suitably. Bayesian upset probabilities can never be larger than the maximum risk, but it seems that they can be arbitrarily smaller. Conversely, Huang et al. [10] discuss finding a threshold for the upset probability in a BA using a nonpartisan prior for a two-candidate, no invalid-vote contest so that using that threshold as a limit on the upset probability yields an RLA (with a larger risk limit).

Sequential RLAs stop as soon as there is strong evidence that the reported result is correct. When the outcome is correct by a wide margin, they generally inspect relatively few ballots. Thus, even though RLAs protect against the worst case, they are relatively efficient when outcomes are correct. (When outcomes are incorrect, they are intended to lead to a full hand tabulation.)

Partisanship, foreign interference, vendor misrepresentations [29], and suspicious results [16] all threaten public trust in elections, potentially destabilizing our democracy. Conducting elections primarily on hand-marked paper ballots (with accessible options for voters with disabilities), routine compliance audits, and RLAs can help ensure that elections deserve public trust.

References

1. American Statistical Association. American Statistical Association statement on risk-limiting post-election audits (2010). www.amstat.org/outreach/pdfs/Risk-Limiting_Endorsement.pdf
2. Appel, A., Stark, P.: Evidence-based elections: create a meaningful paper trail, then audit. Georgetown Law Technol. Rev. 4(2), 523–541 (2020). https://georgetownlaw techreview.org/wp-content/uploads/2020/07/4.2-p523-541-Appel-Stark.pdf
3. Appel, A., DeMillo, R., Stark, P.: Ballot-marking devices cannot assure the will of the voters. Elect. Law J. Rules Polit. Policy (2020). https://papers.ssrn.com/sol3/papers.cfm?abstract_id=3375755

4. Bernhard, M., et al.: Can voters detect malicious manipulation of ballot marking devices? In: 41st IEEE Symposium on Security and Privacy (2020). https://jhalderm.com/pub/papers/bmd-verifiability-sp20.pdf

5. Bickel, P., Doksum, K.: Mathematical Statistics: Basic Ideas and Selected Topics. Pearson (2006)

6. Blom, M., Stuckey, P., Teague, V.: RAIRE: Risk-limiting audits for IRV elections (2019). https://arxiv.org/abs/1903.08804

7. Brennan Center for Justice, Rhode Island RLA Working Group. Pilot implementation study of risk-limiting audit methods in the state of Rhode Island (2019). https://www.brennancenter.org/our-work/research-reports/pilot-implementation-study-risk-limiting-audit-methods-state-rhode-island

8. Colorado Secretary of State. Audit Center (2020). https://www.sos.state.co.us/pubs/elections/auditCenter.html

9. Howard, L., Rivest, R., Stark, P.: A review of robust post-election audits: Various methods of risk-limiting audits and Bayesian audits. Technical report, Brennan Center for Justice (2019). https://www.brennancenter.org/sites/default/files/2019-11/2019_011_RLA_Analysis_FINAL_0.pdf

10. Huang, Z., Rivest, R., Stark, P., Teague, V., Vukcevic, D.: A unified evaluation of two-candidate ballot-polling election auditing methods. In: Proceedings of the 5th Annual Conference on Electronic Voting (E-Vote-ID 2020) (2020)

11. Lindeman, M., Stark, P.: A gentle introduction to risk-limiting audits. IEEE Secur. Priv. 10, 42–49 (2012)

12. McCammon, S.: Virginia Republican David Yancey wins tie-breaking drawing (2018). https://www.npr.org/2018/01/04/573504079/virginia-republican-david-yancey-wins-tie-breaking-drawing

13. Michigan Secretary of State. Pilot audit of march presidential primary results showcases security, accuracy of Michigan elections systems (2020). www.michigan.gov/sos/0,4670,7--127-531561-,00.html

14. Morin, S., McClearn, G., McBurnett, N., Vora, P., Zagorski, F.: A note on risk-limiting Bayesian polling audits for two-candidate elections. In: Voting 2020 (2020, in press)

15. National Academies of Sciences: Engineering, and Medicine. Protecting American Democracy. The National Academies Press, Washington, DC, Securing the Vote (2018). https://doi.org/10.17226/25120. https://www.nap.edu/catalog/25120/securing-the-vote-protecting-american-democracy. ISBN 978-0-309-47647-8

16. Ottoboni, K., Stark, P.: Election integrity and electronic voting machines in 2018 Georgia, USA. In: E-Vote-ID 2019 Proceedings (2019). Preprint: https://ssrn.com/abstract=3426250

17. Ottoboni, K., Bernhard, M., Halderman, A., Rivest, R., Stark, P.: Bernoulli ballot polling: a manifest improvement for risk-limiting audits. In: Proceedings of the 4th Annual Workshop on Advances in Secure Electronic Voting (Voting 2019) (2018). Preprint: http://arxiv.org/abs/1812.06361

18. Ottoboni, K., Stark, P.B., Lindeman, M., McBurnett, N.: Risk-limiting audits by stratified union-intersection tests of elections (SUITE). In: Krimmer, R., et al. (eds.) E-Vote-ID 2018. LNCS, vol. 11143, pp. 174–188. Springer, Cham (2018). https://doi.org/10.1007/978-3-030-00419-4_12

19. Richie, R., Smith, H.: A survey and analysis of statewide election recounts 2000–2015 (2015). https://fairvote.app.box.com/v/recounts

20. Rivest, R., Shen, E.: A Bayesian method for auditing elections. In: Proceedings of the 2012 Electronic Voting Technology Workshop/Workshop on Trustworthy Elections (EVT/WOTE 2012). USENIX, August 2012
21. Rivest, R.L.: Bayesian tabulation audits: Explained and extended, January 1, 2018. https://arxiv.org/abs/1801.00528
22. Select Committee on Intelligence. Russian active measures campaigns and interference in the 2016 U.S. election (2019). https://www.intelligence.senate.gov/sites/default/files/documents/Report_Volume1.pdf
23. Stark, P.: Conservative statistical post-election audits. Ann. Appl. Stat. **2**, 550–581 (2008). http://arxiv.org/abs/0807.4005
24. Stark, P.: Election audits by sampling with probability proportional to an error bound: dealing with discrepancies (2008). https://www.stat.berkeley.edu/~stark/Preprints/ppebwrwd08.pdf
25. Stark, P.: Sets of half-average nulls generate risk-limiting audits: SHANGRLA. In: Voting 2020 (2020, in press). Preprint: http://arxiv.org/abs/1911.10035
26. Stark, P.B., Wagner, D.A.: Evidence-based elections. IEEE Secur. Priv. **10**, 33–41 (2012). https://www.stat.berkeley.edu/ stark/Preprints/evidenceVote12.pdf
27. Verified Voting. The Verifier (2020). https://verifiedvoting.org/verifier/#mode/navigate/map/ppEquip/mapType/normal/year/2020
28. Vora, P.: Risk-limiting Bayesian polling audits for two-candidate elections (2019). https://arxiv.org/abs/1902.00999
29. Zetter, K.: The crisis of election security. The New York Times (2018). https://www.nytimes.com/2018/09/26/magazine/election-security-crisis-midterms.html
30. Zetter, K.: Critical U.S. election systems have been left exposed online despite official denials. Vice (2019). https://www.vice.com/en_us/article/3kzzk9/exclusive-critical-us-election-systems-have-been-left-exposed-online-despite-official-denials
31. Zetter, K.: How close did Russia really come to hacking the 2016 election? Politico (2019). https://www.politico.com/news/magazine/2019/12/26/did-russia-really-hack-2016-election-088171

CHVote: Sixteen Best Practices and Lessons Learned

Rolf Haenni$^{(\boxtimes)}$, Eric Dubuis, Reto E. Koenig, and Philipp Locher

Bern University of Applied Sciences, 2501 Biel, Switzerland
{rolf.haenni,eric.dubuis,reto.koenig,philipp.locher}@bfh.ch

Abstract. The authors of this paper had the opportunity to closely accompany the CHVote project of the State of Geneva during more than two years and to continue the project after its abrupt stop in 2018. This paper is an experience report from this collaboration and the subsequent project continuation. It describes the lessons learned from this project and proposes some best practices relative to sixteen different topics. The goal of the paper is to share this experience with the community.

1 Introduction

Developing a verifiable Internet voting system is a delicate task. While conducting elections over the Internet seems intuitively like a simple matter of counting votes submitted by voters, it actually defines a unique combination of difficult security and privacy problems. As a response to these problems, numerous cryptographic protocols have been proposed to guarantee different combinations of often conflicting security properties. While many aspects of the general problem are solved today in theory, it turned out that transforming them into reliable practical systems is a completely different challenge. In fact, not many projects have been successful so far. In the Switzerland, which played a pioneering role in the early days of Internet voting, three completely untransparent systems were in used for pilot elections with a limited number of voters over more than a decade. They were all black-box system with no verifiability. One of them was the CHVote system from the State of Geneva.

1.1 Project Context

As a response to the third report on *Vote électronique* by the Swiss Federal Council in 2013 and the new requirements of the Swiss Federal Chancellery [1,16], the State of Geneva invited leading scientific researchers and security experts to contribute to the development of their second-generation system *CHVote 2.0*. In this context, a collaboration contract between the State of Geneva and the Bern University of Applied Sciences was signed in 2016. The main goal of this collaboration was the specification of a cryptographic voting protocol that satisfies the new requirements to the best possible degree. The main output of this project is the *CHVote System Specification* document [9], which is publicly available at

© Springer Nature Switzerland AG 2020
R. Krimmer et al. (Eds.): E-Vote-ID 2020, LNCS 12455, pp. 95–111, 2020.
https://doi.org/10.1007/978-3-030-60347-2_7

the *Cryptology ePrint Archive* since April 2017. In the course of the project, updated document versions have been released in regular intervals.

In November 2018, the council of the State of Geneva announced an abrupt stop of the CHVote 2.0 project due to financial reasons.[1] This implied that with the release of Version 2.1 of the specification document in January 2019, the collaboration between the State of Geneva and the Bern University of Applied Sciences came to an end. In June 2019, the State of Geneva released all the public material that have been created during the CHVote 2.0 project, including the Java source code.[2] The implemented cryptographic protocol corresponds to Version 1.4.1 of the specification document.

To continue the CHVote project independently of the support from the State of Geneva, a new funding from *eGovernment Switzerland* has been acquired by the Bern University of Applied Sciences in August 2019. The main goal of this project was to release a final stable version of the specification document and to update the cryptographic core of the protocol based on the code released by the State of Geneva. As a first project deliverable, the current Version 3.0 of the specification document has been released in December 2019 [9]. At the time of writing this paper, the developed *OpenCHVote* software is not yet complete. Since the project is in its final stage, the code is expected to be released soon under a non-proprietary license.[3] The general purpose of the project is to make the achievements available to others for pursuing it further.

1.2   Goals and Paper Overview

This paper presents a retrospective view of the CHVote project over the last four years. The paper is divided into three sections. The two main sections describe our experience and lessons learned from our work related to the specification document and the development of corresponding software, respectively, and the final section discusses some general aspects of the project. The whole paper contains our proposal for best practices on sixteen different topics. We present these topics project in chronological order. While we think that they all have played an important role for the success of our project, we do not claim that the given list is complete or that all points are directly applicable to all similar projects.

Nevertheless, we believe that our experience is worth to be shared with the community, who may struggle with similar problems in other e-voting projects. Sharing our experience with the community is therefore the general goal of this paper. As such, it should been seen as an experience report, which may be helpful in other projects as a guideline for achieving the required quality level in a shorter amount of time. Some of the proposed best practices may even set a certain minimal quality benchmark for e-voting projects in general.

---

[1] For further details about the reasons for abandoning the project, we refer to the State Council's press statement at https://www.ge.ch/document/12832/telecharger.

[2] See https://chvote2.gitlab.io.

[3] See https://gitlab.com/openchvote.

2   Specification

Item 1: Modeling the Electoral Systems
Democracies around the world use very different electoral systems to determine how elections and referendums are conducted. A major challenge in the design of CHVote was to cover the variety of electoral systems that exist in the Swiss context. On a single election day, democratic decisions are sometimes taken simultaneously on federal, cantonal, and communal issues, with election laws that differ from canton to canton. To cope with this complexity, we managed to map all electoral systems into a concise and coherent *electoral model* that is applicable to all possible situations. The core of this model is an *election event*, which consists of several independent *k-out-of-n elections*, in which voters can choose exactly k different candidates from a candidate list of size n. An election event is therefore defined by two vectors of such values k and n.

With this simple model, we were able to cover all electoral systems from the Swiss context with their specific properties, exceptions, and subtleties.[4] Elections of the Swiss National Council turned out to be the most complicated use case, but by splitting them into two independent elections, one 1-out-of-n_p party election and one cumulative k-out-of-n_c candidate election, they fit nicely into the general model [9, Sect. 2.3.2]. By reducing this complexity to essentially two public election parameters and by instantiating them to past election events in all regions of our country, we managed to determine upper limits $k_{max} = 150$ and $n_{max} = 1500$ for the overall problem size.

Defining a general electoral model and keeping it as simple and coherent as possible turned out to be a really important abstraction layer, which allowed us to design the cryptographic protocol independently of the variety of election use cases. The above-mentioned estimation of the maximal problem size defined important cornerstones for judging the suitability of cryptographic techniques and for anticipating potential performance bottlenecks. Therefore, we recommend to carefully design a suitable model of the electoral system as early as possible in projects like this.

Item 2: Modeling the Electorate
For a given election event in the given context of the CHVote project, an additional complication is the possibility that voters may not be eligible in all elections. This can happen for two reasons. First, since cantons are in charge of organizing elections, it may happen that elections are held simultaneously in different communes of a given canton, possibly in conjunction with cantonal and federal elections. In such cases, voters are equally eligible for federal and cantonal issues, but not for communal issues. Second, since non-Swiss citizens are allowed to vote in some canton and communes, they may be part of the electorate for cantonal or communal issues, but not for federal issues.

---

[4] We only had to admit one exception from the general model to allow write-in candidates in some cantons.

To map all possible cases of restricted eligibility into a general model, we introduced in CHVote the concept an *eligibility matrix*, which defines for a given electorate the eligibility of each voter in each election. By connecting this matrix with the two vectors from the general election event model, we can derive for each voter the number of admissible choices in each election. To ensure the correctness of an election outcome, it is absolutely critical for all involved parties to know these values at all times. This includes auditors performing the verification process in the aftermath of an election. The eligibility matrix is therefore a third fundamental public election parameter. Without taking it as additional input, the verification of an election result can not produce a conclusive outcome.

Item 3: Cryptographic Building Blocks

Given the central role of the cryptographic building blocks in a voting protocol, we recommend describing them in the beginning of the specification document. This lays the grounds for the whole document, for example by introducing respective terms and formal notations. By describing the building block next to each other, ambiguities and conflicts in the formal notations can be eliminated in a systematic manner. Given the overall complexity of the CHVote protocol, finding a coherent set of mathematical symbols and using them consistently throughout the whole document was a ongoing challenge during the project. Providing the highest possible degree of disambiguation improves greatly the document's overall readability.

Another important aspect of describing the cryptographic building blocks is to select from the large amount of related literature exactly what is needed for the protocol. Everything can be instantiated to the specific use case and underspecified technical details can be defined to the maximal possible degree. Examples of such technical details are the encoding methods between integers, strings, and byte arrays, or the method of computing hash values of multiple inputs. Another example of an often underspecified building block is the Fiat-Shamir transformation, which is widely applied for constructing non-interactive zero-knowledge protocols [6]. The significance of doing these things right is well documented [4,15]. A separate chapter on these topics helps to present all important cryptographic aspects in a concise form.

Item 4: Cryptographic Parameters

The collection of cryptographic building blocks defines a list of cryptographic parameters for the protocol. This list of parameters is an important input for every participating party. In CHVote, it consists of a total of twenty parameters, which themselves depend on four top-level security parameters [9, Sect. 6.3.1 and Table 6.1]. In theory, proper parameterization is fundamental for defining the protocol's security properties in the computationally bounded adversary model, and in practice, proper parameterization provides the necessary flexibility for adjusting the system's actual security to the desired strength. Given its central role in the security model, we recommend making the cryptographic parameters as clear and visible as possible to everyone.

For building an even more solid basis for an actual CHVote implementation, explicit values are specified for all cryptographic parameters. We introduced four different security levels [9, Sect. 11]. Level 0, which provides only 16 bits of security, has been included for testing purposes. Corresponding mathematical groups are large enough for hosting small elections, but small enough to avoid expensive computations during the tests. Providing a particular security level for testing turned out to be very useful for the software development process. Levels 1, 2, and 3 correspond to current NIST key length recommendations for 80 bits (legacy), 112 bits, and 128 bits of security, respectively [2]. All group parameters are determined deterministically, for example by deriving them from the binary representation of Euler's number. Applying such deterministic procedures demonstrates that the parameters are free from hidden backdoors.

Item 5: Parties and Communication

Parties participating in a cryptographic protocol are usually regarded as atomic entities with distinct, responsibilities, abilities, goals, and attributed tasks. In the design of the protocol, it is important for the parties and their communication abilities to match reality as closely as possible. In CHVote, we decided to consider the voters and their voting devices as two separate types of parties with very different abilities. This distinction turned out to be useful for multiple purposes. First, it enables a more accurate adversary model, because attacks against humans and machines are very different in nature. Second, by including the tasks of the human voters in the abstract protocol description, it provides an accurate model for simulating human voters in a testing environment.

If a voting protocol depends on fully trusted parties, particular care must be applied in the design of their responsibilities and tasks. The *election administrator* and the *printing authority* fall into this category in CHVote. In both cases, we placed great emphasis on limiting their responsibilities to their main role in the protocol. The printing authority, for example, only applies a deterministic algorithm to assemble the inputs from multiple election authorities. The resulting voting cards, which are then printed and sent to the voters, are the only output of this procedure. The procedure itself can be executed in a controlled offline environment. After terminating this task, the printing authority is no longer involved in the protocol, i.e., all its resources can be freed for other tasks. In the aftermath of an election, the voting cards of all participating voters can be reconstructed from the publicly available information. In this way, possible frauds or failures by a corrupt printing authority can be detected. It also means that the printing authority does not need to protect any long-term secrecy.

The definition of the parties in the abstract protocol model includes a description of their communication abilities. Properties of corresponding communication channels need to be specified, again in close accordance with a possible real-world setting. In CHVote, several authenticated and one confidential communication channel are needed to meet to protocol's security requirements [9, Figure 6.1]. This implies the existence of a public-key infrastructure (PKI), which needs to be precisely specified as part of the communication model. To minimize the size of the PKI and the resulting key management overhead, we recommend keeping the number of participating parties (except the voters) as small as possible. Ideally, this PKI can be mapped one-to-one into an implementation of the system.

Item 6: Protocol Structure and Communication Diagrams

A precise and comprehensive description of the voting protocol is the most fundamental system design output. To cope with the overall complexity, we divided the CHVote protocol into three phases and a total of ten sub-phases. We drew protocol diagrams for each of these sub-phases. A portion of one of these diagrams is shown in Fig. 1. Each diagram shows the involved parties, the relevant elements of the acquired knowledge, the messages exchanged between the parties, and all conducted computations. The description of the computations involves calls to algorithms, which are given in a separate section (see Item 11). To optimally connect these diagrams with the remaining parts of the document, we strictly applied our consistent set of mathematical notations and symbols (see Item 3). Keeping these diagrams up-to-date and ensuring their correctness and completeness was a constant challenge during the protocol design. Given their fundamental role in the whole system design, we recommend spending sufficient effort to achieve the best possible result. We see the communication diagrams of the protocol as the core of the system's master plan, which does not permit any lack of clarity or unanswered questions.

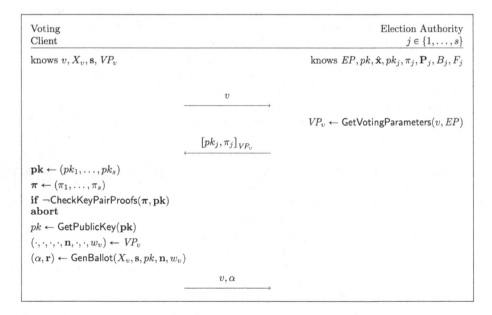

Fig. 1. Exemplary communication diagram: vote casting sub-phase (first part).

Item 7: Pseudo-Code Algorithms

To push the given amount of technical details to the limit, we decided in an early stage of the CHVote project to provide a full set of pseudo-code algorithms for every computational task in the protocol [9, Sect. 8]. The current version of the protocol consists of a total of 79 algorithms and sub-algorithms for very different purposes, including primitives for converting basic data types, for computing hash values of complex mathematical objects, or for generating digital signatures. A large portion of the algorithms deals with the core of the CHVote protocol, which realizes a method for transferring verification codes obliviously to the voters in a distributed manner [8]. Other algorithms describe the verifiable mix-net and the distributed decryption process [10, 12]. By maintaining the consistent set of mathematical symbols and notation, this section of the specification document is smoothly integrated into the big picture of the cryptographic protocol. A tremendous amount of initial work, re-factoring, and housekeeping was necessary to reach the stability of the current set of algorithms. Like in regular code, we applied certain pseudo-code style guides to achieve a maximally consistent result. In Fig. 2, the algorithm for generating a ballot is given as an example.

Algorithm: $\mathsf{GenBallot}(X, \mathbf{s}, pk, \mathbf{n}, w)$

Input: Voting code $X \in A_X^{\ell_X}$
         Selection $\mathbf{s} = (s_1, \ldots, s_k)$, $1 \leqslant s_1 < \cdots < s_k \leqslant n$
         Encryption key $pk \in \mathbb{G}_q$
         Number of candidates $\mathbf{n} = (n_1, \ldots, n_t)$, $n_j \in \mathbb{N}^+$, $n = \sum_{j=1}^{t} n_j$
         Counting circle $w \in \mathbb{N}^+$

$x \leftarrow \mathsf{ToInteger}(X, A_x)$ // see Alg. 4.8

$\hat{x} \leftarrow \hat{g}^x \bmod \hat{p}$

$\mathbf{p} \leftarrow \mathsf{GetPrimes}(n + w)$ // $\mathbf{p} = (p_0, \ldots, p_{n+w})$, see Alg. 8.1

$\mathbf{m} \leftarrow \mathsf{GetEncodedSelections}(\mathbf{s}, \mathbf{p})$ // $\mathbf{m} = (m_1, \ldots, m_k)$, see Alg. 8.24

$m \leftarrow \prod_{j=1}^{k} m_j$

if $p_{n+w} \cdot m \geqslant p$ **then**
     return $\perp$ // $\mathbf{s}$, $\mathbf{n}$, and w are incompatible with p

$(\mathbf{a}, \mathbf{r}) \leftarrow \mathsf{GenQuery}(\mathbf{m}, pk)$ // $\mathbf{a} = (a_1, \ldots, a_k)$, $\mathbf{r} = (r_1, \ldots, r_k)$, see Alg. 8.25

$r \leftarrow \sum_{j=1}^{k} r_j \bmod q$

$\pi \leftarrow \mathsf{GenBallotProof}(x, m, r, \hat{x}, \mathbf{a}, pk)$ // see Alg. 8.26

$\alpha \leftarrow (\hat{x}, \mathbf{a}, \pi)$

return $(\alpha, \mathbf{r})$ // $\alpha \in \mathbb{G}_{\hat{q}} \times (\mathbb{G}_q^2)^k \times (\mathbb{Z}_{2^\tau} \times (\mathbb{Z}_{\hat{q}} \times \mathbb{G}_q \times \mathbb{Z}_q))$, $\mathbf{r} \in \mathbb{Z}_q^k$

Fig. 2. Exemplary pseudo-code algorithm: ballot generation.

To the best of our knowledge, enhancing the specification document of an e-voting system with a complete set of pseudo-code algorithms was a novelty in 2017—and still is today. Our experience with this approach is very positive in almost every respect. First, it added an additional layer to the protocol design, which created an entirely new perspective. Viewing the protocol from this perspective allowed us to recognize certain problems in the protocol design at an early stage. Without detecting them by challenging the protocol from the pseudo-code perspective, they would have come up later during code development.

Another positive effect of releasing pseudo-code algorithms in an early version of the specification document was the possibility of giving third parties the opportunity to inspect, analyze, or even implement the algorithms (see Item 15). Within a few months, we received feedback from two different implementation projects in different programming languages—from the CHVote developers in Geneva and from students of ours [13,14]. This feedback was useful for further improving the quality of the specification document, but more importantly, it demonstrated that we managed to considerably reduce the complexity of developing the core tasks of the protocol in a suitable programming language. Our students, for example, who had only little experience in developing cryptographic applications, managed to fully implement all protocol algorithms from scratch in less than four months time. The resulting code from these projects also demonstrated how to almost entirely eliminate the error-prone gap between code and specification. This gap is a typical problem in comparable projects, especially when it comes to check the correctness of the code by external auditors. Without such a gap, auditors can enforce the focus of their inspection to software-development issues. In the light of these remarks, we learned in this project that providing pseudo-code algorithms defines an ideal interface between cryptographers and software developers.

Item 8: Usability and Performance

During the design of the CHVote protocol, we realized that parts of the overall complexity can be left unspecified without affecting the protocol's security properties. We separated some issues that only affect the usability or the performance of the system from the core protocol and discussed them in separate sections.[5] The general idea is to identify aspects that *can* be implemented in a real system or in a certain way, but with no obligation to do so. The benefit of separating them from the core protocol is a higher degree of decoupling in the specification document, which permits discussing corresponding aspects independently of each other. An example of such an aspect is the strict usage of unspecified alphabets for all the codes delivered or displayed to the voters [9, Sect. 11.1]. Since the actual choice of the alphabets only affects usability (not security), it is something that can be discussed from a pure usability perspective. The situation is similar for various performance improvements, which are optional for an actual implementation. By studying them in a more general context and by publishing the results, our work generated valuable side-products [10,11].

---

[5] The performance section of the specification document is currently under construction. It will be included in one of the next releases.

3   Implementation

Item 9: Mathematical Library

The languages of mathematicians and computer scientists are fairly similar in many respects, but there are also some fundamental differences. One such difference comes from the stateless nature of most mathematical objects, which is very different from mutable data structures in imperative or object-oriented programming languages such as Java. Other differences stem from established conventions. One example of such a convention is the index notation for referring to the elements of a list, vector, or matrix, which usually starts from from 1 in mathematics and from 0 in programming. If a complex cryptographic protocol needs to be translated into programming code, this difference makes the translation process error-prone.

To minimize in our CHVote implementation the difference between specification and code, we introduced a Java library for some additional immutable mathematical objects. The core classes of this library are `Vector`, `Matrix`, `Set`, `ByteArray`, `Alphabet`, and `Tuple` (with sub-classes `Pair`, `Triple`, ...). All of them are strictly generic and immutable. Applying generics in a systematic way greatly improves type-safety, for example in case of complex nested types such as

```
Triple<BigInteger, Vector<String>, Pair<Integer, ByteArray>>.
```

Working with immutable objects has many advantages. They are easier to design, they can always be reused safely, and testing them is much easier [5, P. 80]. `String` and `BigInteger` are examples of given immutable classes in Java. In our mathematical library, we adopted the convention of accessing the elements of a vector of size n with non-zero indices $i \in \{1, \dots, n\}$, and similarly for matrices and tuples. This delegates the translation between different indexing conventions to theses classes and therefore eliminates the error-proneness of this process. It also creates a one-to-one correspondence between indexing variables in the specification and the code, which is beneficial for the overall code readability.

In our experience of implementing the CHVote protocol, the mathematical library turned out to be a key component for achieving the desired level of code quality in a reasonable amount of time. Given its central role in all parts of the system, we put a lot of effort into performance optimizations, rigorous testing, and documentation. We highly recommend the creation and inclusion of such a library in similar projects.

Item 10: Naming Conventions

Most programming languages have a well-established set of naming conventions. Generally, software developers are advised to *"rarely violate them and never without a very good reason"* [5, P. 289]. Not adhering to the conventions usually lowers the code readability and makes code maintenance unnecessarily complicated, especially if multiple developers are involved. In some situations, deviations from common conventions may even lead to false assumptions and programming errors. In Java, the naming convention for variables, fields, and method parameters is to use a connected sequence of words, with the first letter of each subsequent word capitalized (a.k.a. "camel case"), for example `maxVoterIndex`. Abbreviations such as `max` or single letters such as `i` are allowed, as long as their meaning in the given context remains clear.

In our implementation of the cryptographic protocol, we decided to deviate from general Java naming conventions. To achieve our goal of diminishing the gap between specification and code to the maximal possible degree, we decided to adopt the mathematical symbols from the protocol specification as precisely as possible in the code. This includes defining upper-case variable names in Java such as `Set<Integer> X` for a set X of integers. In such cases, we prioritized project-internal naming consistency over general Java naming conventions. Tagged, boldface, or Greek variable names are spelled out accordingly, for example $\hat{\alpha}_{ij}$ as `alpha_hat_ij` or $\mathbf{k}'$ as `bold_k_prime`. We strictly applied this pattern throughout all parts of the code. Code that is written in this way may look quite unconventional at first sight, but it turned out to be a key element for making the Java code look almost exactly the same as the pseudo-code. As an example, consider our implementation of the algorithm GenBallot in Fig. 3, which closely matches with the pseudo-code from Fig. 2.

```java
public class GenBallot extends ch.chvote.algorithms.common.GenBallot {

    public static Pair<Ballot, Vector<BigInteger>>
        run(String X, IntVector bold_s, QuadraticResidue pk, IntVector bold_n, int w, Parameters params) {

        // PREPARATION
        int n = Math.intSum(bold_n);
        Precondition.checkNotNull(X, bold_s, pk, bold_n, params);
        Precondition.check(params.GG_q.contains(pk));
        Precondition.check(IntSet.NN_plus.contains(w));
        Precondition.check(Set.String(params.A_X, params.ell_X).contains(X));
        Precondition.check(Set.IntVector(IntSet.NN_plus).contains(bold_n));
        Precondition.check(Set.IntVector(IntSet.NN_plus(n)).contains(bold_s));
        Precondition.check(bold_s.isSorted());

        // ALGORITHM
        var x = ToInteger.run(X, params.A_X);
        var x_hat = Mod.pow(params.g_hat, x, params.p_hat);
        var bold_p = GetPrimes.run(n + w, params);
        var bold_m = GetEncodedSelections.run(bold_s, bold_p);
        var m = Math.prod(bold_m.map(QuadraticResidue::getValue));
        if (bold_p.getValue(n + w).getValue().multiply(m).compareTo(params.p) >= 0) {
            throw new AlgorithmException(GenBallot.class, AlgorithmException.Type.INCOMPATIBLE_MATRIX);
        }
        var pair = GenQuery.run(bold_m, pk, params);
        var bold_a = pair.getFirst();
        var bold_r = pair.getSecond();
        var r = Mod.sum(bold_r, params.q);
        var pi = GenBallotProof.run(x, Mod.prod(bold_m), r, x_hat, bold_a, pk, params);
        var alpha = new Ballot(x_hat, bold_a, pi);
        return new Pair<>(alpha, bold_r);
    }
}
```

Fig. 3. Exemplary Java code: ballot generation.

Item 11: Implementation of Pseudo-Code Algorithms

We already discussed our view of the pseudo-code algorithms as an ideal interface between cryptographers specifying the protocol and software developers implementing corresponding code (see Item 7). In such a setting, the implementation of the algorithms inherently defines an important bottom layer of the whole system architecture. To strengthen the overall clarity in our implementation of the algorithms, we decided the create separate utility class for all top-level algorithms. Each of them contains exactly one static method `run(<args>)`, which implements the algorithm (plus static nested classes for all sub-algorithms), for example `GenBallot.run(<args>)` for the algorithm GenBallot. This way of structuring the algorithm module establishes direct links to the specification document. These links are clearly visible by inspecting the project's package structure. A section of this package structure is shown in Fig. 4.

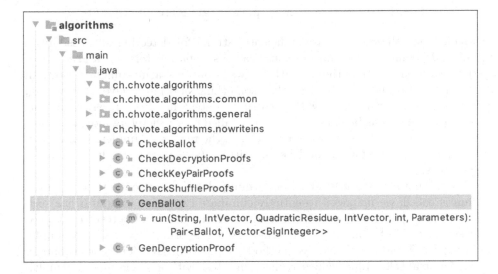

Fig. 4. Package structure of static utility classes for top-level algorithms.

Given the central role of the protocol algorithms for the whole system, we put extra care and effort into developing this part of the code. To obtain the best possible code consistency, we defined a set of project-internal coding style guidelines and applied them strictly to all algorithms. Each algorithm went through an internal reviewing and testing process over multiple rounds, which involved different persons according to the *Four Eyes Principle*. The result is a consistent set of Java methods that are perfectly aligned with the pseudo-code algorithms from the specification. The example shown in Figs. 2 and 3 demonstrates how precisely the algorithms have been translated into code.

We see perfect alignment between specification and code as a quality criterion of highest priority. This implies that even the smallest change in either the specification or the code needs to be updated immediately on the other side. The general idea here is to view them as *the same thing*. This view enables third-party auditors that are familiar with the naming conventions and coding style guidelines to check the translation from specification to programming code at minimal costs. We believe that auditing the implementation of the algorithms remains a diligent (but mostly routine) piece of work, which does not necessarily require the involvement of cryptographic experts.

Item 12: Parameter Validity Checks

An important aspect of the proposed way of implementing the protocol algorithms is the introduction of systematic validity checks of all input parameters. These checks complement the built-in type safety obtained from strictly using the generic mathematical library (see Item 9). The domains of all input parameters are specified in the pseudo-code algorithms, for example $X \in A_X^{\ell_X}$ in GenBallot for a string of characters from the alphabet A_X of length ℓ_X, which translates into the following line of Java code (see Fig. 3, Line 36):

```
Set.Strings(params.A_X, params.ell_X).contains(X)
```

Provided that these checks are sufficiently strong for detecting all possibilities of invalid parameters—or invalid combinations of parameters—of a given algorithm, they ensure that the algorithm always outputs a meaningful result. In case of a failed check, it is clear that something else must have gone wrong, for example that a message with a corrupt content has been received or that some stored data has been modified. Every failed check therefore indicates some deviation from a normal protocol run. This is the reason for implementing them in a systematic way for all top-level algorithms (sub-algorithms do not require such checks).

To minimize the overhead of performing these checks each time an algorithm is called, we managed to entirely eliminate expensive computations such as modular exponentiations. To efficiently perform membership tests $x \in \mathbb{G}_q$ for the set $\mathbb{G}_q \subset \mathbb{Z}_p^*$ of quadratic residue modulo a safe prime $p = 2q + 1$, we implemented the *membership witness* method proposed in [10]. The corresponding class `QuadraticResidue`, which realizes this test with a single modular multiplication, is part of our mathematical library. In Fig. 3, the parameter `pk` is of that type, and its membership test is conducted in Line 38.

Item 13: Implementation of Protocol Parties

To implement the protocol based on the algorithms, we designed a software component for every involved party. These components share some code for various common tasks, but otherwise they are largely independent. For the design of each party, we derived a state diagram from the protocol description in the specification document. This diagram defines the party's behavior during a protocol run. Typically, receiving a message of certain type triggers the party to perform a transition into the next state. The transition itself consist of computations and messages to be sent to other parties. The computations, which we call *tasks*, can be implemented by calling corresponding protocol algorithms.

The left-hand side of Fig. 5 shows the UML state diagram of the printing authority (printer), which consists of two states SP1 and SP2 and one error state EP1. In SP1, the printer expects messages of type MAP1 and MEP1. If all messages are received, the transition into SP2 (or EP1) is triggered. This involves computing task TP1 and sending two types of messages MPV1 and MAX1. The error state EP1 is reached in case of an exception of type AE (algorithm exception) or TE (task exception). This diagram represents the printer's view of the printing sub-phase [9, Protocol 7.2], which is the only sub-phase in which the printer is active. Similar state diagrams exist for all other parties and sub-phases. We defined further naming conventions and strictly applied them to all tasks and message types.

Modeling the parties using the (extended) state machine formalism turned out to be the ideal approach for structuring the parties' implementations in the most natural way. It also allowed us to apply the *state pattern*, one of the well-known "Gang of Four" design patterns [7, P. 305]. This made our implementation very transparent from a general software-engineering perspective. The right-hand side of Fig. 5 shows a section of the package structure, which illustrates for example that the party class `Printer` depends on three state classes SP1, SP2, and EP1, and one task class TE1. Every other party is implemented in exactly this way. Every task and every message type is connected to one of the sub-phase diagrams in the protocol specification, and vice versa.

Using the state pattern, we achieve close correspondence between specification and code also on the abstraction layer representing the parties. Again, we see the code and the specification related to the parties as essentially *the same things*, which means that the slightest change on one side needs to be updated immediately on the other side. In this way, we tried to achieve a similar level of structural clarity and code quality as for the algorithm implementation. The state pattern was also useful for establishing the flexibility of running multiple election events simultaneously (possibly using different protocol versions).

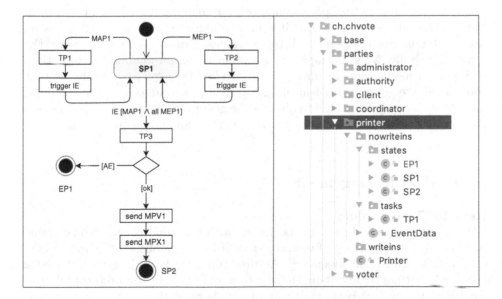

Fig. 5. State diagram of the printer (left) vs. package structure of party classes (right).

Item 14: Cryptographically Relevant Code

Providing code for all algorithms and all parties concludes the implementation of the cryptographically relevant part of the protocol. This is where flaws in the code can cause critical errors or vulnerabilities. Generally, we recommend structuring the software design into *cryptographically relevant* and *cryptographically irrelevant* components and to link them over suitable interfaces. Our current implementation of the CHVote protocol is limited to the cryptographically relevant part of the system, but we provide the required interfaces, for example for connecting our code to concrete high-performance messaging and persistence services.

For testing purposes, we only implemented these interfaces in a rudimentary way, but this turned out to be sufficient for simulating even the most complex election use case from top to bottom. Such a simulation can be conducted on a single machine using any common development environment, i.e., no complex installation of a distributed test environment over multiple servers is required. This is an efficient environment for running all sorts of functional tests with a clear focus on the cryptographic protocol. With almost no communication overhead, it is also ideal for analyzing and optimizing the overall protocol performance. A precondition for establishing a complete test run is the implementation of all protocol parties, including the (human) voters. Even if corresponding code will obviously not be included in a real-world deployment of the system, we see it as an indispensable component of our implementation.

Given its central role in the overall security of the system, we tried to make the cryptographically relevant part of the code accessible to the broadest possible audience. For that, we decided to avoid dependencies to complex third-party libraries or software frameworks as far as possible. We only admitted two dependencies to the widely used native GMP library for efficient computations with large numbers and to the Spock framework for enabling data-driven tests. Both libraries are almost entirely invisible in our implementation, i.e., there is no need to familiarize reviewers with these technologies (except for reviewing the tests). Generally, we see complex frameworks based on annotation, reflection, or injection mechanisms as unsuited for developing cryptographically relevant code. They are great for implementing enterprise software components at minimal costs, but they often tend to obscure the general program flow. This reduces the overall code readability and makes static code analysis more difficult.

4   Project Management

Item 15: Transparency

We started this project from the beginning with the mindset of maximal transparency. At an early stage of the project in 2017, we published the first version of our specification document [9]. At that time, we had already published a peer-reviewed paper describing the cryptographic core of the protocol [8]. The feedback that we received, mostly from members of the e-voting community, was very useful for improving the protocol and its security properties. The most important feedback came from Tomasz Truderung on April 19, 2017, who found a subtle but serious flaw in the construction of our protocol. This flaw had been overlooked by the reviewers of the published paper. After a few weeks, we were able fix the problem to a full extent and update the protocol accordingly. In the meantime, the success of the entire project was at stake.

We recall this anecdote here for making two important points. First, releasing specification documents of an e-voting project usually launches a public examination process in the community. The outcome of this process is sometimes unpredictable, but the received feedback has the potential of greatly improving the quality of the protocol. At the time of writing this document, we have not yet released the source code for public examination, but we expect a similar amount of interest and feedback from the community. Second, a cryptographic protocol without formal security definitions and rigorous proofs provides not a sufficiently solid foundations for building a system. In CHVote, a different group of academics was contracted by the State of Geneva to perform this task. The outcome of this sister project was released in 2018 [3]. The high quality of their work leads one to suppose that the above-mentioned flaw would have been detected in their analysis. Unfortunately, their report has not yet been updated to the current version of the protocol.

In this project, our mindset of maximal transparency always allowed us to openly discuss all aspects of our work with many different people, including students of ours who developed various prototypes [13,14]. This created a permanent challenge for the cryptographic protocol, which forced us to constantly question our design decisions and improve our technical solutions. We conclude that releasing all cryptographically relevant documents as a matter of principle was fundamental for the success of the project. More generally, we see it as an important trust-establishing measure.

Item 16: Verifier

The last point we want to mention in this paper is an important aspect for a verifiable e-voting system. Unfortunately, we were not yet able to cover it in this project. It's about specifying the verification software—sometimes called *the verifier*—for the proposed protocol. In the original project setting of the State of Geneva, it was planned to outsource the specification and development of the verifier to a third-party institution. To establish a certain degree of independence between the protocol and the verifier, this decision of the project owners was perfectly understandable. We never questioned this decision, but it prevented us from paying enough attention to this important topic. When the project was dropped in fall 2018, the outsourced verifier project had started, but it was not yet very advanced. This finally led to the current situation, where the specification and the implementation of the e-voting protocol are both very advanced, but almost nothing is available for the verifier. Even though, the e-voting protocol describes how to verify certain cryptographic aspects, but that is not to be confused with the complete verification of the whole voting process.

We believe that in projects like this, it's best to let the specification of the protocol and the verifier go hand in hand, and to apply the same level of preciseness and completeness to both of them. We see the verifier as the ultimate way of challenging the protocol run, both in the abstract setting of the specification document and in the concrete setting of executing the code on real machines. So far, this challenge is missing in our project.

5   Conclusion

In software development, best practices are available in many areas. They are very useful for developers to avoid bad design decisions and typical programming mistakes. This certainly also holds for developing an e-voting system, but the delicacy of implementing a cryptographic protocol makes the situation a bit more complicated. We therefore believe that the e-voting community should come up with its own set of best practices and define respective minimal standards. This paper makes a first step into this directions based on our experience from the CHVote project. Among the discussed sixteen topics, we believe that the advice of providing all algorithmic details in pseudo-code is the most important one, together with structuring the source code into a cryptographically relevant and a cryptographically irrelevant part.

References

1. Verordnung der Bundeskanzlei über die elektronische Stimmabgabe (VEleS) vom 13. Dezember 2013 (Stand 1. Juli 2018). Die Schweizerische Bundeskanzlei (BK) (2018)
2. Barker, E.: Recommendation for key management. NIST Special Publication 800–57, Part 1, Rev. 5, NIST (2020)
3. Bernhard, D., Cortier, V., Gaudry, P., Turuani, M., Warinschi, B.: Verifiability analysis of CHVote. IACR Cryptology ePrint Archive, 2018/1052 (2018)
4. Bernhard, D., Pereira, O., Warinschi, B.: How not to prove yourself: pitfalls of the Fiat-Shamir heuristic and applications to helios. In: Wang, X., Sako, K. (eds.) ASIACRYPT 2012. LNCS, vol. 7658, pp. 626–643. Springer, Heidelberg (2012). https://doi.org/10.1007/978-3-642-34961-4_38
5. Bloch, J.: Effective Java, 3rd edn. Addison-Wesley (2018)
6. Fiat, A., Shamir, A.: How to prove yourself: practical solutions to identification and signature problems. In: Odlyzko, A.M. (ed.) CRYPTO 1986. LNCS, vol. 263, pp. 186–194. Springer, Heidelberg (1987). https://doi.org/10.1007/3-540-47721-7_12
7. Gamma, E., Helm, R., Johnson, R., Vlissides, J.: Design Patterns - Elements of Reusable Object-Oriented Software. Addison-Wesley (1994)
8. Haenni, R., Koenig, R.E., Dubuis, E.: Cast-as-intended verification in electronic elections based on oblivious transfer. In: Krimmer, R., et al. (eds.) E-Vote-ID 2016. LNCS, vol. 10141, pp. 73–91. Springer, Cham (2017). https://doi.org/10.1007/978-3-319-52240-1_5
9. Haenni, R., Koenig, R.E., Locher, P., Dubuis, E.: CHVote system specification - version 3.0. IACR Cryptology ePrint Archive, 2017/325 (2020)

10. Haenni, R., Locher, P.: Performance of shuffling: taking it to the limits. In: Voting 2020, FC: International Workshops, Kota Kinabalu, Malaysia, p. 2020 (2020)

11. Haenni, R., Locher, P., Gailly, N.: Improving the performance of cryptographic voting protocols. In: Bracciali, A., Clark, J., Pintore, F., Rønne, P.B., Sala, M. (eds.) FC 2019. LNCS, vol. 11599, pp. 272–288. Springer, Cham (2020). https://doi.org/10.1007/978-3-030-43725-1_19

12. Haenni, R., Locher, P., Koenig, R., Dubuis, E.: Pseudo-code algorithms for verifiable re-encryption mix-nets. In: Brenner, M., et al. (eds.) FC 2017. LNCS, vol. 10323, pp. 370–384. Springer, Cham (2017). https://doi.org/10.1007/978-3-319-70278-0_23

13. Häni, K., Denzer, Y.: CHVote prototype in Python. Project report, Bern University of Applied Sciences, Biel, Switzerland (2017)

14. Häni, K., Denzer, Y.: Visualizing Geneva's next generation e-voting system. Bachelor thesis, Bern University of Applied Sciences, Biel, Switzerland (2018)

15. Lewis, S.J., Pereira, O., Teague, V.: How not to prove your election outcome. Technical report (2019)

16. Maurer, U., Casanova, C.: Bericht des Bundesrates zu Vote électronique. 3. Bericht, Schweizerischer Bundesrat (2013)

A Unified Evaluation of Two-Candidate Ballot-Polling Election Auditing Methods

Zhuoqun Huang[1], Ronald L. Rivest[2] (ID), Philip B. Stark[3] (ID),
Vanessa J. Teague[4,5] (ID), and Damjan Vukcevic[1,6(✉)] (ID)

[1] School of Mathematics and Statistics, University of Melbourne,
Parkville, Victoria, Australia
[2] Computer Science and Artificial Intelligence Laboratory,
Massachusetts Institute of Technology, Cambridge, Massachusetts, USA
[3] Department of Statistics, University of California, Berkeley, California, USA
[4] Thinking Cybersecurity Pty. Ltd., Melbourne, Victoria, Australia
[5] College of Engineering and Computer Science, Australian National University,
Canberra, ACT, Australia
[6] Melbourne Integrative Genomics, University of Melbourne,
Parkville, Victoria, Australia
damjan.vukcevic@unimelb.edu.au

Abstract. Counting votes is complex and error-prone. Several statistical methods have been developed to assess election accuracy by manually inspecting randomly selected physical ballots. Two 'principled' methods are risk-limiting audits (RLAs) and Bayesian audits (BAs). RLAs use frequentist statistical inference while BAs are based on Bayesian inference. Until recently, the two have been thought of as fundamentally different.

We present results that unify and shed light upon 'ballot-polling' RLAs and BAs (which only require the ability to sample uniformly at random from all cast ballot cards) for two-candidate plurality contests, that are building blocks for auditing more complex social choice functions, including some preferential voting systems. We highlight the connections between the methods and explore their performance.

First, building on a previous demonstration of the mathematical equivalence of classical and Bayesian approaches, we show that BAs, suitably calibrated, are risk-limiting. Second, we compare the efficiency of the methods across a wide range of contest sizes and margins, focusing on the distribution of sample sizes required to attain a given risk limit. Third, we outline several ways to improve performance and show how the mathematical equivalence explains the improvements.

Keywords: Statistical audit · Risk-limiting · Bayesian

1 Introduction

Even if voters verify their ballots and the ballots are kept secure, the counting process is prone to errors from malfunction, human error, and malicious

The original version of this chapter was revised: this chapter contains mistakes. This has been corrected. The correction to this chapter is available at
https://doi.org/10.1007/978-3-030-60347-2_15

R. Krimmer et al. (Eds.): E-Vote-ID 2020, LNCS 12455, pp. 112–128, 2020.
https://doi.org/10.1007/978-3-030-60347-2_8

intervention. For this reason, the US National Academy of Sciences [4] and the American Statistical Association[1] have recommended the use of risk-limiting audits to check reported election outcomes.

The simplest audit is a manual recount, which is usually expensive and time-consuming. An alternative is to examine a random sample of the ballots and test the result statistically. Unless the margin is narrow, a sample far smaller than the whole election may suffice. For more efficiency, sampling can be done adaptively: stop when there is strong evidence supporting the reported outcome [7].

Risk-limiting audits (RLAs) have become the audit method recommended for use in the USA. Pilot RLAs have been conducted for more than 50 elections in 14 US states and Denmark since 2008. Some early pilots are discussed in a report from the California Secretary of State to the US Election Assistance Commission.[2] In 2017, the state of Colorado became the first to complete a statewide RLA.[3] The defining feature of RLAs is that, if the reported outcome is incorrect, they have a large, pre-specified minimum probability of discovering this and correcting the outcome. Conversely, if the reported outcome is correct, then they will eventually certify the result. This might require only a small random sample, but the audit may lead to a complete manual tabulation of the votes if the result is very close or if tabulation error was an appreciable fraction of the margin.

RLAs exploit frequentist statistical hypothesis testing. There are by now more than half a dozen different approaches to conducting RLAs [8]. Election audits can also be based on Bayesian inference [6].

With so many methods, it may be hard to understand how they relate to each other, which perform better, which are risk-limiting, etc. Here, we review and compare the statistical properties of existing methods in the simplest case: a two-candidate, first-past-the-post contest with no invalid ballots. This allows us to survey a wide range of methods and more clearly describe the connections and differences between them. Most real elections have more than two candidates, of course. However, the methods designed for this simple context are often adapted for more complex elections by reducing them into pairwise contests (see below for further discussion of this point). Therefore, while we only explore a simple scenario, it sheds light on how the various approaches compare, which may inform future developments in more complex scenarios. There are many other aspects to auditing that matter greatly in practice, we do not attempt to cover all of these but we comment on some below.

For two-candidate, no-invalid-vote contests, we explain the connections and differences among many audit methods, including frequentist and Bayesian approaches. We evaluate their efficiency across a range of election sizes and margins. We also explore some natural extensions and variations of the meth-

---

[1] https://www.amstat.org/asa/files/pdfs/POL-ASARecommendsRisk-LimitingAudits.pdf.

[2] https://votingsystems.cdn.sos.ca.gov/oversight/risk-pilot/final-report-073014.pdf.

[3] https://www.denverpost.com/2017/11/22/colorado-election-audit-complete/.

ods. We ensure that the comparisons are 'fair' by numerically calibrating each method to attain a specified risk limit.

We focus on *ballot-polling audits*, which involve selecting ballots at random from the pool of cast ballots. Each sampled ballot is interpreted manually; those interpretations comprise the audit data. (Ballot-polling audits do not rely on the voting system's interpretation of ballots, in contrast to *comparison audits*.)

Paper Outline: Section 2 provides context and notation. Section 3 sketches the auditing methods we consider and points out the relationships among them and to other statistical methods. Section 4 explains how we evaluate these methods. Our benchmarking experiments are reported in Sect. 5. We finish with a discussion and suggestions for future work in Sect. 6.

2   Context and Notation: Two-Candidate Contests

We consider contests between two candidates, where each voter votes for exactly one candidate. The candidate who receives more votes wins. Ties are possible if the number of ballots is even.

Real elections may have invalid votes, for example, ballots marked in favour of both candidates or neither; for multipage ballots, not every ballot paper contains every contest. Here we assume every ballot has a valid vote for one of the two candidates. See Sect. 6.

Most elections have more than two candidates and can involve complex algorithms ('social choice functions') for determining who won. A common tactic for auditing these is to reduce them to a set of pairwise contests such that certifying all of the contests suffices to confirm the reported outcome [1,3,8]. These contests can be audited simultaneously using methods designed for two candidates that can accommodate invalid ballots, which most of the methods considered below do. Therefore, the methods we evaluate form the building blocks for many of the more complex methods, so our results are more widely relevant.

We do not consider *stratified audits*, which account for ballots cast across different locations or by different voting methods within the same election.

2.1   Ballot-Polling Audits for Two-Candidate Contests

We use the terms 'ballot' and 'ballot card' interchangeably, even though typical ballots in the US consist of more than one card (and the distinction does matter for workload and for auditing methods). We consider unweighted *ballot-polling* audits, which require only the ability to sample uniformly at random from all ballot cards.

The sampling is typically sequential. We draw an initial sample and assess the evidence for or against the reported outcome. If there is sufficient evidence that the reported outcome is correct, we stop and 'certify' the winner. Otherwise, we inspect more ballots and try again, possibly continuing to a full manual tabulation. At any time, the auditor can chose to conduct a full hand count rather than continue to sample at random. That might occur if the work of continuing the audit is anticipated to be higher than that of a full hand count or if the audit data suggest that the reported outcome is wrong. One reasonable rule is to set a maximum sample size (number of draws, not necessarily the number of distinct ballots) for the audit; if the sample reaches that size but the outcome has not been confirmed, there is a full manual tabulation. The outcome according to that manual tabulation becomes official.

There are many choices to be made, including:

How to assess evidence. Each stage involves calculating a statistic from the sample. What statistic do we use? This is one key difference amongst auditing methods, see Sect. 3.

Threshold for evidence. The decision of whether to certify or keep sampling is done by comparing the statistic to a reference value. Often the value is chosen such that it limits the probability of certifying the outcome if the outcome is wrong, i.e. limits the risk (see below).

Sampling with or without replacement. Sampling may be done with or without replacement. Sampling without replacement is more efficient; sampling with replacement often yields simpler mathematics. The difference in efficiency is small unless a substantial fraction (e.g. 20% or more) of the ballots are sampled.

Sampling increments. By how much do we increase the sample size if the current sample does not confirm the outcome? We could enlarge the sample one ballot at a time, but it is usually more efficient to have larger 'rounds'. The methods described here can accommodate rounds of any size.

We assume that the auditors read votes correctly, which generally requires retrieving the correct ballots and correctly applying legal rules for interpreting voters' marks.

2.2   Notation

Let $X_1, X_2, \cdots \in \{0,1\}$ denote the sampled ballots, with $X_i = 1$ representing a vote in favour of the reported winner and $X_i = 0$ a vote for the reported loser.

Let n denote the number of (not necessarily distinct) ballots sampled at a given point in the audit, m the maximum sample size (i.e. number of draws) for the audit, and N the total number of cast ballots. We necessarily have $n \leqslant m$ and if sampling without replacement we also have $m \leqslant N$.

Each audit method summarizes the evidence in the sample using a statistic of the form $S_n(X_1, X_2, \ldots, X_n, n, m, N)$. For brevity, we suppress n, m and N in the notation.

Let $Y_n = \sum_{i=1}^{n} X_i$ be the number of sampled ballots that are in favour of the reported winner. Since the ballots are by assumption exchangeable, the statistics used by most methods can be written in terms of Y_n.

Let T be the *true* total number of votes for the winner and $p_T = T/N$ the true proportion of such votes. Let p_r be the *reported* proportion of votes for the winner. We do not know T nor p_T, and it is not guaranteed that $p_r \simeq p_T$.

For sampling with replacement, conditional on n, Y_n has a binomial distribution with parameters n and p_T. For sampling without replacement, conditional on n, Y_n has a hypergeometric distribution with parameters n, T and N.

2.3 Risk-Limiting Audits as Hypothesis Tests

Risk-limiting audits amount to statistical hypothesis tests. The null hypothesis H_0 is that the reported winner(s) did *not* really win. The alternative H_1 is that the reported winners really won. For a single-winner contest,

$$H_0 : p_T \leqslant \tfrac{1}{2}, \quad \text{(reported winner is false)}$$
$$H_1 : p_T > \tfrac{1}{2}. \quad \text{(reported winner is true)}$$

If we reject H_0, we certify the election without a full manual tally. The *certification rate* is the probability of rejecting H_0. Hypothesis tests are often characterized by their *significance level* (false positive rate) and *power*. Both have natural interpretations in the context of election audits by reference to the certification rate. The power is simply the certification rate when H_1 is true. Higher power reduces the chance of an unnecessary recount. A false positive is a *miscertification*: rejecting H_0 when in fact it is true. The probability of miscertification depends on p_T and the audit method, and is known as the *risk* of the method. In a two-candidate plurality contest, the maximum possible risk is typically attained when $p_T = \tfrac{1}{2}$.

For many auditing methods we can find an upper bound on the maximum possible risk, and can also set their evidence threshold such that the risk is limited to a given value. Such an upper bound is referred to as a *risk limit*, and methods for which this is possible are called *risk-limiting*. Some methods are explicitly designed to have a convenient mechanism to set such a bound, for example via a formula. We call such methods *automatically risk-limiting*.

Audits with a sample size limit m become full manual tabulations if they have not stopped after drawing the mth ballot. Such a tabulation is assumed to find the correct outcome, so the power of a risk-limiting audit is 1. We use the term 'power' informally to refer to the chance the audit stops after drawing m or fewer ballots.

3 Election Auditing Methods

We describe Bayesian audits in some detail because they provide a mathematical framework for many (but not all) of the other methods. We then describe the other methods, many of which can be viewed as Bayesian audits for a specific choice of the prior distribution. Some of these connections were previously described by [11]. These connections can shed light on the performance or interpretation of the other methods. However, our benchmarking experiments are frequentist, even for the Bayesian audits (for example, we calibrate the methods to limit the risk).

Table 1 lists the methods described here; the parameters of the methods are defined below.

Table 1. Summary of auditing methods. The methods in the first part of the table are benchmarked in this report.

Method	Quantities to set	Automatically risk-limiting
Bayesian	$f(p)$	—
Bayesian (risk-max.)	$f(p)$, for $p > 0.5$	✓
BRAVO	p_1	✓
MaxBRAVO	None	—
ClipAudit	None	—a
KMart	$g(\gamma)$b	✓
Kaplan–Wald	γ	✓
Kaplan–Markov	γ	✓
Kaplan–Kolmogorov	γ	✓

a Provides a pre-computed table for approximate risk-limiting thresholds.
b Extension introduced here.

3.1 Bayesian Audits

Bayesian audits quantify evidence in the sample as a posterior distribution of the proportion of votes in favour of the reported winner. In turn, that distribution induces a (posterior) probability that the outcome is wrong, $\Pr(H_0 \mid Y_n)$, the *upset probability*.

The posterior probabilities require positing a *prior distribution*, f for the reported winner's vote share p. (For clarity, we denote the fraction of votes for the reported winner by p when we treat it as random for Bayesian inference and by p_T to refer to the actual true value.)

We represent the posterior using the posterior odds,

$$\frac{\Pr(H_1 \mid X_1, \ldots, X_n)}{\Pr(H_0 \mid X_1, \ldots, X_n)} = \frac{\Pr(X_1, \ldots, X_n \mid H_1)}{\Pr(X_1, \ldots, X_n \mid H_0)} \times \frac{\Pr(H_1)}{\Pr(H_0)}.$$

The first term on the right is the *Bayes factor* (BF) and the second is the prior odds. The prior odds do not depend on the data: the information from the data is in the BF. We shall use the BF as the statistic, S_n. It can be expressed as,

$$S_n = \frac{\Pr(X_1, \ldots, X_n \mid H_1)}{\Pr(X_1, \ldots, X_n \mid H_0)} = \frac{\int_{p>0.5} \Pr(Y_n \mid p)\, f(p)\, dp}{\int_{p\leqslant 0.5} \Pr(Y_n \mid p)\, f(p)\, dp}.$$

The term $\Pr(Y_n \mid p)$ is the *likelihood*. The BF is similar to a likelihood ratio, but the likelihoods are integrated over p rather than evaluated at specific values (in contrast to classical approaches, see Sect. 3.2).

Understanding Priors. The prior f determines the relative contributions of possible values of p to the BF. It can be continuous, discrete, or a combination of the two. A *conjugate prior* is often used [6], which has the property that the posterior distribution is in the same family, which has mathematical and practical advantages. For sampling with replacement the conjugate prior is beta (which is continuous), while for sampling without replacement it is a beta-binomial (which is discrete).

Vora [11] showed that a prior that places a probability mass of 0.5 on the value $p = 0.5$ and the remaining mass on $(1/2, 1]$ is *risk-maximizing*. For such a prior, limiting the upset probability to v also limits the risk: for the specific type of Bayesian audits considered by Vora [11], the risk limit is v; however, for the Bayesian audits described here (see below), the risk limit is $\frac{v}{1-v} > v$.

We explore several priors below, emphasizing a uniform prior (an example of a 'non-partisan prior' [6]), which is a special case within the family of conjugate priors used here.

Bayesian Audit Procedure. A Bayesian audit proceeds as follows. At each stage of sampling, calculate S_n and then:

$$\begin{cases} \text{if } S_n > h, & \text{terminate and certify,} \\ \text{if } S_n \leqslant h, & \text{continue sampling.} \end{cases} \tag{$*$}$$

If the audit does not terminate and certify for $n \leqslant m$, there is a full manual tabulation of the votes.

The threshold h is equivalent to a threshold on the upset probability: $\Pr(H_0 \mid Y_n) < v$ corresponds to $h = \frac{1-v}{v} \frac{\Pr(H_0)}{\Pr(H_1)}$. If the prior places equal probability on the two hypotheses (a common choice), this simplifies to $h = \frac{1-v}{v}$.

Interpretation. The upset probability, $\Pr(H_0 \mid Y_n)$, is **not** the risk, which is $\Pr(\text{certify} \parallel p_T)$. The procedure outlined above limits the upset probability. This is not the same as limiting the risk. Nevertheless, in the election context considered here, Bayesian audits are risk-limiting, but with a risk limit that is in general larger than the upset probability threshold.[4]

For a given prior, sampling scheme, and risk limit α, we can calculate a value of h for which the risk of the Bayesian audit with threshold h is bounded by α. For risk-maximizing priors, taking $h = \frac{1}{\alpha}$ (which is equivalent to a threshold of $v = \frac{\alpha}{(1+\alpha)}$ on the upset probability) yields an audit with risk limit α.

3.2 SPRT-Based Audits

The basic sequential probability ratio test (SPRT) [12], adapted slightly to suit the auditing context here,[5] tests the simple hypotheses

$$H_0 \colon p_T = p_0,$$
$$H_1 \colon p_T = p_1,$$

---

[4] This is a consequence of the fact that the risk is maximized when $p_T = 0.5$, a fact that we can use to bound the risk by choosing an appropriate value for the threshold. We include the mathematical details of this result in a technical appendix available at: https://arxiv.org/abs/2008.08536.

[5] The SPRT allows rejection of either H_0 or H_1, but we only allow the former here. This aligns it with the broader framework for election audits described earlier. Also, we impose a maximum sample size, as we do for the other methods.

using the likelihood ratio:

$$\begin{cases} \text{if } S_n = \frac{\Pr(Y_n \| p_1)}{\Pr(Y_n \| p_0)} > \frac{1}{\alpha}, & \text{terminate and certify (reject } H_0), \\ \text{otherwise,} & \text{continue sampling.} \end{cases}$$

This is equivalent to (*) for a prior with point masses of 0.5 on the values p_0 and p_1 with $h = 1/\alpha$. This procedure has a risk limit of α.

The test statistic can be tailored to sampling with or without replacement by using the appropriate likelihood. The SPRT has the smallest expected sample size among all level α tests of these same hypotheses. This optimality holds only when no constraints are imposed on the sampling (such as a maximum sample size).

The SPRT statistic is a nonnegative martingale when H_0 holds; Kolmogorov's inequality implies that it is automatically risk-limiting. Other martingale-based tests are discussed in Sect. 3.4.

The statistic from a Bayesian audit can also be a martingale, if the prior is the true data generating process under H_0. This occurs, for example, for a risk-maximizing prior if $p_T = 0.5$.[6]

BRAVO. In a two-candidate contest, BRAVO [3] applies the SPRT with:

$$p_0 = 0.5,$$
$$p_1 = p_r - \epsilon,$$

where ϵ is a pre-specified small value for which $p_1 > 0.5$.[7] Because it is the SPRT, BRAVO has a risk limit no larger than α.

BRAVO requires picking p_1 (analogous to setting a prior for a Bayesian audit). The recommended value is based on the reported winner's share, but the SPRT can be used with any alternative. Our numerical experiments do not involve a reported vote share; we simply set p_1 to various values.

MaxBRAVO. As an alternative to specifying p_1, we experimented with replacing the likelihood, $\Pr(Y_n \| p_1)$, with the maximized likelihood, $\max_{p_1} \Pr(Y_n \| p_1)$, leaving other aspects of the test unchanged. This same idea has been used in other contexts, under the name MaxSPRT [2]. We refer to our version as *MaxBRAVO*. Because of the maximization, the method is not automatically risk-limiting, so we calibrate the stopping threshold h numerically to attain the desired risk limit, as we do for Bayesian audits.

3.3 ClipAudit

Rivest [5] introduces *ClipAudit*, a method that uses a statistic that is very easy to calculate, $S_n = (A_n - B_n)/\sqrt{A_n + B_n}$, where $A_n = Y_n$ and $B_n = n - Y_n$. Approximately risk-limiting thresholds for this statistic were given (found numerically),

---

[6] Such a prior places all its mass on $p = 0.5$ when $p \leqslant 0.5$.

[7] The SPRT can perform poorly when $p_T \in (p_0, p_1)$; taking $\epsilon > 0$ protects against the possibility that the reported winner really won, but not by as much as reported.

along with formulae that give approximate thresholds. We used ClipAudit with the 'best fit' formula [5, Eq. (6)].

As far as we can tell, ClipAudit is not related to any of the other methods we describe here, but S_n is the test statistic commonly used to test the hypothesis $H_0: p_T = 0.5$ against $H_1: p_T > 0.5$:

$$S_n = \frac{A_n - B_n}{\sqrt{A_n + B_n}} = \frac{Y_n - n + Y_n}{\sqrt{n}} = \frac{Y_n/n - 0.5}{\sqrt{0.5 \times (1 - 0.5)/n}} = \frac{\hat{p}_T - p_0}{\sqrt{p_0 \times (1 - p_0)/n}}.$$

3.4   Other Methods

Several martingale-based methods have been developed for the general problem of testing hypotheses about the mean of a non-negative random variable. SHANGRLA exploits this generality to allow auditing of a wide class of elections [8]. While we did not benchmark these methods in our study (they are better suited for other scenarios, such as comparison audits, and will be less efficient in the simple case we consider here), we describe them here in order to point out some connections among the methods.

The essential difference between methods is in the definition of the statistic, S_n. Given the statistic, the procedure is the same: certify the election if $S_n > 1/\alpha$; otherwise, keep sampling. All of the procedures can be shown to have risk limit α.

All the procedures involve a parameter γ that prevents degenerate values of S_n. This parameter either needs to be set to a specific value or is integrated out.

The statistics below that are designed for sampling without replacement depend on the order in which ballots are sampled. None of the other statistics (in this section or earlier) have that property.

We use t to denote the value of $\mathbb{E}(X_i)$ under the null hypothesis. In the two-candidate context discussed in this paper, $t = p_0 = 0.5$.

We have presented the formulae for the statistics a little differently to highlight the connections among these methods. For simplicity of notation, we define $Y_0 = 0$.

KMart. This method was described online under the name *KMart*[8] and is implemented in SHANGRLA [8]. There are two versions of the test statistic, designed for sampling with or without replacement,[9] respectively:

$$S_n = \int_0^1 \prod_{i=1}^n \left(\gamma \left[\frac{X_i}{t} - 1 \right] + 1 \right) d\gamma, \text{ and } S_n = \int_0^1 \prod_{i=1}^n \left(\gamma \left[X_i \frac{\left(\frac{N-i+1}{N} \right)}{t - \frac{1}{N} Y_{i-1}} - 1 \right] + 1 \right) d\gamma.$$

This method is related to Bayesian audits for two-candidate contests: for sampling with replacement and no invalid votes, we have shown that KMart

---

[8] https://github.com/pbstark/MartInf/blob/master/kmart.ipynb.
[9] When sampling without replacement, if we ever observe $Y_n > Nt$ then we ignore the statistic and terminate the audit since H_1 is guaranteed to be true.

is equivalent to a Bayesian audit with a risk-maximizing prior that is uniform over $p > 0.5$.[10] The same analysis shows how to extend KMart to be equivalent to using an arbitrary risk-maximizing prior, by inserting an appropriately constructed weighting function $g(\gamma)$ into the integrand (see Footnote 10).

There is no direct relationship of this sort for the version of KMart that uses sampling without replacement, since this statistic depends on the order the ballots are sampled but the statistic for Bayesian audits does not.

Kaplan–Wald. This method is similar to KMart but involves picking a value for γ rather than integrating over γ [10]. The previous proof (see Footnote 10) shows that for sampling with replacement, Kaplan–Wald is equivalent to BRAVO with $p_1 = (\gamma + 1)/2$; while for sampling without replacement, there is no such relationship.

Kaplan–Markov. This method applies Markov's inequality to the martingale $\prod_{i \leq n} X_i / \mathbb{E}(X_i)$, where the expectation is calculated assuming sampling with replacement [9]. This gives the statistic $S_n = \prod_{i=1}^{n} (X_i + \gamma) / (t + \gamma)$.

Kaplan–Kolmogorov. This method is the same as Kaplan–Markov but with the expectation calculated assuming sampling without replacement [8]. This gives the statistic $S_n = \prod_{i=1}^{n} \left[(X_i + \gamma) \left(\frac{N-i+1}{N} \right) \right] / \left[t - \frac{1}{N} Y_{i-1} + \frac{N-i+1}{N} \gamma \right]$.[11]

4   Evaluating Auditing Methods

We evaluated the methods using simulations; see the first part of Table 1.

For each method, the termination threshold h was calibrated numerically to yield maximum risk as close as possible to 5%. This makes comparisons among the methods 'fair'. We calibrated even the automatically risk-limiting methods, resulting in a slight performance boost. We also ran some experiments without calibration, to quantify this difference.

We use three quantities to measure performance: maximum risk and 'power', defined in Sect. 2.3, and the mean sample size.

Choice of Auditing Methods. Most of the methods require choosing the form of statistics, tuning parameters, or a prior. Except where stated, our benchmarking experiments used sampling without replacement. Except where indicated, we used the version of each statistic designed for the method of sampling used. For example, we used a hypergeometric likelihood when sampling without replacement. For Bayesian audits we used a beta-binomial prior (conjugate to

---

[10] We include the mathematical details of these results in a technical appendix available at: https://arxiv.org/abs/2008.08536.

[11] As for KMart, if $Y_n > Nt$, the audit terminates: the null hypothesis is false.

the hypergeometric likelihood) with shape parameters a and b. For BRAVO, we tried several values of p_1.

The tests labelled 'BRAVO' are tests of a method related to but not identical to BRAVO, because there is no notion of a 'reported' vote share in our experiments. Instead, we set p_1 to several fixed values to explore how the underlying test statistic (from the SPRT) performs in different scenarios.

For MaxBRAVO and Bayesian audits with risk-maximizing prior, due to time constraints we only implemented statistics for the binomial likelihood (which assumes sampling with replacement). While these are not exact for sampling without replacement, we believe this choice has only a minor impact when $m \ll N$ (based on our results for the other methods when using different likelihoods).

For Bayesian audits with a risk-maximizing prior, we used a beta distribution prior (conjugate to the binomial likelihood) with shape parameters a and b.

ClipAudit only has one version of its statistic. It is not optimized for sampling without replacement (for example, if you sample **all** of the ballots, it will not 'know' this fact), but the stopping thresholds are calibrated for sampling without replacement.

Election Sizes and Sampling Designs. We explored combinations of election sizes $N \in \{500, 1000, 5000, 10000, 20000, 30000\}$ and maximum sample sizes $m \in \{500, 1000, 2000, 3000\}$. Most of our experiments used a sampling increment of 1 (i.e. check the stopping rule after each ballot is drawn). We also varied the sampling increment (values in $\{2, 5, 10, 20, 50, 100, 250, 500, 1000, 2000\}$) and tried sampling with replacement.

Benchmarking via Dynamic Programming. We implemented an efficient method for calculating the performance measures using dynamic programming.[12] This exploits the Markovian nature of the sampling procedure and the low dimensionality of the (univariate) statistics. This approach allowed us to calculate—for elections with up to tens of thousands of votes—exact values of each of the performance measures, including the tail probabilities of the sampling distributions, which require large sample sizes to estimate accurately by Monte Carlo. We expect that with some further optimisations our approach would be computationally feasible for larger elections (up to 1 million votes). The complexity largely depends on the maximum sample size, m. As long as this is moderate (thousands) our approach is feasible. For more complex audits (beyond two-candidate contests), a Monte Carlo approach is likely more practical.

---

[12] Our code is available at: https://github.com/Dovermore/AuditAnalysis.

5   Results

5.1   Benchmarking Results

Sample Size Distributions. Different methods have different distributions of sample sizes; Fig. 1 shows these for a few methods when $p_T = 0.5$. Some methods tend to stop early; others take many more samples. Requiring a minimum sample size might improve performance of some of the methods; see Sect. 5.3.

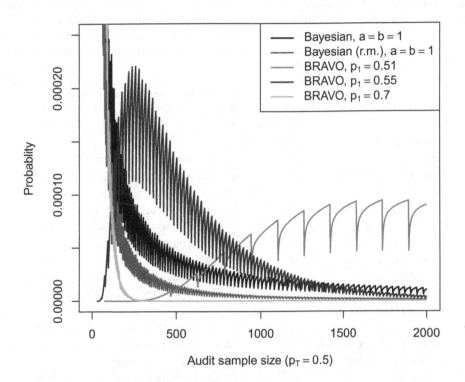

Fig. 1. Sample size distributions. Audits of elections with $N = 20,000$ ballots, maximum sample size $m = 2,000$, and true vote share a tie ($p_T = 0.5$). Each method is calibrated to have maximum risk 5%. The depicted probabilities all sum to 0.05; the remaining 0.95 probability in each case is on the event that the audit reaches the full sample size ($n = m$) and progresses to a full manual tabulation. 'Bayesian (r.m.)' refers to the Bayesian audit with a risk-maximizing prior. The sawtooth pattern is due to the discreteness of the statistics.

Mean Sample Sizes. We focus on average sample sizes as a measure of audit efficiency. Table 2 shows the results of experiments with $N = 20,000$ and $m = 2,000$. We discuss other experiments and performance measures below.

No method was uniformly best. Given the equivalence of BRAVO and Bayesian audits, the comparisons amount to examining dependence on the prior.

Table 2. Results from benchmarking experiments. Audits of elections with $N = 20,000$ ballots and a maximum sample size $m = 2,000$. The numeric column headings refer to the value of p_T; the corresponding margin of victory (MOV) is also reported. Each row refers to a specific auditing method. For calibrated methods, we report the threshold obtained. For easier comparison, we present these on the nominal risk scale for BRAVO, MaxBRAVO and ClipAudit (e.g. $\alpha = 1/h$ for BRAVO), and on the upset probability scale for the Bayesian methods ($v = 1/(h + 1)$). For the experiments without calibration, we report the maximum risk of each method when set to a 'nominal' risk limit of 5%. We only report uncalibrated results for methods that are automatically risk-limiting, as well as ClipAudit using its 'best fit' formula to set the threshold. 'Bayesian (r.m.)' refers to the Bayesian audit with a risk-maximizing prior. The numbers in bold are those that are (nearly) best for the given experiment and choice of p_T. The section labelled '$n \geqslant 300$' refers to experiments that required the audit to draw at least 300 ballots.

Method		Power (%)			Mean sample size				
	p_T (%) $\rightarrow$	52	55	60	52	55	60	64	70
	MOV (%) $\rightarrow$	4	10	20	4	10	12	28	40
Calibrated	α or v (%)								
Bayesian, $a = b = 1$	0.2	35	**99**	**100**	1623	637	**172**	**90**	46
Bayesian, $a = b = 100$	1.2	48	**100**	**100**	**1551**	616	232	150	97
Bayesian, $a = b = 500$	3.6	**53**	**100**	**100**	1582	709	318	219	149
Bayesian (r.m.), $a = b = 1$	6.1	19	94	**100**	1742	813	185	**89**	41
BRAVO, $p_1 = 0.7$	5.8	9	21	84	1828	1592	530	95	**37**
BRAVO, $p_1 = 0.55$	5.3	37	**99**	**100**	**1549**	**562**	196	129	85
BRAVO, $p_1 = 0.51$	22.7	**55**	**100**	**100**	1617	791	384	272	190
MaxBRAVO	1.6	30	**98**	**100**	1660	680	177	**91**	45
ClipAudit	4.7	33	**98**	**100**	1630	639	**169**	**89**	45
Calibrated, $n \geqslant 300$	α or v (%)								
Bayesian, $a = b = 1$	0.6	45	**99**	**100**	1547	601	**311**	**300**	**300**
Bayesian (r.m.), $a = b = 1$	34.4	39	**99**	**100**	1554	587	**307**	**300**	**300**
BRAVO, $p_1 = 0.7$	100.0	0	6	83	1994	1900	708	309	**300**
BRAVO, $p_1 = 0.55$	6.0	38	**99**	**100**	**1545**	**583**	309	**300**	**300**
BRAVO, $p_1 = 0.51$	22.7	**55**	**100**	**100**	1617	791	392	313	**300**
MaxBRAVO	5.0	44	**99**	**100**	1546	595	**310**	**300**	**300**
ClipAudit	11.4	44	**99**	**100**	**1545**	595	**310**	**300**	**300**
Uncalibrated	Risk (%)								
Bayesian (r.m.), $a = b = 1$	3.7	17	93	**100**	1785	864	198	95	44
BRAVO, $p_1 = 0.7$	4.3	8	20	83	1846	1621	552	99	**38**
BRAVO, $p_1 = 0.55$	4.7	**37**	**98**	**100**	**1561**	**572**	200	131	86
BRAVO, $p_1 = 0.51$	0.029	6	89	**100**	1985	1505	760	542	377
ClipAudit	5.1	**34**	**98**	**100**	1618	628	**167**	**88**	45

In general, methods that place more weight on close elections, such as BRAVO with $p_1 = 0.55$ or a Bayesian audit with a moderately constrained prior ($a = b = 100$) were optimal when p_T was closer to 0.5. Methods with substantial prior weight on wider margins, such as BRAVO with $p_1 = 0.7$ and Bayesian audits with the risk-maximizing prior, perform poorly for close elections.

Consistent with theory, BRAVO was optimal when the assumptions matched the truth ($p_1 = p_T$). However, our experiments violate the theoretical assumptions because we imposed a maximum sample size, m. (Indeed, when $p_1 = p_T = 0.51$, BRAVO is no longer optimal in our experiments.)

Two methods were consistently poor: BRAVO with $p_1 = 0.51$ and a Bayesian audit with $a = b = 500$. Both place substantial weight on a very close election.

MaxBRAVO and ClipAudit, the two methods without a direct match to Bayesian audits, performed similarly to a Bayesian audit with a uniform prior ($a = b = 1$). All three are 'broadly' tuned: they perform reasonably well in most scenarios, even when they are not the best.

Effect of Calibration on the Uncalibrated Methods. For most of the automatically calibrated methods, calibration had only a small effect on performance. BRAVO with $p_1 = 0.51$ is an exception: it was very conservative because it normally requires more than m samples.

Other Election Sizes and Performance Measures. The broad conclusions are the same for a range of values of m and N, and when performance is measured by quantiles of sample size or probability of stopping without a full hand count rather than by average sample size.

Sampling with vs Without Replacement. There are two ways to change our experiments to explore sampling with replacement: (i) construct versions of the statistics specifically for sampling with replacement; (ii) leave the methods alone but sample with replacement. We explored both options, separately and combined; differences were minor when $m \ll N$.

5.2   Choosing Between Methods

Consider the following two methods, which were the most efficient for different election margins: (i) BRAVO with $p_1 = 0.55$; (ii) ClipAudit. For $p_T = 0.52$, the mean sample sizes are 1,549 vs 1,630 (BRAVO saved 81 draws on average). For $p_T = 0.7$, the equivalent numbers are 85 vs 45 (ClipAudit saved 40 draws on average).

Picking a method requires trade-offs involving resources, workload predictability, and jurisdictional idiosyncrasies in ballot handling and storage—as well as the unknown true margin. Differences in expected sample size across ballot-polling methods might be immaterial in practice compared to other desiderata.

5.3   Exploring Changes to the Methods

Increasing the Sampling Increment ('Round Size'). Increasing the number of ballots sampled in each 'round' increases the chance that the audit will stop without a full hand count but increases mean sample size. This is as expected; the limiting version is a single fixed sample of size $n = m$, which has the highest power but loses the efficiency that early stopping can provide.

Increasing the sampling increment had the most impact on methods that tend to stop early, such as Bayesian audits with $a = b = 1$, and less on methods that do not, such as BRAVO with $p_1 = 0.51$. Increasing the increment also decreases the differences among the methods. This makes sense because when the sample size is m, the methods are identical (since all are calibrated to attain the risk limit).

Considering the trade-off discussed in the previous section, since increasing the sampling increment improves power but increases mean sample size, it reduces effort when the election is close, but increases it when the margin is wide.

Increasing the Maximum Sample Size (m). Increasing m has the same effect as increasing the sampling increment: higher power at the expense of more work on average. This effect is stronger for closer elections, since sampling will likely stop earlier when the margin is wide.

Requiring/Encouraging More Samples. The Bayesian audit with $a = b = 1$ tends to stop too early, so we tried two potential improvements, shown in Table 2.

The first was to impose a minimum sample size, in this case $n \geqslant 300$. This is very costly if the margin is wide, since we would not normally require this many samples. However, it boosts the power of this method and reduces its expected sample size for close contests.

A gentler way to achieve the same aim is to make the prior more informative, by increasing a and b. When $a = b = 100$, we obtain largely the same benefit for close elections with a much milder penalty when the margin is wide. The overall performance profile becomes closer to BRAVO with $p_1 = 0.55$.

6   Discussion

We compared several ballot-polling methods both analytically and numerically, to elucidate the relationships among the methods. We focused on two-candidate contests, which are building blocks for auditing more complex elections. We explored modifications and extensions to existing procedures. Our benchmarking experiments calibrated the methods to attain the same maximum risk.

Many 'non-Bayesian' auditing methods are special cases of a Bayesian procedure for a suitable prior, and Bayesian methods can be calibrated to be risk-limiting (at least, in the two-candidate, all-valid-vote context investigated here). Differences among such methods amount to technical details, such as choices of tuning parameters, rather than something more fundamental. Of course, upset probability *is* fundamentally different from risk.

No method is uniformly best, and most can be 'tuned' to improve performance for elections with either closer or wider margins—but not both simultaneously. If the tuning is not extreme, performance will be reasonably good for a wide range of true margins. In summary:

1. If the true margin is known approximately, BRAVO is best.
2. Absent reliable information on the margin, ClipAudit and Bayesian audits with a uniform prior (calibrated to attain the risk limit) are efficient.
3. Extreme settings, such as $p_1 \approx 0.5$ or an overly informative prior may result in poor performance even when the margin is small. More moderate settings give reasonable or superior performance if the maximum sample size is small compared to the number of ballots cast.

Choosing a method often involves a trade-off in performance between narrow and wide margins.

There is more to auditing than the choice of statistical inference method. Differences in performance across many 'reasonable' methods are small compared to other factors, such as how ballots are organized and stored.

Future Work: While we tried to be comprehensive in examining ballot-polling methods for two-candidate contests with no invalid votes, there are many ways to extend the analysis to cover more realistic scenarios. Some ideas include: (i) more than two candidates and non-plurality social choice functions; (ii) invalid votes; (iii) larger elections; (iv) stratified samples; (v) batch-level audits; (vi) multipage ballots.

References

1. Blom, M., Stuckey, P.J., Teague, V.J.: Ballot-polling risk limiting audits for IRV elections. In: Krimmer, R., et al. (eds.) Electronic Voting. E-Vote-ID 2018. Lecture Notes in Computer Science, vol. 11143, pp. 17–34. Springer, Cham (2018). https://doi.org/10.1007/978-3-030-00419-4_2
2. Kulldorff, M., Davis, R.L., Kolczak, M., Lewis, E., Lieu, T., Platt, R.: A maximized sequential probability ratio test for drug and vaccine safety surveillance. Seq. Anal. **30**(1), 58–78 (2011). https://doi.org/10.1080/07474946.2011.539924
3. Lindeman, M., Stark, P.B., Yates, V.S.: BRAVO: ballot-polling risk-limiting audits to verify outcomes. In: 2012 Electronic Voting Technology Workshop/Workshop on Trustworthy Elections, EVT/WOTE 2012 (2012)
4. National Academies of Sciences, Engineering, and Medicine: Securing the Vote: Protecting American Democracy. The National Academies Press, Washington, D.C. (September 2018). https://doi.org/10.17226/25120
5. Rivest, R.L.: ClipAudit: A simple risk-limiting post-election audit. arXiv e-prints arXiv:1701.08312 (January 2017)
6. Rivest, R.L., Shen, E.: A Bayesian method for auditing elections. In: 2012 Electronic Voting Technology/Workshop on Trustworthy Elections, EVT/WOTE 2012 (2012)

7. Stark, P.: Conservative statistical post-election audits. Ann. Appl. Stat. **2**, 550–581 (2008). http://arxiv.org/abs/0807.4005
8. Stark, P.: Sets of half-average nulls generate risk-limiting audits: SHANGRLA. Voting 2020 (2020, in press). http://arxiv.org/abs/1911.10035
9. Stark, P.B.: Risk-limiting postelection audits: conservative P-values from common probability inequalities. IEEE Trans. Inf. Forensic. Secur. **4**(4), 1005–1014 (2009). https://doi.org/10.1109/TIFS.2009.2034190
10. Stark, P.B., Teague, V.: Verifiable European elections risk-limiting audits for D'Hondt and its relatives. USENIX J. Election Technol. Syst. (JETS) **1**(3), 18–39 (2014). https://www.usenix.org/jets/issues/0301/stark
11. Vora, P.L.: Risk-Limiting Bayesian Polling Audits for Two Candidate Elections. arXiv e-prints arXiv:1902.00999 (Feburary 2019)
12. Wald, A.: Sequential tests of statistical hypotheses. Ann. Math. Statist. **16**(2), 117–186 (1945). https://doi.org/10.1214/aoms/1177731118

Towards Model Checking of Voting Protocols in UPPAAL

Wojciech Jamroga[1,2]([envelope]), Yan Kim[1], Damian Kurpiewski[2],
and Peter Y. A. Ryan[1]

[1] Interdisciplinary Centre for Security, Reliability, and Trust, SnT, University of
Luxembourg, Esch-sur-Alzette, Luxembourg
{wojciech.jamroga,yan.kim,peter.ryan}@uni.lu
[2] Institute of Computer Science, Polish Academy of Sciences, Warsaw, Poland
kurpiewski@ipipan.waw.pl

Abstract. The design and implementation of a trustworthy e-voting system is a challenging task. Formal analysis can be of great help here. In particular, it can lead to a better understanding of how the voting system works, and what requirements on the system are relevant. In this paper, we propose that the state-of-art model checker UPPAAL provides a good environment for modelling and preliminary verification of voting protocols. To illustrate this, we demonstrate how to model a version of Prêt à Voter in UPPAAL, together with some natural extensions. We also show how to verify a variant of receipt-freeness, despite the severe limitations of the property specification language in the model checker.

The aim of this work is to open a new path, rather then deliver the ultimate outcome of formal analysis. A comprehensive model of Prêt à Voter, more accurate specification of requirements, and exhaustive verification are planned for the future.

1 Introduction

The design and implementation of a good e-voting system is highly challenging. Real-life systems are notoriously complex and difficult to analyze. Moreover, elections are *social* processes: they are run by humans, with humans, and for humans, which makes them unpredictable and hard to model. Last but not least, it is not always clear what *good* means for a voting system. A multitude of properties have been proposed by the community of social choice theory (such as Pareto optimality and nonmanipulability), as well as researchers who focus on the security of voting (cf. ballot secrecy, coercion-resistance, voter-verifiability, and so on). The former kind of properties are typically set for a very abstract view of the voting procedure, and consequently miss many real-life concerns. For the latter ones, it is often difficult to translate the informal intuition to a formal definition that will be commonly accepted.

In a word, we deal with processes that are hard to understand and predict, and seek to evaluate them against criteria for which we have no clear consensus. Formal analysis can be of great help here: perhaps not in the sense of providing

© Springer Nature Switzerland AG 2020
R. Krimmer et al. (Eds.): E-Vote-ID 2020, LNCS 12455, pp. 129–146, 2020.
https://doi.org/10.1007/978-3-030-60347-2_9

the ultimate answers, but rather to strengthen our understanding of both how the voting system works and how it should work. The main goal of this paper is to propose that model checkers from distributed and multi-agent systems can be invaluable tools for such an analysis.

Model Checkers and UPPAAL. Much research on model checking focuses on the design of logical systems for a particular class of properties, establishing their theoretical characteristics, and development of verification algorithms. This obscures the fact that a model checking framework is valuable as long as it is actually *used* to analyze something. The analysis does not have to result in a "correctness certificate". A readable model of the system, and an understandable formula capturing the requirement are already of substantial value.

In this context, two features of a model checker are essential. On the one hand, it should provide a *flexible model specification language* that allows for modular and succinct specification of processes. On the other hand, it must offer a *good graphical user interface*. Paradoxically, tools satisfying both criteria are rather scarce. Here, we suggest that the state of the art model checker UPPAAL can provide a nice environment for modelling and preliminary verification of voting protocols and their social context. To this end, we show how to use UPPAAL to model a voting protocol of choice (in our case, a version of Prêt à Voter), and to verify some requirements written in the temporal logic **CTL**.

Contribution. The main contribution of this paper is methodological: we demonstrate that specification frameworks and tools from distributed and multi-agent systems can be useful in analysis and validation of voting procedures. An additional, technical contribution consists in a reduction from model checking of temporal-epistemic specifications to purely temporal ones, in order to verify a variant of receipt-freeness despite the limitations of UPPAAL.

We emphasize that this is a preliminary work, aimed at exploring a path rather then delivering the ultimate outcome of formal analysis. A comprehensive model of Prêt à Voter, more accurate specification of requirements, and exhaustive verification are planned for the future. We also plan to cover social engineering-style attacks involving interactions between coercers (or vote-buyers) and voters. This will require, however, a substantial extension of the algorithms in UPPAAL or a similar model checker.

Structure of the Paper. We begin by introducing the main ideas behind modelling and model checking of multi-agent systems, including a brief introduction to UPPAAL (Sect. 2). In Sect. 3, we provide an overview of Prêt à Voter, the voting protocol that we will use for our study. Section 4 presents a multi-agent model of the protocol; some interesting extensions of the model are proposed in Sect. 6. We show how to specify simple requirements on the voting system, and discuss the output of model checking in Sect. 5. The section also presents our main technical contribution, namely the model checking reduction that recasts knowledge-related statements as temporal properties. We discuss related work in Sect. 7, and conclude in Sect. 8.

2   Towards Model Checking of Voting Protocols

Model checking is the decision problem that takes a model of the system and a formula specifying correctness, and determines whether the model satisfies the formula. This allows for a natural separation of concerns: the model specifies how the system is, while the formula specifies how it should be. Moreover, most model checking approaches encourage systematic specification of requirements, especially for the requirements written in modal and temporal logic. In that case, the behavior of the system is represented by a transition network, possibly with additional modal relations to capture e.g. the uncertainty of agents. The structure of the network is typically given by a higher-level representation, e.g., a set of agent templates together with a synchronization mechanism.

We begin with a brief overview of UPPAAL, the model checker that we will use in later sections. A more detailed introduction can be found in [5].

2.1   Modelling in UPPAAL

An UPPAAL model consists of a set of concurrent processes. The processes are defined by templates, each possibly having a set of parameters. The templates are used for defining a large number of almost identical processes. Every template consists of *nodes*, *edges*, and optional local declarations. An example template is shown in Fig. 2; we will use it to model the behavior of a voter.

Nodes are depicted by circles and represent the local states of the module. *Initial* nodes are marked by a double circle. *Committed* nodes are marked by circled C. If any process is in a committed node, then the next transition must involve an edge from one of the committed nodes. Those are used to create atomic sequences or encode synchronization between more than two components.

Edges define the local transitions in the module. They are annotated by selections (in yellow), guards (green), synchronizations (teal), and updates (blue). The syntax of expressions mostly coincides with that of C/C++. *Selections* bind the identifier to a value from the given range in a nondeterministic way. *Guards* enable the transition if and only if the guard condition evaluates to true. *Synchronizations* allow processes to synchronize over a common channel ch (labeled ch? in the receiver process and ch! for the sender). Note that a transition on the side of the sender can be fired only if there exists an enabled transition on the receiving side labeled with the same channel identifier, and vice versa. *Update* expressions are evaluated when the transition is taken. Straightforward value passing over a channel is not allowed; instead, one has to use shared global variables for the transmission.

For convenience, we will place the selections and guards at the top or left of an edge, and the synchronizations and updates at the bottom/right.

2.2   Specification of Requirements

To specify requirements, UPPAAL uses a fragment of the temporal logic **CTL** [14]. **CTL** allows for reasoning about the possible execution paths of the system by means of the *path quantifiers* E ("there is a path") and A ("for every path"). A path is a maximal[1] sequence of states and transitions. To address the temporal pattern on a path, one can use the *temporal operators* $\bigcirc$ ("in the next moment"), $\square$ ("always from now on"), $\diamond$ ("now or sometime in the future"), and U ("until"). For example, the formula $\mathsf{A}\square(\mathsf{has\_ballot}_i \rightarrow \mathsf{A}\diamond(\mathsf{voted}_{i,1} \vee \cdots \vee \mathsf{voted}_{i,k}))$ expresses that, on all paths, whenever voter i gets her ballot form, she will eventually cast her vote for one of the candidates $1, \ldots, k$. Another formula, $\mathsf{A}\square\neg\mathsf{punished}_i$ says that voter i will never be punished by the coercer.

More advanced properties usually require a combination of temporal modalities with *knowledge operators* K_a, where $K_a\phi$ expresses "agent a knows that ϕ holds." For example, formula $\mathsf{E}\diamond(\mathsf{results} \wedge \neg\mathsf{voted}_{i,j} \wedge \neg K_c\neg\mathsf{voted}_{i,j})$ says that the coercer c might not know that voter i hasn't voted for candidate j, even if the results are already published. Moreover, $\mathsf{A}\square(\mathsf{results} \rightarrow \neg K_c\neg\mathsf{voted}_{i,j})$ expresses that, when the results are out, the coercer won't know that the voter refused to vote for j. Intuitively, both formulas capture different strength of receipt-freeness for a voter who has been instructed to vote for candidate j.

3   Outline of Prêt à Voter

In this paper, we use UPPAAL for modelling and analysis of a voting protocol. The protocol of choice is a version of Prêt à Voter. We stress that this is not an up to date version of Prêt à Voter but it serves to illustrate how some attacks can be captured with UPPAAL. A short overview of Prêt à Voter is presented here; the full details can be found, for example, in [32] or [19].

Most voter-verifiable voting systems work as follows: at the time of casting, an encryption or encoding of the vote is created and posted to a secure public bulletin board (BB). The voter can later check that her encrypted ballot appears correctly. The set of posted ballots are then processed in some verifiable way to reveal the tally or outcome. Much of this is effectively a secure distributed computation, and as such is well-established and understood in cryptography. The really challenging bit is the creation of the encrypted ballots, because it involves interactions between the users and the system. This has to be done in a way that assures the voter that her vote is correctly embedded, while avoiding introducing any coercion or vote buying threats.

The key innovation of the Prêt à Voter approach is to encode the vote using a randomised candidate list. This contrasts with earlier verifiable schemes that involved the voter inputting her selection to a device that then produces an encryption of the selection. Here what is encrypted is the candidate order which can be generated and committed in advance, and the voter simply marks her choice on the paper ballot in the traditional manner.

Suppose that our voter is called Anne. At the polling station, Anne is authenticated and registered and she chooses at random a ballot form sealed in an envelope and saunters over to the booth. An example of such a form is shown in

---

[1] I.e., infinite or ending in a state with no outgoing transitions.

(a)	Discard	Retain
	Obelix	
	Idefix	
	Asterix	
	Panoramix	
		7304944

(b)	Retain
	X
	7304944

Fig. 1. (a) Prêt à Voter ballot form; (b) Receipt encoding a vote for "Idefix"

Fig. 1a. In the booth, she extracts her ballot form from the envelope and marks her selection in the usual way by placing a cross in the right hand column against the candidate (or candidates) of her choice. Once her selection has been made, she separates the left and right hand strips and discards the left hand strip. She keeps the right hand strip which now constitutes her *privacy protected receipt*, as shown in Fig. 1b.

Anne now exits the booth clutching her receipt, returns to the registration desk, and casts the receipt: it is placed over an optical reader or similar device that records the string at the bottom of the strip and registers which cells are marked. Her original paper receipt is digitally signed and franked and returned to her to keep and later check that her vote is correctly recorded on the bulletin board. The randomisation of the candidate list on each ballot form ensures that the receipt does not reveal the way she voted, thus ensuring the secrecy of her vote. Incidentally, it also removes any bias towards the candidate at the top of the list that can occur with a fixed ordering.

The value printed on the bottom of the receipt is what enables extraction of the vote during the tabulation phase: buried cryptographically in this value is the information needed to reconstruct the candidate order and so extract the vote encoded on the receipt. This information is encrypted with secret keys shared across a number of tellers. Thus, only a threshold set of tellers acting together are able to interpret the vote encoded in the receipt. In practice, the value on the receipt will be a pointer (e.g. a hash) to a ciphertext committed to the bulletin board during the setup phase.

After the voting phase, voters can visit the Bulletin Board and confirm that their receipts appear correctly. Once any discrepancies are resolved, the tellers take over and perform anonymising mixes and decryption of the receipts. At the end, the plaintext votes will be posted in secret shuffled order, or in the case of homomorphic tabulation, the final result is posted. All the processing of the votes can be made universally verifiable, i.e., any observer can check that no votes were manipulated.

Prêt à Voter brings several advantages in terms of privacy and dispute resolution. Firstly, it avoids side channel leakage of the vote from the encryption device. Secondly, it improves on dispute resolution: ballot assurance is based on random audits of the ballot forms, which can be performed by the voter or independent observers. A ballot form is either well-formed, i.e. the plaintext order matches the encrypted order, or not. This is independent of the voter or her choice, hence there can be no dispute as to what choice the voter provided. Such disputes can arise in Benaloh challenges and similar cut-and-choose style audits. Furthermore, auditing ballots does not impinge on ballot privacy, as nothing about the voter or the vote can be revealed at this point.

4 Modelling Prêt à Voter in UPPAAL

In this section, we present how the components and participants of Prêt à Voter can be modelled in UPPAAL. To this end, we give a description of each module template, its elements, and their interactions. The templates represent the behavior of the following types of agents: *voters, coercers, mix tellers, decryption tellers, auditors*, and the *voting infrastructure*. For more than one module of a given type, an identifier $i = 0, 1, \ldots$ will be associated with each instance.

The code of the model is available at https://github.com/pretvsuppaal/model. Here, we present in detail only the Voter template. The details of the other modules can be found in the extended version of the paper, available at https://arxiv.org/abs/2007.12412.

To facilitate readability and manageability of the model code, we define some data structures and type name aliases based on the configuration variables:

- **Ciphertext**: a pair (y_1, y_2). For the simplicity of modeling, we assume that ElGamal encryption is used.
- **Ballot**: a pair (θ, cl) of onion $\theta = E_{PK}(s, *)$ and candidate list $cl = \pi(s)$, where s is a seed associated with the ballot, and $\pi : \mathbb{R} \to Perm_C$ is a function that associates a seed with a permutation of the candidates. To allow absorption of the index of a marked cell into the onion, we use cyclic shifts of the base candidate order. This means that we just have simple ElGamal ciphertexts to mix.
- **Receipt**: a pair (θ, r) of onion θ and an index r of marked cell. It can be used to verify if a term was recorded and if it was done correctly.
- **c_t**: an integer with range [0, c_total), a candidate;
- **v_t**: an integer with range [0, v_total), a voter;
- **z_t**: an integer with range [0, z_total), an element of $\mathbb{Z}_p^*$.

4.1 Voter Template

The structure of the Voter template is shown in Fig. 2. The idea is that while the voter waits for the start of election she might be subject to coercion. When the ballots are ready, the voter selects a candidate, and transmits the receipt to the system. Then she decides if she wants to check how her vote has been recorded, and if she wants to show the receipt to the coercer. If coerced, she also waits for the coercer's decision to punish her or refrain from punishment. The module includes the following private variables:

- **receipt**: an instance of **Receipt**, obtained after casting a vote;

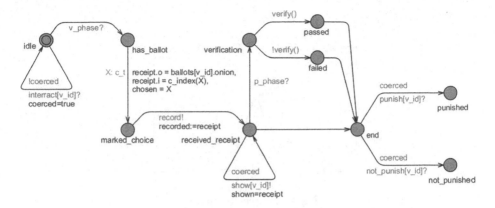

Fig. 2. Voter template for the model of Prêt à Voter (Color figure online)

- `coerced[=false]`: a Boolean value, indicating if coercer has established a contact;
- `chosen`: integer value of chosen candidate.

Moreover, the following procedures are included:

- `c_index(target)`: returns an index, at which `target` can be found on the candidate list of a ballot;
- `verify()`: returns *true* if the voter's `receipt` can be found on the Web Bulletin Board, else it returns *false*.

Local states:

- *idle*: waiting for the election, might get contacted by coercer;
- *has_ballot*: the voter has already obtained the ballot form;
- *marked_choice*: the voter has marked an index of chosen candidate (and destroyed left hand side with candidate list);
- *received_receipt*: the receipt is obtained and might be shown to the coercer;
- *verification*: the voter has decided to verify the receipt;
- *passed*: the voter got a confirmation that the receipt appears correctly;
- *failed*: the voter obtains evidence that the receipt does not appear on BB or appears incorrectly;
- *end*: the end of the voting ceremony;
- *punished*: the voter has been punished by the coercer;
- *not_punished*: the coercer refrained from punishing the voter.

Transitions:

- *idle→ idle*: if was not already coerced, enable transition; if taken, then set `coercion` to *true*;
- *idle→has_ballot*: always enabled; if taken, the voter acquires a ballot form;
- *has_ballot→ marked_choice*: mark the cell with the selected candidate;

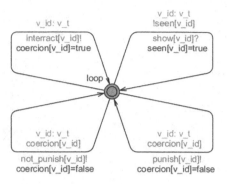

Fig. 3. Coercer template

- *marked_choice→received_receipt*: send **receipt** to the Sys process over channel **record** using shared variable **recorded**;
- *received_receipt→received_receipt*: if was coerced, enable transition; if taken, then pass the **receipt** to the coercer using shared variable **shown**;
- *received_receipt→verification*: always enabled; if taken, the voter decides to verify whether the receipt appears on the BB;
- *(received_receipt || passed || failed)→end*: voting ceremony ends for the voter;
- *end→punished*: if was coerced, enable transition; if taken, then the voter has been punished by the coercer;
- *end→not_punished*: if was coerced, enable transition; if taken, the coercer has refrained to punish the voter.

4.2 Coercer

The coercer can be thought of as a party that tries to influence the outcome of the vote by forcing voters to obey certain instructions. To enforce this, the coercer can punish the voter. The structure of the Coercer module is presented in Fig. 3; see the extended version of the paper at https://arxiv.org/abs/2007. 12412 for the technical details.

4.3 Mix Teller (Mteller)

Once the mixing phase starts, each mix teller performs two re-encryption mixes. The order of turns is ascending and determined by their identifiers. The randomization factors and permutation of each mix are selected in a nondeterministic way and stored for a possible audit of re-encryption mixes. When audited, the mix teller reveals the requested links and the associated factors, thus allowing Auditor to verify that the input ciphertext maps to the output. The structure of the mix teller is shown in Fig. 4.

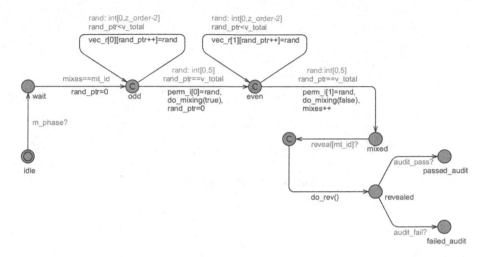

Fig. 4. Mteller template

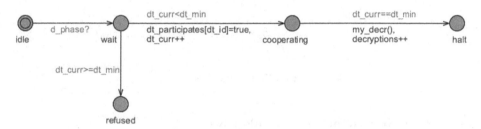

Fig. 5. Dteller template

4.4 Decryption Teller (Dteller)

In this module, after the re-encryption mixes are done, a subset of cooperating decryption tellers is chosen nondeterministically. Note that if a subset has less than two elements (e.g. when two or more decryption tellers refused to cooperate), then they should not be able to reconstruct a secret key, which would lead to a deadlock. In order to avoid that, only subsets with cardinality of 2 are considered in our simplified model (Fig. 5).

4.5 Auditor

In order to confirm that the mix tellers performed their actions correctly, the auditor conducts an audit. In this paper, we assume that the audit is based on the randomized partial checking technique, RPC in short [20]. To this end, each mix teller is requested to reveal the factors for the selected half of an odd-mix batch, and verify whether the input corresponds to the output. The control flow of the Auditor module is presented in Fig. 6. In the future, we plan to extend the model with auditing techniques that rely on zero-knowledge proofs.

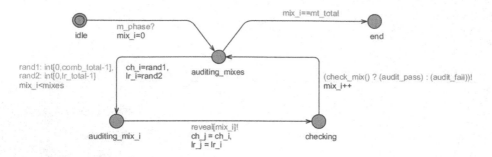

Fig. 6. Auditor template

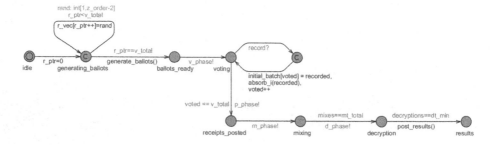

Fig. 7. Module Sys

4.6 Voting Infrastructure Module (Sys)

This module represents the behavior of the election authority that prepares the ballot forms, monitors the current phase, signals the progress of the voting procedure to the other components, and at the end posts the results of the election. In addition, the module plays the role of a server that receives receipts and transfers them to the database throughout the election. We assume that all the ballots were properly generated and thus omit procedures (e.g. ballot audits) which can ensure that. Capturing related attacks and possible defences remains a subject for future work (Fig. 7).

5 Verification

We chose UPPAAL for this study mainly because of its modelling functionality. Interestingly, the model checking capabilities of UPPAAL turned out rather limited for analysis of voting protocols, due to the limitations of its requirement specification language. First, UPPAAL admits only a fragment of **CTL**: it excludes the "next" and "until" modalities, and does not allow for nesting of operators (with one exception that we describe below). Thus, the supported properties fall into the following categories: simple *reachability* (E◇p), *liveness* (A◇p), and *safety* (A□p and E□p). The only allowed nested formulas come in the form of the *p leads to q* property, written p $\leadsto$ q, and being a shorthand for A$\Box$(p $\rightarrow$ A$\Diamond$q).

Nonetheless, UPPAAL allows to model-check some simple properties of Prêt à Voter, as we show in Sect. 5.1. Moreover, by tweaking models and formulas, one can also verify some more sophisticated requirements, see Sect. 5.2.

5.1 Model Checking Temporal Requirements

It is difficult to encode meaningful requirements on voting procedures in the input language of UPPAAL. We managed to come up with the following properties:

1. E$\Diamond$failed_audit$_0$: the first mix teller might eventually fail an audit;
2. A$\Box$¬punished$_i$: voter i will never be punished by the coercer;
3. has_ballot$_i$ $\leadsto$ marked_choice$_i$: on all paths, whenever voter i gets a ballot form, she will eventually mark her choice.

We verified each formula on the parameterized model in Sect. 4. Several configurations were used, with the number of voters ranging from 1 to 5. For the first property, the UPPAAL verifier returns 'Property is satisfied' for the configurations with 1, 2, 3 and 4 voters. In case of 5 voters, we get 'Out of memory' due to the state-space explosion. This is a well-known problem in verification of distributed systems; typically, the blow-up concerns the system states to be explored in model checking and proof states in case of theorem proving. Formula (2) produces the answer 'Property is not satisfied' and pastes a counter-example into the simulator for all the five configurations. Finally, formula (3) ends with 'Out of memory' regardless of the number of voters.

Optimizations. To keep the model manageable and in attempt to reduce the state space, every numerical variable is defined as a bounded integer in a form of int[min,max], restricting its range of values.[2] The states violating the bounds are discarded at run-time. For example, transition *has_ballot→marked_choice* of the Voter (Fig. 2) has a selection of value X in the assignment of variable chosen. The type of X is c_t, which is an alias to int[0,c_total-1], i.e., the range of meaningful candidate choices.

We also tried to keep the number of used variables minimal, as it plays an important role in the model checking procedure.

5.2 How to Make Model Checker Do More Than it Is Supposed to

Many important properties of voting refer to the knowledge of its participants. For example, receipt-freeness expresses that the coercer should never know how the voter has voted. Or, better still, that the coercer will never know if the voter disobeyed his instructions. Similarly, voter-verifiability says that the voter

---

[2] Without the explicit bounds, the range of values would be [−32768,32768].

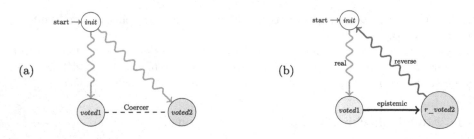

Fig. 8. (a) Epistemic bisimulation triangle; (b) turning the triangle into a cycle by reversing the transition relation

will eventually know whether her vote has been registered and tallied correctly (assuming that she follows the verification steps).

A clear disadvantage of UPPAAL is that its language for specification of requirements is restricted to purely temporal properties. Here we show that, with some care, one can use it to embed the verification of more sophisticated properties. In particular, we show how to enable model checking of some knowledge-related requirements by a technical reconstruction of models and formulas. The construction has been inspired by the reduction of epistemic properties to temporal properties, proposed in [17, 21]. Consequently, UPPAAL and similar tools can be used to model check some formulas of **CTLK** (i.e., **CTL** + Knowledge) that express variants of receipt-freeness and voter-verifiability.

In order to simulate the knowledge operator K_a under the **CTL** semantics, the model needs to be modified. The first step is to understand how the formula $\neg K_c \neg \mathsf{voted}_{i,j}$ (saying that the coercer doesn't know that the particular voter i hasn't voted for candidate j) is interpreted. Namely, if there is a reachable state in which $\mathsf{voted}_{i,j}$ is true, there must also exist another reachable state, which is indistinguishable from the current one, and in which $\neg \mathsf{voted}_{i,j}$ holds. The idea is shown in Fig. 8a. We observe that to simulate the epistemic relation we need to create copies of the states in the model (the "real" states). We will refer to those copies as the *reverse states*. They are the same as the real states, but with reversed transition relation. Then, we add transitions from the real states to their corresponding reverse states, that simulate the epistemic relation between the states. This is shown in Fig. 8b.

To illustrate how the reconstruction of the model works on a concrete example, we depict the augmented Coercer template in Fig. 9.

In order to effectively modify the model and verify the selected properties according to the previously defined procedure, the model was first simplified. In the simplified version there are two voters and the coercer can interact only with one of them. Furthermore we removed the verification phase and the tallying phase from the model.

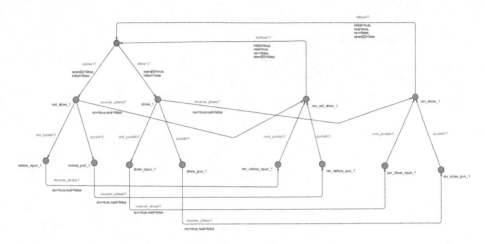

Fig. 9. Coercer module augmented with the converse transition relation

The next step is the reconstruction of formulas. Let us take the formula for the weak variant of receipt-freeness from Sect. 2.2, i.e., $E\Diamond(\text{results} \wedge \neg\text{voted}_{i,j} \wedge \neg K_c\neg\text{voted}_{i,j})$. In order to verify the formula in UPPAAL, we need to replace the knowledge operator according to our model reconstruction method (see Fig. 8 again). This means that the verifier should find a path that closes the cycle: from the initial state, going through the real states of the voting procedure to the vote publication phase, and then back to the initial state through the reversed states. In order to "remember" the relevant facts along the path, we use persistent Boolean variables $\text{voted}_{i,j}$ and $\text{negvoted}_{i,j}$: once set to true they always remain true. We also introduce a new persistent variable $\text{epist\_voted}_{i,j}$ to refer to the value of the vote after an epistemic transition. Once we have all that, we can propose the reconstructed formula: $E\Diamond(\text{results}\wedge\text{negvoted}_{i,j}\wedge\text{epist\_voted}_{i,j}\wedge\text{initial})$. UPPAAL reports that the formula holds in the model.

A stronger variant of receipt-freeness is expressed by another formula of Sect. 2.2, i.e., $A\Box(\text{results} \rightarrow \neg K_c\neg\text{voted}_{i,j})$. Again, the formula needs to be rewritten to a pure **CTL** formula. As before, the model checker should find a cycle from the initial state, "scoring" the relevant propositions on the way. More precisely, it needs to check if, for every real state in which election has ended, there exist a path going back to the initial state through a reverse state in which the voter has voted for the selected candidate. This can be captured by the following formula: $A\Box((\text{results} \wedge \text{real}) \rightarrow E\Diamond(\text{voted}_{i,j} \wedge \text{init}))$. Unfortunately, this formula cannot be verified in UPPAAL, as UPPAAL does not allow for nested path quantifiers. In the future, we plan to run the verification of this formula using another model checker LTSmin [23] that accepts UPPAAL models as input, but allows for more expressive requirement specifications.

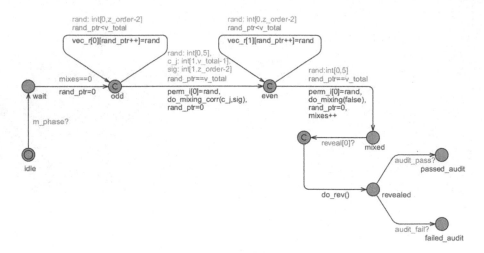

Fig. 10. Corrupted Mix Teller module

6 Replicating Pfitzmann's Attack

A version of *Pfitzmann's attack* is known to compromise mix-nets with random-ized partial checking [25]. It can be used to break the privacy of a given vote with probability $1/2$ of being undetected. The leaked information may differ depending on both the implementation of the attack and the voting protocol.

The idea is that the first mix teller, who is corrupted, targets a ciphertext c_i from the odd mix input, and replaces some output term. c_j with c_i^δ, After the decryption results are posted, a pair of decrypted messages m and m' satisfying equation $m' = m^\delta$ can be used to identify the corresponding input terms.

Clearly, the model presented in Sect. 4 is too basic to allow for detection of the attack. Instead, we can examine attacker's behavior by a simple extension of the model. For that, we change the Mteller template as shown in Fig. 10. The only difference lies in how the first re-encryption mix is done: the corrupted mix teller targets c_0, chooses a random non-zero δ, and uses c_0^δ instead of some other output term. We assume that the corrupt mix teller will always try to cheat. In all other respects, the teller behaves honestly.

Using UPPAAL, it can be verified that there exist executions where the corrupt mix teller's cheating behaviour is not detected during the audit. That is, both $E\Diamond\text{failed\_audit}_0$ and $E\Diamond\text{passed\_audit}_0$ produce 'Property satisfied' as the output. We note that, in order to successfully verify those properties in our model of Prêt à Voter, the search order option in UPPAAL had to be changed from the (default) **Breadth First** to either **Depth First** or **Random Depth First**.

7 Related Work

Over the years, the properties of *ballot secrecy*, *receipt-freeness*, *coercion resis-tance*, and *voter-verifiability* were recognized as important for an election to

work properly, see also [29] for an overview. More recently, significant progress
has been made in the development of voting systems that would be coercion-
resistant and at the same time allow the voter to verify "her" part of the election
outcome [12,31]. A number of secure and voter-verifiable schemes have been proposed, notably Prêt à Voter for supervised elections [32], Pretty Good Democracy for internet voting [34], and Selene, a coercion mitigating form of tracking
number-based, internet scheme [33].

Such schemes are starting to move out of the laboratory and into use in
real elections. For example, (a variant of) Prêt à Voter has been successfully
used in one of the state elections in Australia [9] while the Scantegrity II system [10] was used in municipal elections in the Takoma Park county, Maryland.
Moreover, a number of verifiable schemes were used in non-political elections.
E.g., Helios [1] was used to elect officials of the International Association of
Cryptologic Research and the Dean of the University of Louvain la Neuve. This
underlines the need for extensive analysis and validation of such systems.

Formal analysis of selected voting protocols, based on theorem proving in
first-order logic or linear logic, includes attempts at verification of vote counting
in [3,30]. The Coq theorem prover [6] was used to implement the STV counting scheme in a provably correct way [16], and to produce a provably voter-
verifiable variant of the Helios protocol [18]. Moreover, Tamarin [28] was used
to verify receipt-freeness in Selene [8] and Electryo [35]. Approaches based on
model checking are fewer and include the analysis of risk-limiting audits [4] with
the CBMC model checker [11]. Moreover, [22] proposed and verified a simple
multi-agent model of Selene using MCMAS [27]. Related research includes the
use of multi-agent methodologies to specify and verify properties of authentication and key-establishment protocols [7,26] with MCMAS. In particular, [7] used
MCMAS to obtain and verify models, automatically synthesized from high-level
protocol description languages such as CAPSL, thus creating a bridge between
multi-agent and process-based methods.

In all the above cases, the focus is on the verification itself. Indeed, all the
tools mentioned above provide only a text-based interface for specification of
the system. As a result, their model specifications closely resemble programming code, and insufficiently protect from the usual pitfalls of programming:
unreadability of the code, lack of modularity, and opaque control structure. In
this paper, we draw attention to tools that promote modular design of the model,
emphasize its control structure, and facilitate inspection and validation.

8   Conclusions

Formal methods are well established in proving (and disproving) the correctness of cryptographic protocols. What makes voting protocols special is that
they prominently feature human and social aspects. In consequence, an accurate
specification of the behaviors admitted by the protocol is far from straightforward. An environment that supports the creation of modular, compact, and –
most of all – readable specifications can be an invaluable help.

In this context, the UPPAAL model checker has a number of advantages. Its
modelling language encourages modular specification of the system behavior. It

provides flexible data structures, and allows for parameterized specification of states and transitions. Last but not least, it has a user-friendly GUI. Clearly, a good graphical model helps to understand how the voting procedure works, and allows for a preliminary validation of the system specification just by looking at the graphs. Anybody who ever inspected a text-based system specification or the programming code itself will know what we mean.

In this paper, we try to demonstrate the advantages of UPPAAL through a case study based on a version of Prêt à Voter. The models that we have obtained are neat, easy to read, and easy to modify. On the other hand, UPPAAL has not performed well with the verification itself. This was largely due to the fact that its requirement specification language turned out to be very limited – much more than it seemed at the first glance. We managed to partly overcome the limitations by a smart reconstruction of models and formulas. In the long run, however, a more promising path is to extend the implementation of verification algorithms in UPPAAL so that they handle nested path quantifiers and knowledge modalities, given explicitly in the formula.

The model proposed here is far from complete. We intend to refine and expand it to capture a broader range of attacks, in particular coercion (or vote-buying attacks) that involve subtle interactions between coercer and voters. Prime examples include chain voting and randomisation attacks, where the coercer requires the voter to place an "X" in, say, the first position. Such an attack does not violate any privacy property – the coercer does not learn the vote – but it does deny the voter the freedom to cast her vote as intended. Still more subtle styles of attack have been identified against many verifiable schemes by Kelsey, [24]. Essentially any freedom the voter may have in executing the voting ceremony can potentially be exploited by a coercer.

A comprehensive discussion of coercion-resistance and its possible formalizations is also planned for future work. Another important line of research concerns data independence and saturation results. It is known that, to verify some properties, it suffices to look for small counterexamples [2]. It is also known that such results are in general impossible [15] or incur prohibitive blowup [13]. We will investigate what saturation can be achieved for the verification of Prêt à Voter.

Acknowledgements. The authors acknowledge the support of the Luxembourg National Research Fund (FNR) and the National Centre for Research and Development Poland (NCBiR) under the INTER/PolLux projects VoteVerif (POLLUX-IV/1/2016) and STV (POLLUX-VII/1/2019).

References

1. Adida, B.: Helios: web-based open-audit voting. In: Proceedings of the 17th Conference on Security Symposium, SS 2008, USENIX Association, Berkeley, CA, USA, pp. 335–348 (2008)
2. Arapinis, M., Cortier, V., Kremer, S.: When are three voters enough for privacy properties? In: Askoxylakis, I., Ioannidis, S., Katsikas, S., Meadows, C. (eds.) ESORICS 2016. LNCS, vol. 9879, pp. 241–260. Springer, Cham (2016). https://doi.org/10.1007/978-3-319-45741-3_13

3. Beckert, B., Goré, R., Schürmann, C.: Analysing vote counting algorithms via logic. In: Bonacina, M.P. (ed.) CADE 2013. LNCS (LNAI), vol. 7898, pp. 135–144. Springer, Heidelberg (2013). https://doi.org/10.1007/978-3-642-38574-2_9
4. Beckert, B., Kirsten, M., Klebanov, V., Schürmann., C.: Automatic margin computation for risk-limiting audits. In: Krimmer, R. et al. (eds.) Electronic Voting. Proceedings of E-Vote-ID, Lecture Notes in Computer Science, vol. 10141, pp. 18–35. Springer, Cham (2016). https://doi.org/10.1007/978-3-319-52240-1_2
5. Behrmann, G., David, A., Larsen, K.G.: A tutorial on UPPAAL. In: Bernardo, M., Corradini, F. (eds.) Formal Methods for the Design of Real-Time Systems: SFM-RT. LNCS, vol. 3185, pp. 200–236. Springer, Heidelberg (2004). https://doi.org/10.1007/978-3-540-30080-9_7
6. Bertot, Y., Casteran, P., Huet, G., Paulin-Mohring, C.: Interactive Theorem Proving and Program Development. Coq'Art: The Calculus of Inductive Constructions. Springer, Heidelberg (2004). https://doi.org/10.1007/978-3-662-07964-5
7. Boureanu, I., Kouvaros, P., Lomuscio, A.: Verifying security properties in unbounded multiagent systems. In: Proceedings of International Joint Conference on Autonomous Agents and Multiagent Systems (AAMAS), pp. 1209–1217 (2016)
8. Bruni, A., Drewsen, E., Schürmann, C.: Towards a mechanized proof of selene receipt-freeness and vote-privacy. In: Krimmer, R., Volkamer, M., Braun Binder, N., Kersting, N., Pereira, O., Schürmann, C. (eds.) E-Vote-ID 2017. LNCS, vol. 10615, pp. 110–126. Springer, Cham (2017). https://doi.org/10.1007/978-3-319-68687-5_7
9. Burton, C., et al.: Using Prêt à Voter in Victoria state elections. In: Proceedings of EVT/WOTE. USENIX (2012)
10. Chaum, D., et al.: Scantegrity II: end-to-end verifiability by voters of optical scan elections through confirmation codes. IEEE Trans. Inf. Forensics Secur. 4(4), 611–627 (2009)
11. Clarke, E., Kroening, D., Lerda, F.: A tool for checking ANSI-C programs. In: Jensen, K., Podelski, A. (eds.) TACAS 2004. LNCS, vol. 2988, pp. 168–176. Springer, Heidelberg (2004). https://doi.org/10.1007/978-3-540-24730-2_15
12. Cortier, V., Galindo, D., Küsters, R., Müller, J., Truderung, T.: SoK: verifiability notions for e-voting protocols. In: IEEE Symposium on Security and Privacy, pp. 779–798 (2016)
13. Czerwiński, W., Lasota, S., Lazić, R., Leroux, J., Mazowiecki, F.: The reachability problem for petri nets is not elementary. In: Proceedings of the 51st Annual ACM SIGACT Symposium on Theory of Computing STOC, pp. 24–33. Association for Computing Machinery (2019)
14. Emerson, E.A.: Temporal and modal logic. In: van Leeuwen, J. (ed.) Handbook of Theoretical Computer Science, vol. B, pp. 995–1072. Elsevier, Amsterdam (1990)
15. German, S.M., Sistla, A.P.: Reasoning about systems with many processes. J. ACM 39(3), 675–735 (1992)
16. Ghale, M.K., Goré, R., Pattinson, D., Tiwari, M.: Modular formalisation and verification of STV algorithms. In: Krimmer, R., et al. (eds.) E-Vote-ID 2018. LNCS, vol. 11143, pp. 51–66. Springer, Cham (2018). https://doi.org/10.1007/978-3-030-00419-4_4
17. Goranko, V., Jamroga, W.: Comparing semantics of logics for multi-agent systems. Synthese 139(2), 241–280 (2004)
18. Haines, T., Goré, R., Tiwari, M.: Verified verifiers for verifying elections. In: Proceedings of CCS, pp. 685–702. ACM (2019)
19. Hao, F., Ryan, P.Y.A.: Real-World Electronic Voting: Design, Analysis and Deployment, 1st edn. Auerbach Publications, Boca Raton (2016)

20. Jakobsson, M., Juels, A., Rivest, R.L.: Making mix nets robust for electronic voting by randomized partial checking. In: USENIX Security Symposium, pp. 339–353 (2002)
21. Jamroga, W.: Knowledge and strategic ability for model checking: a refined approach. In: Bergmann, R., Lindemann, G., Kirn, S., Pěchouček, M. (eds.) MATES 2008. LNCS (LNAI), vol. 5244, pp. 99–110. Springer, Heidelberg (2008). https://doi.org/10.1007/978-3-540-87805-6_10
22. Jamroga, W., Knapik, M., Kurpiewski, D.: Model checking the SELENE e-voting protocol in multi-agent logics. In: Krimmer, R., et al. (eds.) E-Vote-ID 2018. LNCS, vol. 11143, pp. 100–116. Springer, Cham (2018). https://doi.org/10.1007/978-3-030-00419-4_7
23. Kant, G., Laarman, A., Meijer, J., van de Pol, J., Blom, S., van Dijk, T.: LTSmin: high-performance language-independent model checking. In: Baier, C., Tinelli, C. (eds.) TACAS 2015. LNCS, vol. 9035, pp. 692–707. Springer, Heidelberg (2015). https://doi.org/10.1007/978-3-662-46681-0_61
24. Kelsey, J., Regenscheid, A., Moran, T., Chaum, D.: Attacking Paper-Based E2E Voting Systems, pp. 370–387. Springer, Heidelberg (2010). https://doi.org/10.1007/978-3-642-12980-3_23
25. Khazaei, S., Wikström, D.: Randomized partial checking revisited. In: Dawson, E. (ed.) CT-RSA 2013. LNCS, vol. 7779, pp. 115–128. Springer, Heidelberg (2013). https://doi.org/10.1007/978-3-642-36095-4_8
26. Lomuscio, A., Penczek, W.: LDYIS: a framework for model checking security protocols. Fundamenta Informaticae 85(1–4), 359–375 (2008)
27. Lomuscio, A., Qu, H., Raimondi, F.: MCMAS: an open-source model checker for the verification of multi-agent systems. Int. J. Softw. Tools Technol. Transfer. 19(1), 9–30 (2017)
28. Meier, S., Schmidt, B., Cremers, C., Basin, D.: The TAMARIN prover for the symbolic analysis of security protocols. In: Sharygina, N., Veith, H. (eds.) CAV 2013. LNCS, vol. 8044, pp. 696–701. Springer, Heidelberg (2013). https://doi.org/10.1007/978-3-642-39799-8_48
29. Meng, B.: A critical review of receipt-freeness and coercion-resistance. Inf. Technol. J. 8(7), 934–964 (2009)
30. Pattinson, D., Schürmann, C.: Vote counting as mathematical proof. In: Pfahringer, B., Renz, J. (eds.) AI 2015. LNCS (LNAI), vol. 9457, pp. 464–475. Springer, Cham (2015). https://doi.org/10.1007/978-3-319-26350-2_41
31. Ryan, P.Y.A., Schneider, S.A., Teague, V.: End-to-end verifiability in voting systems, from theory to practice. IEEE Secur. Priv. 13(3), 59–62 (2015)
32. Ryan, P.Y.A.: The computer ate my vote. In: Boca, P., Bowen, J., Siddiqi, J. (eds.) Formal Methods: State of the Art and New Directions, pp. 147–184. Springer, London (2010). https://doi.org/10.1007/978-1-84882-736-3_5
33. Ryan, P.Y.A., Rønne, P.B., Iovino, V.: Selene: voting with transparent verifiability and coercion-mitigation. In: Clark, J., et al. (eds.) Financial Cryptography and Data Security. Lecture Notes in Computer Science, vol. 9604, pp. 176–192. Springer, Heidelberg (2016)
34. Ryan, P.Y.A., Teague, V.: Pretty good democracy. In: Christianson, B., Malcolm, J.A., Matyáš, V., Roe, M. (eds.) Security Protocols 2009. LNCS, vol. 7028, pp. 111–130. Springer, Heidelberg (2013). https://doi.org/10.1007/978-3-642-36213-2_15
35. Zollinger, M.-L., Roenne, P., Ryan, P.Y.A.: Mechanized proofs of verifiability and privacy in a paper-based e-voting scheme. In: Proceedings of 5th Workshop on Advances in Secure Electronic Voting (2020)

E-Voting System Evaluation Based on the Council of Europe Recommendations: *n*Votes

David Yeregui Marcos del Blanco[1]([⊠]) [iD], David Duenas-Cid[2,3] [iD], and Héctor Aláiz Moretón[1,2,3] [iD]

[1] University of Leon, Campus de Vegazana, s/n, 24071 León, Spain
dmarcb01@estudiantes.unileon.es, hector.moreton@unileon.es
[2] Tallinn University of Technology, Akadeemia tee 3, 12618 Tallinn, Estonia
david.duenas@taltech.ee, dduenas@kozminski.edu.pl
[3] Kozminski University, Jagiellonska 57/59, 03-301 Warsaw, Poland

Abstract. E-voting implantation has been facing important challenges in recent years. Several incidents, together with a lack of evaluation methodologies social and cultural customs hinder a broader application. In this work, the authors aim to contribute to a safer introduction of e-voting tools by applying a practical evaluation framework strongly based on the security requirements issued by the Council of Europe (CoE) in 2017 to *n*votes, a system that has been utilized to cast over 2 million votes over the last 6 years.

The ultimate goal of the analysis is not to judge from a rigid, "infallible" but to contribute to a gradual and secure implementation of e-voting solutions in the democratic processes. The authors believe it can constitute a useful source of information for election officials, researchers and voters.

Keywords: E-democracy · E-voting · System evaluation · nvotes

1 Introduction

Since the first implementation of remote electronic voting in the 90s [4], the process of dissemination of internet voting did not meet the initial and promised expectations. Several countries experimented with the possibility of adding internet voting systems to their elections[1], but it just turned into a reality in a reduced number of them: Estonia, Canada, Australia, Switzerland or Norway, amongst others. The Estonian case is the most prominent success story, using Internet Voting uninterruptedly since 2005 in all elections [1] an reaching high levels of acceptation [2] and cost efficiency [3, 4].

The dissemination of internet voting technologies is challenged by a complex set of factors that affect different layers of administration, law, society and technology [5] and that should be achieved in a constant dialogue between themselves: dealing with

---

[1] For a better understanding, see International IDEA's database on use of ICT in Elections: https://www.idea.int/data-tools/data/icts-elections (last accessed 4 June 2020).

© Springer Nature Switzerland AG 2020
R. Krimmer et al. (Eds.): E-Vote-ID 2020, LNCS 12455, pp. 147–166, 2020.
https://doi.org/10.1007/978-3-030-60347-2_10

complexity in electoral management, reforming electoral laws, ensuring transparency, neutrality and participation and ensuring secure and risk-free technological apparatus. The latter factor, has been constantly labelled as an important element not only for the correct functioning of the internet voting and its integration in the electoral systems, but also as an element projecting trust in the society where the system is being implemented [6–8].

Pursuing the same goal, the creation of trust as a key element for the adoption of internet voting systems, the Council of Europe (CoE) proposes a set of recommendations to guide the process of implementation of electronic remote voting systems [9]. The CM/Rec(2017)5 updates the previous Recommendations from 2004 and integrates lessons learned from previous experiences and developments in the electoral field to create a useful and up-to-date document. Specifically, proposes a set of Principles, Standards and Requirements that every electronic voting system should fulfil for the development of elections and for reinforcing the democratic principles that are the common heritage of its member states [10]: Elections should be Universal, Equal, Free and Secret, should meet a set of regulatory and organizational requirements, should be transparent and allow observation and should be accountable, and should use reliable and secure systems.

In view of the aforementioned list, this paper presents an analysis on how the system *nVotes* fits within the CoE requirements. The ultimate goal of the authors is not to judge from a rigid *immovable* or *infallible* point of view for the sake of pin pointing shortcomings, but to establish a comprehensive, multi-faceted evaluation in order to improve the knowledge and security level in the deployment of e-voting systems.

2 Related Works

The research work of Bräunlich, Grimm and Richter in 2013 [111] is considered one of the most relevant to date. The authors presented the first interdisciplinary collaboration which has transformed legal requirements into technical criteria. Specifically, they established thirty Technical Design Goals (TDG), using the KORA methodology (*Konkretis-ierung Rechtlicher Inforderungen, Concretization of Legal Requirements*) [12]. This methodology had been used previously for mobile devices amongst others.

Neumann combined the previous methodology of Bräunlich, Grimm and Richter with the *Common Criteria for IT-Security Evaluation* [13] and established sixteen technical requirements to relate the legal criteria to Bräunlich's TDGs.

While Neumann's work [14] has critically contributed to constructing a very valuable framework, it still had room for improvement from a practical standpoint:

On the one hand, the security evaluation framework is aimed at schemes rather than entire systems, with the author himself coming across an example of a structural flaw that would not be identified using his evaluation scheme: *"for instance, the Vote Forwarding Server and the Vote Storage Server of the Estonian Internet voting scheme are developed and maintained by the same vendor"* [14, p. 135].

Additionally, the security evaluation assumes that the voters will use the authentication tools sufficiently. Unfortunately, the tendency of the voters is not to verify: for instance, one of the largest electoral e-voting initiatives which took place in New South Wales in 2015, showed that only 1.7% of 283.669 votes were verified [15].

Furthermore, Neumann's framework is based on probabilistic attack strategies through Monte-Carlo simulations [14]. While represeting an interesting approach indeed, it is less useful for a practical evaluation standpoint. As a result, the author concludes: "we therefore recommend to incorporate the security evaluation framework into a larger decision-support system for elections officials" [14, p. 138].

Following with the above recommendation, a decision-support system was proposed by Marcos, et al. as a practical evaluation framework [16]. It is in accordance with the guidelines from the 2017 Council of Europe's (*"Guidelines on the implementation of the provisions of Recommendation CM/Rec(2017)5 on standards for e-voting"*) [17] and deals with the five key principles of a democratic election (universal, free, equal, direct and secret) detailed in the same document.

3 Evaluation Methodology

As previously stated, while Neumann's work set out an irrefutable improvement, it constitutes a scheme evaluation tool with probabilistic proofs as its core with Monte-Carlo simulations rather than a practical evaluation framework tool for election officials and other stakeholders involved in the democratic processes.

In 2018, Panizo et al. proposed an extended evaluation approach [19] in the context of the Spanish Constitution [18] and the CoE's e-voting recommendations [17]:

1. Defining an homogeneous series of e-voting requirements with the KORA methodology [12] as its basis, together with the CC and ISO 27001-IT Grundschutz guideline [13], their assimilation by Simic-Draws et al. [20], the Guidelines of the Council of Europe [17] and Neumann's methodology [14].
2. Formal conformity between point 1 and Bräunlich's TDG's [11], as in Fig. 1.
3. Consultation with more than 30 international experts in e-voting (Research and Industry Experts or RIE, selected using the snowball [21] and judgement [22] sampling methodologies) to review the evaluation framework and add weighting factors.
4. Formal definition of the practical evaluation framework, including two sine-qua-non requirements (E2Ev and Coercion Resistance) and 41 evaluation items.

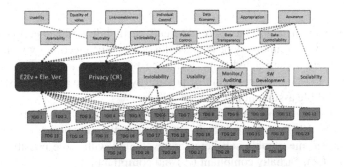

Fig. 1. Integration of Panizo [19] and Bräunlich [11]

The work in [16] established for the first time a correlation between the end to end verifiability (E2Ev) and coercion resistance (CR) to the legal requirements for a democratic process and the Council of Europe: *"The five key principles of electoral law are: universal, equal, free, direct and secret suffrage and they are at the root of democracy"* (article 68 of the Spanish Constitution [18]).

Specifically, Marcos et al. Set out the equivalence of the aforementioned five key principles, into a formal authentication of the E2Ev the universal, free, equal and direct properties and its coercion resistance for the secrecy prerequisite (based on the findings by Hirt and Sako on the matter in [46]).

The methodology presented to this point is solid from a legal point of view but still lacks the technical and practical approach necessary for a complete evaluation.

In order to solve the shortcomings, five practical requisites were introduced, partially based on the research by Benaloh, Rivest, Ryan and Volkamer [23, 24]. Subsequently, the requisites were codified, refined and subdivided into 73 specific items by means of a partial application of Zissis and Lekkas [25] and New Zealand's Department of Internal Affair's Communication on e-voting [26][2].

As a final step, e-voting RIEs from Canada, France, Norway, Switzerland, Germany and Spain among other countries were consulted to assign a weighting factors.

The following Fig. 2 visually represents the complete evaluation methodology:

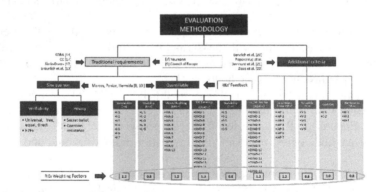

Fig. 2. Complete evaluation framework [16]

The sine-qua-non requirements (end-to-end verifiability and coercion resistance, representing the five compulsory principles of a democratic election), which evaluation is not a numerical value related to performance but instead in terms of "holds" (○) or "does not hold" (×). There is a third possibility, when the property "stands under determined, credible assumptions" (△).

The second quantifiable and additional criteria, totaling 10 requirements, are evaluated from 0 to 10. In order to obtain the numerical evaluation for each criterion, the corresponding measurable sub-items are evaluated with three possible outcomes: non-compliant (×), partially compliant (△) and compliant (○).

---

[2] For a complete explanation of the previous process, please refer to the original work in [6, 8].

Due to space constraints, the evaluation framework design, implementation and constituent requirements has been simplified. For a full explanation, the reader can refer to Dr. Marcos' Ph.D. thesis which originated the methodology [27].

It is relevant to mention that this practical evaluation methodology has also been applied to Helios Voting and published by the IEEE [19].

4 nVotes Analysis

4.1 Introduction

nVotes [28] is a remote e-voting system developed by the Spanish company Agora Voting SL in 2014. Its roots trace back to 2009 and the Internet Party, although the developing team has since then dropped any political affiliation and nVotes is currently an apolitical project.

Until 2017, nVotes was known as Agora Voting and under such moniker it was one of the 18 European start-ups to be accepted in the Impact Accelerator project, and awarded with 100,000 EUR [29].

According to their website, nVotes has been used to cast over 2 million votes for over 150 clients, including Public Administrations like the Barcelona Provincial Council, Madrid City Council; Political Parties like Podemos, Ahora Madrid and Barcelona en Comú, as well as Education Institutions like UNED University in Spain.

4.2 Main Characteristics

As previously mentioned, the methodology presented in Sect. 3 has been already applied to other relevant e-voting tools, including Helios Voting [19] or iVote by Scytl [30]; in both cases with numerous bibliography and research resources available:

- Helios Voting is a very well-known open source e-voting system [31], which has been used as blueprint for several variations and improvements such as Helios KTV [32] or Belenios [33].
- Scytl is probably the most widely used e-voting system at a global level, including numerous legally-binding elections and pilots for a total of over 100,000 processes managed and more than 200 employees. The information available ranges from research papers to Government reports and corporate presentations.

In the case of of nVotes, the available bibliography is much more limited due to the fact that they are neither a research standard tool, nor a global company. In order to complement the publicly available information, the authors of this document got in touch with nVotes and they key people have always been open and supporting in providing all the available information and answers to the questions raised.

Additionally, the authors were provided with two documents named *"Technical Overview"* and *"Client Action Protocol"*, which have been extremely useful for conducting the analysis. They are at the reader's disposal upon request to the authors since they have not been published before.

nVotes Scheme Components and Cryptographic Primitives. According to the information included in the *"Technical Overview"* and complemented with a Q/A with nVotes technical team, the key elements are:

- Registry: The registration database programmed in Python. It includes the SMS service platform Esendex [34], server certificate with TSL support, Cloudfare [35] and Fail2ban [36] for protection against DDoS attacks and hardware redundancy $1 + 1$.
- Virtual Polling Station: TLS server validation, *cast-or-audit* voting javascript (similar to that of Helios Voting [31]), random number generator (not specified), HMAC client authentication, Election Manager with Scala REST API, Postgresql database and similar to the Registry case, Cloudfare and Fail2ban DDoS protection.
- Electoral Authority: HTTP distributed queue, TLS client/server authentication, mixnet library *Verificatum* [37] and tabulation library OpenSTV [38].
- Election Verificator: a Python/Java.

With regards to the main cryptographic primitives, they are the following:

- El Gamal Homomorphic Encryption [39]
- Pedersen Threshold Distributed Key Generator [40]
- *Verificatum* verifiable mixnet [37]
- Fiat-Shamir heuristic to convert Zero Knowledge Proofs into Non-Iterative Zero Knowledge Proofs [41]
- Schnorr Signature [42] to make the ElGamal Encryption IND-CCA2.

nVotes Voting Sequence. As presented in the *"Technical Review"* and *"Client Action Protocol"* documents, the voting procedure is as follows:

1. Authorities distributedly generate the Election's Public Key with Pedersen [40].
2. Eve (voter) access the Registry site and provides the required personal information, including a security code which has been sent independently by SMS.
3. The Registry system compares the information provided with the census. If it is correct, Eve is forwarded to the Virtual Polling Station.
4. Eve fills her vote, encrypts it and sends it. Alternatively, she can audit it but in such case, the cast vote is no longer valid and will not be tallied. This *cast-or-audit* approach is also implemented in Helios Voting [31].
5. Once the vote casting period ends, the authorities jointly proceed with the mix and decryption of the ballots.
6. The decrypted votes are tallied.
7. The election results are published, together with the tally results, the vote's ciphertexts as well as the mixnet and decryption Zero Knowledge Proofs.
8. Voters and third parties can download and execute the election verificator.

Once nVotes has been introduced, together with its associated scheme components, cryptographic primitives and voting process, the practical evaluation methodology for e-voting systems [16] can be applied.

The analysis is intended to be a sort of a guideline, which introduces strengths and potential weaknesses in order to establish a safe range if utilization and to offer directions as to how to improve the voting system.

4.3 End to End Verifiability

Unfortunately, there is no formal, universal definition for end-to-end verifiability (E2Ev). Additionally, symbolic analysis of security protocols still find associative and commutative operators are out of reach. It is then not possible to analyze a homomorphic property [43] such as:

$$enc(pk; v_1) * enc(pk; v_2) = enc(pk; v_1 + v_2) \tag{1}$$

and therefore, a case by case analysis has to be conducted for each system.

Currently, probably the most widely accepted definition of E2Ev is the one by Benaloh et al. in [23] and is comprised of the properties: "Cast as intended", "Recorded as cast" and "Tallied as recorded".

For the first and second items, nVotes presents a similar approach to that of Helios Voting: the voter can audit her vote until she is convinced that it is trustable. Once cast, she receives a hash of the encrypted vote, which she can check on public bulletin board. Finally, for the tallied as recorded condition, ElGamal together with *Verificatum* mixnet [37] and Schnorr [42] are implemented.

Consequently, on the question of nVotes being E2Ev or not and similar to the analysis in [18] for Helios Voting, it can be considered end to end verifiable assuming that:

- The cast and audit mechanism is used by a large enough number of voters so that ballot alteration will not go unnoticed.
- The Election Authorities and the Bulletin Board (BB) are honest.
- An attack which gains control of the Registry/Ballot is detected.

For the first precondition, Acemyan in [44] and the New South Wales case [15] have shown that voters' ballot verification percentage is quite low and they should not be responsible of part of the security of an e-voting system.

As for the other two prerequisites, in a perfect scenario nVotes would be compliant but in real elections, both the Election Authorities and/or the BB can illegally introduce votes (ballot stuffing). For public, legally binding elections, it is not acceptable.

To sum up, provided that nVotes implementation is limited to elections with a low risk of corruption such as student government bodies, local clubs, online groups, and other education-related organizations, the pre-assumptions could be acceptable. For other, more demanding types of elections, E2Ev cannot be recommended.

Evaluation: Δ. E2Ev holds if the preconditions set in nVotes' *Technical Overview* document are accepted and its use is limited to low corruption risk elections.

4.4   Coercion Resistance

Assuming probably the most accepted definition of privacy levels by Juels et al. [45] and the proof by Hirt and Sako [46] that receipt-freeness is not enough for preserving it in electronic elections, the required level is Coercion Resistance. It implies that a voter cannot provide to an attacker any proof of her vote or even whether she voted or nor, even if she is willing to cooperate.

As for nVotes, the voter receives a verification code after casting the ballot, therefore she can prove it to a potential attacker.

Additionally, the Election Administrator of an Election can verify whether an specific person in the census has voted or not, which clearly compromises the privacy.

Evaluation: X. Does not hold.

4.5   Inviolability (I-n)

nVotes' *Technical Overview* document includes an integrity, privacy and availability analysis. The authors include the possibility of "ballot stuffing" if the Election Administrators are corrupt and of DDoS attacks despite implementing specific tools [35, 36].

There have also been questions raised about the census integrity used in consultative referenda [47, 48] and the separation between the tally administrator and the census administrator, which can be the same person and thus lead to potential collusions (I-4).

Safe authentication protocols, tracking tools, Risk Assessment and modularity principles are partially compliant, with room for improvement (Table 1).

Table 1. Inviolability in nVotes

I-n	Definition	Val
I-1	Software and auxiliary system's protection w/safe authentication protocols. Access via third-parties/vulnerable-servers not permitte	Δ
I-2	Action protocols in the event of compromised inviolability	X
I-3	Tracking tools and offline backup copies available	Δ
I-4	Distributed control in the critical nodes with division of responsibilities to minimize collusion risks	X
I-5	Existence of *Risk Assessment* and *Threat Modelling* protocols	Δ
I-6	Modularity principles to confine potential attacks and coding bugs	Δ
I-7	Proper updating of items I-1...I-6	Δ

Evaluation: 4/10 Points. The inviolability policy presents vulnerabilities which, for private elections (while being very serious), are ultimately up to the organizer whether to take the risk or not. For legally binding public elections, they are not acceptable and nVotes inviolability should be improved before being used in such environment.

4.6   Usability (U-n)

nVotes presents a satisfactory performance in terms of simplicity and clarity in the voting process (U-1, U-3) as well as in intuitiveness and lexicon choice both for the voter and the administrators.

Concerning the aspects to be improved, there is no version adapted to collectives with special needs, the SMS authentication might prove challenging for the elders and the verification codes are too long and "imposing" voters with no technical background. An intermediate usability layer might be advisable. Overall, usability is satisfactory while it could be enhance with some simple, easy to implement changes (Table 2).

Table 2.   Usability in nVotes

U-*n*	Definition	Val
U-1	Simplicity in the authentication, voting and verification	O
U-2	Special attention to vulnerable groups pursuant to the Council of Europe and the United Nations' resolutions on the matter	X
U-3	Transparency & clarity communicating the voter that the voting process has successfully ended/vote has been received	O
U-4	Privacy and integrity preference over usability in a compromise	X
U-5	Intuitive/user-friendly admin interface for setup and management	O

Evaluation: 6/10 points.

4.7   Monitoring/Auditing (MA-n)

This aspect is especially relevant for nVotes due to the possibility of *Ballot Stuffing* if the Administrators are corrupt or collide or due to DDoS attacks.

Probably due to the nature and scope of the elections managed, the Monitoring and Auditing Protocol is based on the Administrators training. According to nVotes' team, a unified protocol including all the auditing activities is currently being generated.

Until then, nVotes generates retrievable logs, and provides information and data in an easily understandable format. Even so, at this point the Monitoring/Auditing Protocol is still largely to be developed and implemented; therefore not satisfactory (Table 3).

Table 3. Monitoring/Auditing in nVotes

MA-n	Definition	Val
MA-1	External, independent and distributed	X
MA-2	MA protocol from the design phase, to assure a correct development throughout the whole lifecycle of the project	X
MA-3	*Specific control on Risk Assess* and *Thread Modelling strategies*	X
MA-4	Generation of periodical, tamper-proof, indelible logs; stored offline in premises guarded by different personnel from other critical nodes	Δ
MA-5	Implementation from census collecting to post-electoral maintenance	Δ
MA-6	Well-documented, detailed information in the appropriate format	Δ
MA-7	Existence of a test bench to verify that the system is working correctly	X
MA-8	The members of the monitoring/auditing team must be independent from the rest of authorities/administrators involved	X
MA-9	Auditing protocol for previous attacks and the MA protocol itself	X
MA-10	In the event of a successful attack, the system will give total priority to the vote/voter's privacy, even calling off the elections	X

Evaluation: 3/10 points.

4.8 Software Development (SWD-n)

nVotes displays an overall solid Software Development (partly because of its open source approach), with a satisfactory performance in usual software engineering practices (SWD-1), FAQ (SWD-4), impartiality (SWD-5), ballot cast termination (SWD-8), compatibility (SWD-9), third party access (SWD-10), and protocolized application (SWD-13).

Regarding the distributed approach (SWD-2), it has been correctly implemented for key generation and encryption/decryption but there is no separation between the census and the bulletin board. If the same person is responsible for both of them, there is an important risk of collusion.

Finally, the primitives are well implemented but some of them have been already been proven flawed and should be reviewed (SWD-11). Additionally, more frequent updates would be preferable (SWD-14) (Table 4).

Table 4. Software Development in nVotes

SWD-*n*	Definition	Val
SWD-1	Usual software engineering requirements in terms of design, implementation and documentation	O
SWD-2	Distributed approach on critical operations. No authority should have attributions to single-handedly modify critical parameters	Δ
SWD-3	User-friendly approach. User's guide and administrator's guide well documented and available well in advance	Δ
SWD-4	Secure and accessible website, with a well-documented FAQ	O
SWD-5	The voting options must be presented in a totally objective and unbiased way, showing no preference whatsoever	O
SWD-6	System must not provide the voter with evidence to proof her vote	X
SWD-7	The system must guarantee the voter's privacy throughout the whole voting process, not being possible to rebuild the vote/voter link	Δ
SWD-8	The voting process must offer the possibility to be terminated at any time, not saving any information compromising the voter's privacy	O
SWD-9	SW to be tested in every platform, operational system and browser with a market share ≥ 1%	O
SWD-10	Software must neither allow for third-party access (incl. social media) nor include links to programs/sites outside the e-voting infrastructure	O
SWD-11	The cryptographic primitives shall be tested in advance under conditions more demanding than the ones expected during the elections in order to avoid breakdowns and foresee shortages	Δ
SWD-12	Access to the source code by independent experts to reinforce security. The code developer can demand an NDA to protect its IP	Δ
SWD-13	Use of protocolized systems/open standards to improve interoperability	O
SWD-14	Update policy, against new e-voting attacks as they are discovered	X

Evaluation: 7/10 points.

4.9 Scalability (S-n)

nVotes has managed elections up to 150,000 votes in consultative referenda of political parties, although they didn't managed many of the ex_software activities, which were handled by the Party itself.

So far, the system has proved to be scalable to the amount of votes already managed in private elections. The shortcomings related to monitoring, ex-software development and potential collusion request a further in-depth improvement before being considered for introduction in public binding elections (Table 5).

Table 5. Scalability in nVotes

S-n	Definition	Val
S-1	Maximum capacity tests both from a SW and a HW standpoint in environments more demanding than the elections to be managed	Δ
S-2	Ad-hoc performance tests for the most critical operations (authentication, encryption/decryption, cryptographic primitives, tallying …)	X
S-3	Existence of test benches more demanding than the actual elections	X
S-4	Clear indicators and metrics on the max manageable size and complexity from a SW (cryptographic capabilities, number of voters) and ex_SW (infrastructure, costs, logistics, second channels etc.) standpoints	Δ
S-5	Clear definition of election which can be adequately handled by the *e-voting* system (from consultative referenda to politically binding elections)	Δ

Evaluation: 5.5/10 points.

4.10   Ex-Software Development (ESWD-n)

Ex_Software development is intimately related to the increased complexity of public binding elections. The lower the score in this category, the less recommended it is for the analyzed e-voting system to be implemented for such type of elections.

In the case of nVotes, it has been deployed only for private elections and referenda, and therefore has not implemented ESWD1-4, ESWD6-7, and ESWD-10.

The aspects in which the development is satisfactory are: authentication by alternative channels (ESWD-11) and the master initialization protocol (ESWD-12).

As for the communication/problem solving/back up policy (ESWD5, 6, 8, 9, 14, 15), nVotes stated that they offer different levels of services according to the needs and budget of each election. They can even let the client handle most of the activities related to back-up protocols, responsibilities attributions etc.

While that could make sense from a business perspective, the security implications in case of a misuse or a scandal, and the potential impact in the reputation of nVotes, advice against allowing the election organizer to handle such sensitive actions (Table 6).

Table 6. Ex_Software Development in nVotes

ESWD-*n*	Definition	Val
ESWD-1	Design, development & update of SWD/ESWD protocols in parallel	N/A
ESWD-2	Safe protocol for credential, permission & responsib. distribution	N/A
ESWD-3	Automated access control and infrastructure surveillance	N/A
ESWD-4	Auditing and independent observers' protocol	X
ESWD-5	Distributed *back-up* protocol	Δ
ESWD-6	Distribution of attributions and responsibilities throughout the whole ex_sw development to minimize collusion risk	X
ESWD-7	Availability of complementary, non e-voting systems	X
ESWD-8	Voters must be informed about the e-voting process in advance, through websites, telephone, information stands…	Δ
ESWD-9	If re-voting is permitted, provide a reinforced information campaign to explain the prevalence of paper ballot	Δ
ESWD-10	Organize opinion polls on selected cohorts to gather reliable feedback on usability, tendencies and improvements	X
ESWD-11	Authentication of credential submission by alternative channels	O
ESWD-12	Master initialization protocol to be executed right before the start of the e-voting period to verify the correct operation/readiness	O
ESWD-13	Implementation, to the extent possible, of protocolized and standardized systems to improve interoperability	Δ
ESWD-14	Free assistance phone service available before/during the election	
ESWD-15	Complete PR strategy to promote e-voting and train voters, including: webinars, stands, demos, open days etc.	Δ

Evaluation: 4/10 points.

4.11 Incidents and Attacks Protocol (IAP-n)

Due to the track record of elections managed by nVotes, they do not have a proper protocol in place, presenting only partial compliance in distributed/modular approach and actions taken towards limiting the risk of an attack with the introduction of Cloudfare [35] and Fail2Ban services [36].

In conclusion, nVotes needs to develop a proper Incidents and Attacks Protocol before being used for legally binding, public elections (Table 7).

Table 7. Incidents and Attacks protocol in nVotes

IAP-n	Definition	Val
IAP-1	*Risk Assessment (RA), Privacy Impact Assessment (PIAS), Penetration Testing (PT), Control Validation Plan (CVP)* and *Control Validation Audit (CVA)* protocols	Δ
IAP-2	Specific prevention protocols for each cryptographic scheme	X
IAP-3	All the information shall be kept to the extent possible in the country's National soil	O
IAP-4	Implementation of protocols and reinforcement operations to minimize the risk of permanent losses of information	Δ
IAP-5	Reinforced distributed approach to contribute to the absence of critical nodes which undermine the e-voting system's viability	Δ
IAP-6	Training and awareness campaigns to minimize the risk of voter-driven attacks (*phishing*, social engineering, etc.)	X
IAP-7	Hackers/indep. experts to test and compromise the system beforehand	X

Evaluation: 4/10 points.

4.12 Versatility (V-n)

nVotes can be used by the voter with a standard internet connection, hardware and Operative System. While it works in most of the available browsers and devices, there is no compatibility study available.

Regarding the existence of different versions depending on the type of election (yes/no, 1/N, N/M, order etc.) there are no adapted versions but according to the data in *Verificatum* [37], its performance is satisfactory enough to not require adapted versions. The authors believe that such statement is only partially true and largely depends on the range of the election.

Finally, the score against the WCAG 2.0 standard was good but not brilliant (A) (Table 8).

Table 8. Versatility in nVotes

V-n	Definition	Val
V-1	Versions adapted to different election typologies (yes/no, 1/N...	Δ
V-2	Specific solutions for vulnerable groups (disabilities, illiterates etc.)	X
V-3	The voter shall be able to vote using her personal device, through a standard internet connection without installing any additional SW	O
V-4	E-voting system tested in browsers/devices w/a market share ≥1%	Δ
V-5	The interface is WCAG 2.0 AA complain	Δ

Evaluation: 5/10 points.

4.13 Cost (C-n)

Cost in a sensitive issue for e-voting systems. Most of them are not transparent in their pricing policy. That is understandable to a certain point, but even the cheapest option should offer a sufficient security level.

nVotes used to have a very clear, direct policy with 3 plans with a fix cost of 0.2 EUR per voter plus other associated costs. In its simplest version, it was possible to organize a 1.000 voter election with all the required elements for a little over 1.000 EUR. Currently, the policy has changed and there is no clear indication of the cost for the organization of an election.

While probably still an affordable option, the authors believe that the previous, more transparent approach was better from a user's point of view (Table 9).

Table 9. Cost in nVotes

C-*n*	Definition	Val
C-1	Transparency and clarity in the cost breakdown	
C-2	System cost related to quality and performance. Comparison with other e-voting solution	

Evaluation: Review (6/10 points).

4.14 Maintenance (M-n)

Both from a software and ex-software perspective. On the software side, nVotes is an open source project and therefore very open and verifiable. It is regularly updated. Regarding the ex_software aspect, there is not much improvement and it would be very advisable in order to extend the safe utilization range of the system.

As for everlasting privacy and post-quantum security, nVotes team is working on it but there is no expected imminent announcement.

Finally, the maintenance cost is quite limited and performed internally (Table 10).

Table 10. Maintenance in nVotes

M-*n*	Definition	Val
M-1	Covering both SW and ex_SW aspects. Frequency, thoroughness and existence of security logs to check the maintenance process are also evaluated	Δ
M-2	Maintenance as *everlasting privacy*	N/A
M-3	Maintenance cost itself	Δ

Evaluation: 6.5/10 points.

5 Final Results and Conclusion

nVotes [218] is a remote e-voting system developed by the Spanish company Agora Voting SL and active since 2014. It has managed a total of 2 million votes with up to 150.000 votes in the same election.

In order to complement the relatively limited publicly available information for the analysis in this article, they have been diligent and helpful and the authors with like to extend their gratitude for their availability.

The ultimate goal of the analysis is not to judge from a rigid, "infallible" perspective for the sake of it, but to try contribute to a gradual and secure implementation of e-voting solutions in the democratic processes.

The formula and table below summarize the findings and scores of nVotes (Table 11):

Table 11. Practical Evaltuation Methodology [16] applied to nVotes

Requirement	Code	Weight	nVotes
E2Ev	E2Ev	N.A.	Δ
Coerc. Resistance	CR	N.A.	X
Inviolability	(I-n)	1.2	4 * 1.2 = 4.8
Usability	(U-n)	0.8	6 * 0.8 = 4.8
Monitoring/Audit	(MA-n)	1.2	3 * 1.2 = 3.6
Software Devel.	(SWD-n)	1.2	7 * 1.2 = 8.4
Scalability	(S-n)	0.8	5.5 * 0.8 = 4.4
Ex_Soft. Develop.	(ESWD-n)	1.2	4 * 1.2 = 4.8
Incid./AttackProt.	(IAP-n)	1.2	4 * 1.2 = 4.8
Versatility	(V-n)	0.6	5 * 0.6 = 3
Cost	(C-n)	1.0	7 * 1.0 = 7
Maintenance	(M-n)	0.8	6.5 * 0.8 = 5.2
Total		10	50.8

$$\sum_{i=1}^{n} \frac{f_1 \cdot w_1 + \cdots + f_n \cdot w_n}{n} \cdot \frac{n}{t} = \sum_{i=1}^{n} \frac{f_1 \cdot w_1 + \cdots + f_n \cdot w_n}{t} \qquad (2)$$

Due to the nature of the elections in which nVotes has been deployed, it is in an intermediate position between Helios Voting and Scytl's iVote systems. nVotes can manage elections with a number of voters that Helios Voting has not been able to proof so far while showing serious shortcomings in legally binding elections, where a strong infrastructure, ex-software policies and monitoring/auditing protocols are a must.

Therefore, currently nVotes' safe range of use is that of private elections.

The areas in which nVotes presents a stronger performance are:

- Open source approach, with good software engineering and possibility of review by researchers/academia.
- Intuitive, simple and user-friendly interface for both the voter and the administrators.
- Compatibility.
- Open standards, modularity.
- Support service during the elections.

Conversely, the aspects which should be improved include:

- No proper Audit/Monitoring or Incidents/Attacks protocols in place
- Policy for credential, access and permit distribution. Currently allows for collusion to happen between the census administrator and the election administrator
- Ex_software development
- Certain cryptographic primitives implemented are vulnerable [41]
- No version for voters with special needs

Additionally, the election administrator can know whether a voter has voted or not and a voter with a fake ID might be able to authenticate to vote. Even for private elections, it should be an issue to be solved.

In short and considering all the points reviewed in the analysis, the authors estimate that nVotes is currently not ready to be introduced for public, politically binding elections due to the limitations in auditing, monitoring, backup and potential collusion. Its current secure rage is that of private elections, always taking into account the highly recommended distribution of administrative roles.

To conclude, the authors hope that it can contribute, even if modestly, to improve the knowledge and security level in the deployment of e-voting systems, through the comprehensive, multi-faceted results presented. Nonetheless, in order to make the best possible decision, Elections Officials should also consider complementing the information contained in this document with other inputs from different, more atomistic and cryptographically formal analyses.

Acknowledgements. The contribution of Dr. David Duenas-Cid is based upon work supported by the Estonian Research Council grant (PUT 1361 "Internet Voting as Additional Channel for Legally Binding Elections: Challenges to Voting Processes Reengineering", 2017–2020); and by the Polish National Research Center grant (Miniatura 3 - 2019/03/X/HS6/01688 "Zaufanie do technologii w e-administracji: Powtórna analiza nieudanego wdrożenia elektronicznych maszyn do głosowania w Holandii (2006-07)").

References

1. Vinkel, P., Krimmer, R.: The how and why to internet voting an attempt to explain e-stonia. In: Krimmer, R., et al. (eds.) E-Vote-ID 2016. LNCS, vol. 10141, pp. 178–191. Springer, Cham (2017). https://doi.org/10.1007/978-3-319-52240-1_11

2. Solvak, M., Vassil, K.: Could internet voting halt declining electoral turnout? new evidence that e-voting is habit forming. Policy Internet **10**(1), 4–21 (2018)

3. Krimmer, R., Duenas-Cid, D., Krivonosova, I., Vinkel, P., Koitmae, A.: How much does an e-vote cost? Cost comparison per vote in multichannel elections in estonia. In: Krimmer, R., et al. (eds.) E-Vote-ID 2018. LNCS, vol. 11143, pp. 117–131. Springer, Cham (2018). https://doi.org/10.1007/978-3-030-00419-4_8

4. Krimmer, R. et al.: New methodology for calculating cost-efficiency of different ways of voting: is internet voting cheaper? Public Money Manage. 1–10 (2020)

5. Trechsel, A.H., et al.: Potential and Challenges of E-Voting in the EU Study. Bruss (2016)

6. Gjøsteen, K.: Analysis of an internet voting protocol. IACR Cryptol. ePrint Arch. 1–16 (2010). https://doi.org/10.1007/978-3-642-32747-6_1

7. Kulyk, O., et al.: Electronic voting with fully distributed trust and maximized flexibility regarding ballot design. In: EVOTE 2014. pp. 139–149. TUT Press, Bregenz (2014)

8. Oostveen, A.-M., Van den Besselaar, P.: Security as belief user's perceptions on the security of electronic voting systems. Electron. Voting Eur. Technol. **47**, 73–82 (2004)

9. Council of Europe: Recommendation CM/Rec(2017)5 of the Committee of Ministers to member States on standards for e-voting (2017)

10. Driza Maurer, A.: Updated European standards for e-voting. In: Krimmer, R., Volkamer, M., Braun Binder, N., Kersting, N., Pereira, O., Schürmann, C. (eds.) E-Vote-ID 2017. LNCS, vol. 10615, pp. 146–162. Springer, Cham (2017). https://doi.org/10.1007/978-3-319-68687-5_9

11. Bräunlich, K., Grimm, R., Richter, P.: Sichere Internetwahlen Ein rechtswissenschaftlich-informatisches Modell. Nomos (2013)

12. Hammer, V., Pordesch, U.: KORA (Konkretisierung Rechtlicher Inforderungen). Betriebliche Telefon und ISDN-Anlagen rechtsgemäss gestaltet (1993)

13. Common Criteria for Information Technology Security Evaluation Part 1 : Introduction and general model July 2009 Revision 3 Final Foreword. Nist, vol. 49, 93, July 2009

14. Neumann, S.R.: Evaluation and Improvement of Internet Voting Schemes Based on Legally-Founded Security Requirements. Technische Universität Darmstadt (2016)

15. Electoral Commission New South Gales. http://www.elections.nsw.gov.au/voting/ivote. Accessed 12 May 2020

16. Marcos del Blanco, D.Y., Panizo Alonso, L., Hermida Alonso, J.A.: The need for Harmonization in the online voting field: towards an European Standard for edemocracy. In: E-Vote-ID 2016, Bregenz, Austria, 18-21 October 2016, Proceedings, pp. 339–340 (2016)

17. Standards: Guidelines on the implementation of the provisions of Recommendation CM/Rec(2017)5 on standards for e-voting. 1289 th Meet., 14 June 2017 2. 3 Ad hoc Comm. Expert. Leg., Oper. Tech. Stand. e- voting (CAHVE), June, pp. 1–19 (2017)

18. Constitución Española, pp. 101931–101941. https://www.boe.es/legislacion/documentos/ConstitucionCASTELLANO.pdf. Accessed 12 May 2020

19. Panizo Alonso, L., Gasco, M., Marcos del Blanco, D.Y., Hermida Alonso, J.A., Alaiz Moreton, H.: E-voting system evaluation based on the Council of Europe recommendations: Helios Voting. IEEE Trans. Emerg. Top. Comput. (2018)

20. Simić-Draws, D., et al.: Holistic and law compatible IT security evaluation: integration of common criteria, ISO 27001/IT- and KORA. Int. J. Inf. Secur. Priv. **7**, 16–35 (2013)

21. Goodman, L.: Snowball sampling. Ann. Math. Stat. **32**, 148–170 (1961)

22. Kish, L.: Sample Design in Business Research. American Statistical Association, Ltd

23. Benaloh, J.D.C., Rivest, R., Ryan, et al.: End-to-end verifiability. arXiv e-prints (2014)
24. Bernhard, D., Neumann, S., Volkamer, M.: Towards a practical cryptographic voting scheme based on malleable proofs. In: Heather, J., Schneider, S., Teague, V. (eds.) Vote-ID 2013. LNCS, vol. 7985, pp. 176–192. Springer, Heidelberg (2013). https://doi.org/10.1007/978-3-642-39185-9_11
25. Zissis, D., Lekkas, D.: Design, Development, and Use of Secure Electronic Voting Systems (2014). http://services.igiglobal.com/resolvedoi/resolve.aspx?
26. Taiwhenua, T.T.: The Department of Internal Affairs - Online voting. https://www.dia.govt.nz/online-voting. Accessed 12 May 2020
27. Marcos del Blanco, D.Y.: Cybersecurity applied to e-democracy: cryptographic analysis and development of a practical evaluation methodology for remote electronic voting systems and its application to the most relevant solutions. University of Leon (2018). http://riasc.unileon.es/archivos/documentos/tesis/Tesis_David_Y_Marcos.pdf
28. nVotes. https://nvotes.com/. Accessed 14 May 2020
29. Impact Accelerator. https://www.impact-accelerator.com/. Accessed 14 May 2020
30. Marcos del Blanco, D.Y., Gascó, M.: A protocolized, comparative study of helios voting and Scytl/iVote. In: International Conference on eDemocracy & eGovernment (ICEDEG), pp. 31–38 IEEE (2019)
31. Adida, B.: Helios: web-based open-audit voting. In: Proceedings of the 17th Conference on Security Symposium, pp. 335–348. USENIX Association, Berkeley (2008)
32. Kulyk, O., Teague, V., Volkamer, M.: Extending helios towards private eligibility verifiability. In: Haenni, R., Koenig, Reto E., Wikström, D. (eds.) VOTELID 2015. LNCS, vol. 9269, pp. 57–73. Springer, Cham (2015). https://doi.org/10.1007/978-3-319-22270-7_4
33. Cortier, V., Gaudry, P., Glondu, S.: Belenios: a simple private and verifiable electronic voting system. In: Foundations of Security, Protocols, and Equational Reasoning, pp. 214–238 (2019)
34. Esendex. https://www.esendex.es/. Accessed 14 May 2020
35. Cloudfare. https://www.cloudflare.com. Accessed 15 May 2020
36. Fail2ban. https://www.fail2ban.org. Accessed 14 May 2020
37. Verificatum. https://www.verificatum.org/. Accessed 14 May 2020
38. Open STV. https://www.opavote.com/?openstv=1. Accessed 14 May 2020
39. ElGamal, T.: A public key cryptosystem and a signature scheme based on discrete logarithms. In: Blakley, G.R., Chaum, D. (eds.) CRYPTO 1984. LNCS, vol. 196, pp. 10–18. Springer, Heidelberg (1985). https://doi.org/10.1007/3-540-39568-7_2
40. Pedersen, T.P.: A threshold cryptosystem without a trusted party. In: Davies, Donald W. (ed.) EUROCRYPT 1991. LNCS, vol. 547, pp. 522–526. Springer, Heidelberg (1991). https://doi.org/10.1007/3-540-46416-6_47
41. Fiat, A., Shamir, A.: How to prove yourself: practical solutions to identification and signature problems. In: Odlyzko, Andrew M. (ed.) CRYPTO 1986. LNCS, vol. 263, pp. 186–194. Springer, Heidelberg (1987). https://doi.org/10.1007/3-540-47721-7_12
42. Schnorr, C.P.: Efficient identification and signatures for smart cards. In: Brassard, G. (ed.) CRYPTO 1989. LNCS, vol. 435, pp. 239–252. Springer, New York (1990). https://doi.org/10.1007/0-387-34805-0_22
43. Cortier, V.: Formal verification of e-voting: solutions and challenges. ACM SIGLOG News 2(1), 25–34 (2015)
44. Acemyan, C.Z., Kortum, P., et al.: From error to error: why voters could not cast a ballot and verify their vote with Helios, Pret a Voter and Scantegrity II. Usenix J. Elect. Technol. Syst. (2015)
45. Juels, A., Catalano, D., Jakobsson, M.: Coercion-resistant electronic elections. In: Chaum, D., Jakobsson, M., Rivest, Ronald L., Ryan, Peter Y.A., Benaloh, J, Kutylowski, M., Adida, B. (eds.) Towards Trustworthy Elections. LNCS, vol. 6000, pp. 37–63. Springer, Heidelberg (2010). https://doi.org/10.1007/978-3-642-12980-3_2

46. Hirt, M., Sako, K.: Efficient receipt-free voting based on homomorphic encryption. In: Preneel, B. (ed.) EUROCRYPT 2000. LNCS, vol. 1807, pp. 539–556. Springer, Heidelberg (2000). https://doi.org/10.1007/3-540-45539-6_38
47. El Español. https://www.elespanol.com/espana/20160511/123987880_0.html. Accessed 15 May 2020
48. Minutos.   https://www.20minutos.es/noticia/2419700/0/podemos-defiende-fiabilidad/sistema-votacion-acusaciones/primarias/. Accessed 15 May 2020

My Vote, My (Personal) Data: Remote Electronic Voting and the General Data Protection Regulation

Adrià Rodríguez-Pérez[1,2](✉) (iD)

[1] Scytl Secure Electronic Voting, S.A., 08008 Barcelona, Spain
`adria.rodriguez@scytl.com`
[2] Universitat Rovira i Virgili, 43002 Tarragona, Spain

Abstract. On 19 September 2019, the Data Protection Authority of the Åland Islands (in Finland) published its findings on the data processing audit for the autonomous region's parliamentary election special internet voting procedure. It claimed that there were faults in the documentation provided by the processor, which in turn meant that the election's integrity could not be guaranteed without further precautions from the government of the Åland Islands. Since the European Union's General Data Protection Regulation (GDPR) entered into force in May 2018, it has set new critical requirements for remote electronic voting projects. Yet, to date, no specific guidance nor research has been conducted on the impact of GDPR on remote electronic voting. Tacking stock of two recent internet voting experiences in the Åland Islands and France, this paper aims at identifying and understanding these new requirements. More specifically, based on these two case studies it analyses four different challenges on the processing of personal data in remote electronic voting under the GDPR: the definitions and categories of personal data processed in online voting projects; the separation of duties between data controllers and data processors; the secure processing of (sensitive) personal data, including the use of anonymisation and pseudonymisation techniques; as well as post-election processing of personal data, and possible limits to (universal) verifiability and public access to personal data.

Keywords: Internet voting · Data protection law · GDPR

1 Introduction

Since the European Union (EU)'s General Data Protection Regulation (GDPR) entered into force in May 2018, it has set new critical requirements for the processing of personal data in remote electronic voting projects. In some countries where internet voting is widely used, both in public as well as in private elections, data protection authorities have adopted or updated their regulations on i-voting. This is the case, for instance, of the Recommendation on the security of e-voting systems by the French *Commission Nationale de l'Informatique et des Libertés* (CNIL). Yet, this case is rather the exception

© Springer Nature Switzerland AG 2020
R. Krimmer et al. (Eds.): E-Vote-ID 2020, LNCS 12455, pp. 167–182, 2020.
https://doi.org/10.1007/978-3-030-60347-2_11

than the rule. In turn, no specific guidance at the European level has been provided on this matter.

Tacking stock of two recent internet voting experiences in the Åland Islands (an autonomous region in Finland) and France, this paper aims at identifying the nature of these new requirements, to understand how they have been translated into practice, and to comprehend how they have impacted the implementation of i-voting. More specifically, it addresses the four following aspects: (i) the definitions and categories of personal data processed in these two experiences; (ii) the separation of duties between data controllers and data processors; (iii) the secure processing of (sensitive) personal data, including anonymisation and pseudonymisation techniques; and (iv) post-election processing of personal data, including its destruction, as well as possible limits to (universal) verifiability and public access to personal data. To the best of our knowledge, this one is the first academic paper on the topic. Thus, our goal is to identify some critical aspects in the implementation of GDPR's requirements in online voting, rather than to come up with solutions on how to guarantee compliance with its provision.

To do so, we start by providing an overview of the legal framework governing the use of personal data in elections (Sect. 2). First, we analyse the wider, overarching principle of secret suffrage (Sect. 2.1). In the framework of remote electronic voting, it helps us identify the requirement of data minimisation, as well as that of respect with provisions on data protection. We then move to study the main provisions on personal data protection at the European level (Sect. 2.2). More specifically, we study data protection by comparing it to the international right to respect for private life, and then we move to analyse the more recent provisions on European data protection law, with a specific focus on the EU's GDPR, which was adopted in May 2016 and entered into force two years later. This analysis will allow us to argue that the requirements for personal data processing are independent of and complementary to those of secret suffrage. Following (Sect. 3), the actual implementation of the GDPR's provisions in real internet voting projects is studied. We focus on the extent to which the (planned) use of internet voting in the Åland Islands (Sect. 3.1) and France (Sect. 3.2) complied with the provisions of the new EU Regulation. Drawing from these two projects, we have identified the four above-mentioned trends, which we consider specifically relevant when it comes to the processing of personal data in i-voting under the GDPR (Sect. 3.3). After this analysis, the fourth and final section provides the conclusion of the paper, attempts to draw some lessons learned, acknowledges limitations in our study, and outlines potential future research.

2 Beyond Secret Suffrage: European Data Protection Law

2.1 The Right to Vote and Secret Suffrage

Secret suffrage is one of the key principles of the right to free elections. The obligation to guarantee the secrecy of the ballot features in both Article 21(3) of the Universal Declaration on Human Rights (UDHR) as 'secret vote', as well as in Article 25(b) of the International Covenant on Civil and Political Rights (ICCPR) as elections held by 'secret ballot' (International IDEA 2014: 43). In Europe, the right to free elections is enshrined in Article 3 of the Protocol (no. 1) to the Convention for the Protection of

Human Rights and Fundamental Freedoms (ECHR). Article 3 of the Protocol explicitly recognises that democratic elections are to be held by secret vote or by equivalent free voting procedures. In this sense, "the secrecy of the vote is [considered] an aspect of free suffrage, which aims to shield voters from any pressure that might result from the knowledge of his [sic] choice by third parties and, in fine, to ensure the honesty and sincerity of the vote" (Lécuyer 2014: 76).

As part of secret suffrage, the Council of Europe's recently updated Recommendation CM/Rec(2017)5 on standards for e-voting specifies that "[p]rovisions on data protection shall be respected" (Council of Europe, 2017a: 20). More specifically, it states that "[t]he e-voting system shall process and store, as long as necessary, only the personal data needed for the conduct of the e-election" (2017a: 20), and that "[t]he e-voting system and any authorised party shall protect authentication data so that unauthorised parties cannot misuse, intercept, modify, or otherwise gain knowledge of this data" (Council of Europe 2017a: 21). The Guidelines on implementation of the Recommendation also state that "[t]he legal framework should include procedures for the process of data destruction, in particular to align processing, storing and destruction of the data (and equipment) of voting technology with the personal data protection legislation" (Council of Europe 2017c: 28.d), and that "printing of voter identification data such as polling cards should be reviewed to ensure security of sensitive data" (Council of Europe 2017c: 48.a).

These standards are related to the requirement of 'data minimisation', which refers to "data necessary for fulfilling legal requirements of the voting process" (Council of Europe 2017b: 65). Interestingly enough, this provision of the Recommendation's Explanatory Memorandum states that it is "[t]he electoral management body in charge of organising e-voting [who] identifies such data and should be able to explain what are the underlying legal provisions and considerations that render them necessary" (Council of Europe 2017b: 65). The Explanatory Memorandum concludes that "data minimisation aims at ensuring data protection and is part of vote secrecy" (Council of Europe 2017b: 65). However, and as we will see now, we should consider personal data protection requirements as protecting a distinct, independent legal asset.

2.2 The Rights to Respect for Private Life and to Personal Data Protection

From the Right to Respect for Private Life to the Right to Personal Data Protection. The right to privacy (article 12 of the UDHR and art. 17 of the ICCPR), also known as the right to respect for private life (article 8 of the ECHR), provides that "everyone has the right to respect for his or her private and family life, home and correspondence." Interference with this right by a public authority is prohibited, except where the interference is in accordance with the law, pursues important and legitimate public interests and is necessary in a democratic society (EU Agency for Fundamental Rights and Council of Europe 2018: 18). The development of computers and the Internet presented new risks to the right to respect for private life. In response to the need for specific rules governing the collection and use of personal information, a new concept of privacy emerged, known as 'information privacy' or the 'right to informational self-determination' (EU Agency for Fundamental Rights and Council of Europe 2018: 18).

Data protection in Europe began in the seventies at the national level, and afterwards, data protection instruments were established at the European level: first, in the Council of Europe's Convention for the Protection of Individuals with regard to Automatic Processing of Personal Data (Convention 108), adopted in 1981; and then in the European Union's Directive 95/46/EC on the protection of individuals with regards to the processing of personal data and on the free movement of such data. Over the years, data protection developed into a distinctive value that is not subsumed by the right to respect for private life (EU Agency for Fundamental Rights and Council of Europe 2018: 19).

While both rights strive to protect similar values (i.e., the autonomy and human dignity of individuals) the two differ in their formulation and scope: while the right to respect for private life consists of a general prohibition on interference, the protection of personal data is viewed as a modern and active right, putting in place a system of checks and balances to protect individuals whenever their personal data are processed. The right to personal data protection thus comes into play whenever personal data are processed. Therefore, it is broader than the right to respect for private life. Any processing operation of personal data is subject to appropriate protection. Data protection concerns all kinds of personal data and data processing, irrespective of the relationship and impact on privacy. Processing of personal data may infringe on the right to private life. However, it is not necessary to demonstrate an infringement on private life for data protection rules to be triggered (EU Agency for Fundamental Rights and Council of Europe 2018: 20). In our opinion, the same could be argued for personal data protection and secret suffrage: the former cannot be subsumed by this latter principle.

Data Protection Regulations in the EU. From 1995 until May 2018, the principal EU legal instrument on data protection was the Directive 95/46/EC (EU Agency for Fundamental Rights and Council of Europe 2018: 29). In 2009, debates on the need to modernise EU data protection rules began, with the Commission launching a public consultation about the future legal framework for the fundamental right to personal data protection. The proposal for the regulation was published by the Commission in January 2012, starting a long legislative process of negotiations between the European Parliament and the Council of the EU. After adoption, the GDPR provided for a two-year transition period. It became fully applicable on 25 May 2018, when the Directive 95/46/EC was repealed (EU Agency for Fundamental Rights and Council of Europe 2018: 30).

The adoption of GDPR in 2016 modernised EU data protection legislation, making it fit for protecting fundamental rights in the context of the digital age's economic and social challenges. The GDPR preserves and develops the core principles and rights of the data subject provided for in the Directive 95/46/EC. In addition, it has introduced new obligations requiring organisations to implement data protection by design and default, to appoint a Data Protection Officer in certain circumstances, to comply with a new right to data portability, and to comply with the principle of accountability (EU Agency for Fundamental Rights and Council of Europe 2018: 30). Furthermore, under EU law regulations are directly applicable and there is no need for national implementation. Therefore, the GDPR provides for a single set of data protection rules to the whole EU. Finally, the regulation has comprehensive rules on territorial scope: it applies both to businesses established in the UE, as well as to controllers and processors not established in the EU that offer goods or services to data subjects in the EU or monitor their behaviour (EU Agency for Fundamental Rights and Council of Europe 2018: 31).

Ahead of the elections to the European Parliament of 2019, the European Commission released a guidance document on the application of the Union's data protection law in the electoral context. The goal of the document was to "provide clarity to the actors involved in election processes – such as national electoral authorities, political parties, data brokers and analysts [and] highlight the data protection obligations of relevance for elections" (European Commission 2018: 2). Specifically, the document addressed key obligations for the various actors, the role as data controller or data processor, principles, lawfulness of processing and special conditions for the processing sensitive data, security and accuracy of personal data, and data protection impact assessment, to name just a few examples. Yet, it is worth noticing that the guidance document does not make specific reference to the use of (remote) electronic voting technologies.

3   Remote Electronic Voting Experiences Under the GDPR

3.1   The Parliamentary Elections in the Åland Islands, Finland

In 2014, the Government of the Åland Islands started studying how to amend the Election Act for Åland. Among other issues, they wanted to know whether internet voting could be introduced for the elections to their parliament. Work on a new Election Act for Åland started in 2017. A draft law was approved by the Government in 2018, and the Parliament passed it in January 2019. The law was then signed by the President of Finland by mid-May. Thus, the Election Act for Åland, together with the Act on the Autonomy of Åland, provide the basic electoral framework for the autonomous region. The law provides that "[a]dvance voting via the internet shall be organised in parliamentary elections if a reliable system for electronic voting via the internet is available" (Election Act for Åland, section 78).

The Government of Åland started to work on the procurement of an internet voting system for the 2019 parliamentary elections in 2018. In March, they published a Request for Information. They received answers from five different providers, but they realised that only two providers would meet the requirements of their tender. The tender was published in October 2018 and two offers were received (from the two vendors that they expected that would bid). Scytl Secure Electronic Voting, S.A. (Scytl) was awarded the project. The contract with Scytl was signed in early January 2019.

On 19 June, the Åland Data Protection Authority (DPA) decided to conduct a data protection audit for the 2019 Election Special Internet Voting Procedure (2019a)[1]. The goal was to "identify potential risks with the treatment before the election would take place" (DPA 2019c). The audit was conducted by TechLaw Sweden AB (TechLaw). While the object of the audit was the Government of the Åland Islands' treatment of i-voters' personal data, "Scytl [the processor] got the questions asked directly from the Data Inspectorate [as] a practical solution to save time" (DPA 2019c). The report was concluded on 12 September and the findings were published on the 19 of September, together with another report by the DPA. The DPA criticised, "inter alia, the lack of clarity

---

[1] All translations from the original reports in Swedish by the author, using an online tool.

of contracts between the Government, ÅDA[2] and Scytl, as well as, the issue regarding the personal data of i-voters" (Krimmer et al.2019: 11). The report also identified faults in the documentation provided by the processor (Scytl), which in turn meant that the election's integrity could not be guaranteed without further precautions from the government of the Åland Islands (DPA 2019b). On 13 December, the DPA also published a report with comments from Scytl. The purpose of the comment from Scytl was "to find out any misunderstandings that may have arisen regarding their security measures by the reporter employed by the Data Inspectorate" (DPA 2019b).

3.2 The Consular Elections in France

Internet voting in France dates back to 2003, with the passing of the first law allowing the use of internet voting for the elections to the Assembly of French Citizens Abroad (Sénat 2014: 38)[3]. Subsequently, the Ministry of Foreign and European Affairs (MEAE) carried out three pilot projects during the 2003, 2006, and 2009 elections (OSCE/ODIHR 2012b: 9). Nowadays, internet voting is foreseen as an additional voting channel for French voters abroad. They can cast an i-vote for the elections to the National Assembly (the country's directly elected lower house, with 577 seats) and for the election of the Consular Advisers and Delegates. For the elections to the National Assembly, a constitutional amendment of 2008 introduced 11 seats to be elected by voters residing abroad (OSCE/ODIHR 2012a: 3). In 2012, voters had the possibility to vote online for these seats (Sénat 2014: 37) for the first time (OSCE 2012a: 1). However, in 2017 this possibility was halted due to "concerns of foreign cyber threats as well as over certain technical issues" (OSCE/ODIHR 2017c: 6). On their side, Consular Advisers and Delegates are based at each embassy with a consular district and at each consular post. They are elected for a six-year period during the month of May, their first elections taking place in 2014 (Sénat 2014: 37). The next elections were scheduled on May 2020. Yet, the MEAE decided to post-pone these elections due to the Covid-19 pandemic. Scytl was also the technology provider for these two elections, having signed a contract with the MEAE for a four-year period in May 2016 (Sénat 2018: 38).

In France, and since internet voting requires the set-up of data files with the citizens enrolled on consular lists (Sénat 2014: 43; 2018: 29), this technology is under the legal supervision of the CNIL. In 2010, the CNIL adopted a Recommendation on the security of e-voting systems (CNIL 2010). The Recommendation provides "general guidelines regarding minimal privacy, secrecy and security requirements for any internet voting" (OSCE/ODIHR 2012b: 12). The CNIL prescribes both 'physical' measures (such as access controls to the servers or rules for the clearance of authorized employees), as well as software-related ones (i.e., firewalls) (Sénat 2014: 37). The Recommendation was updated in 2019, precisely to take stock of the new requirements introduced by the GDPR after it entered into force (CNIL 2019b). The goal of the update was for it to apply to future developments in internet voting, "with a view to better respect the principles

---

[2] According to Krimmer et al. (2019: 9): "In Åland, it is not the government itself, but a particular agency, ÅDA, which is acting as the procurement agent being in charge of the procurement process with the Government as the "real" customer".

[3] All translations from the original reports in French by the author.

of personal data protection, and to inform data controllers on their choice for an online voting system" (CNIL 2019a). Furthermore, a General Security Regulatory Framework (RGS) is established by the *Agence nationale de la sécurité des systèmes d'information* (ANSSI) to regulate minimal requirements on "electronic certificates, encryption levels, and authentication mechanisms" (OSCE/ODIHR 2012b: 12).

3.3 Comparing Remote Electronic Elections Under GDPR

In what follows, we provide an overview of the most relevant issues in these two experiences concerning the application of the GDPR. More specifically, we will focus on (i) the definitions and categories of personal data processed; (ii) the separation of duties between data controllers and data processors; (iii) the secure processing of (sensitive) personal data, including the use of anonymisation and pseudonymisation techniques; and (iv) the post-election processing of personal data, including its destruction, as well as possible limits to (universal) verifiability and public access to personal data.

This list of issues is not exhaustive, since these aspects have been identified as relevant in the two experiences studied here. It is likely that additional issues could be raised in different cases, or after the implementation of these two specific projects.

Definition and Categories of Personal Data. According to EU law, data are personal if they relate to an identified or identifiable person, the 'data subject' (EU Agency for Fundamental Rights and Council of Europ 2018: 83). The GDPR defines personal data as information relating to an identified or identifiable natural person (GDPR, art. 4.1). Any kind of information can be personal data provided that it relates to an identified and identifiable person[4]. Personal data covers information pertaining to the private life of a person, as well as information about their public life (EU Agency for Fundamental Rights and Council of Europe 2018: 86).

The GDPR stipulates that a natural person is identifiable when he or she "can be identified, directly or indirectly, in particular by reference to an identifier such as a name, an identification number, location data, and online identifier or to one or more factors specific to the physical, physiological, genetic, mental, economic, cultural or social identity of that person" (GDPR, art. 4.1). Yet, according to the Article 29 Data Protection Working Party (Article 29 Working Party), it is also "possible to categorise [a] person on the basis of socio-economic, psychological, philosophical or other criteria and attribute certain decisions to him or her since the individual's contact point (a computer) no longer requires the disclosure of his or her identity in the narrow sense" (2007: 15). Identification, thus, requires elements which describe a person in such a way that he or she is distinguishable from all other persons and recognisable as an individual (EU Agency for Fundamental Rights and Council of Europe 2018: 89). Establishing the identity of a person may need additional attributes to ensure that a person is not mistaken for someone else. Sometimes, direct and indirect attributes may have to be combined to identify the individual to whom the information relates. Date and place of birth are often used. In addition, personalised numbers have been introduced in some countries to

---

[4] For the applicability of European data protection law there is no need for actual identification of the data subject: it is sufficient that the person concerned is identifiable.

better distinguish between citizens. Biometric data, such as fingerprints, digital photos or iris scans, location data and online attributes are increasingly used to identify persons in the technological age (EU Agency for Fundamental Rights and Council of Europe 2018: 90).

Personal Data About Candidates. Based on the above, it is clear that data about candidates is personal data and thus falls under the scope of the right to personal data protection and of the GDPR. It goes without saying that candidates are to be described in such a way that they are distinguishable from all other persons and recognisable as individuals. How was personal data about candidates processed in these two experiences? In Åland, the online voting process was similar to the paper-based one (Krimmer et al. 2019: 11), where voters do not mark or select a candidate in the ballot but write their number on a blank ballot paper. Likewise, in the Åland's voting platform, voters were not "able to select a candidate by clicking on it in the list of candidates displayed. [Instead, a] voter will need to insert the number of a candidate, exactly like it is done when a voter cast a vote on paper" (Krimmer et al. 2019: 11). On the other hand, in France, the Election Management System service used by the election managers to configure the election (GUES), includes personal data about each candidate. This data includes their name, surname, sex, birth date, phone, e-mail, etc. Similar information is also processed for candidates' substitutes.

Authentication Data. Authentication means proving that a certain person possesses a certain identity and/or is authorized to carry out certain activities (EU Agency for Fundamental Rights and Council of Europe 2018: 83). This is a procedure by which a person is able to prove that they possess a certain identity and/or is authorised to do certain things, such as enter a security area, withdraw money from a banking account or, as in this case: cast an i-vote. Authentication can be achieved by comparing biometric data, such as a photo or fingerprints in a passport, with the data of the person presenting themselves. However, this kind of authentication can only be conducted face-to-face (i.e., when voters cast a paper ballot in polling stations). An alternative for the remote setting is to ask for information which should be known only to the person with a certain identity or authorisation, such as a personal identification number (PIN) or a password. In addition to these, electronic signatures are an instrument especially capable of identifying and authenticating a person in electronic communications (EU Agency for Fundamental Rights and Council of Europe 2018: 95).

Voter authentication was similar in both the Åland Islands and in France. In Åland, the voters had to go to a website provided by ÅDA and authenticate via BankID (TechLaw 2019: 9). Upon successful authentication, the voter received a KeyStore with the election public key (to encrypt the vote) and their voter private key (to digitally sign the encrypted vote). The voter is identified internally by the voting platform using a randomly generated pseudonymous (VoterID) "that is used to ensure that a vote has been cast by an eligible voter and that no voter has voted twice" (Scytl 2019: 24). According to Scytl (2019: 24), "under no circumstances can Scytl correlate this voter identifier with the real identity of the voter".

In addition to the vote and the voterID, Scytl's voting system also stores the voters' IP addresses (TechLaw 2019: 8). In a 2011 ruling, the Court of Justice of the EU (CJEU) held that users' IP addresses "are protected personal data because they allow those users to be precisely identified" (CJEU 2011: para. 51). The CJEU has also considered that a dynamic IP address, which an online media services provider registers when a person accesses a website that the provider has made accessible to the public, constitutes personal date where only a third party (i.e., the internet service provider) has the additional data necessary to identify the person (EU Agency for Fundamental Rights and Council of Europe 2018: 91). According to Scytl (2019: 24), it is not possible to link the vote or the voter with the IP because they have "no information to correlate IP addresses with the real identity of the voter".

Encrypted and Digitally Signed Electronic Ballots. There are special categories of data, so-called 'sensitive data', which require enhanced protection and, therefore, are subject to a special legal regime (EU Agency for Fundamental Rights and Council of Europe 2018: 83). These are special categories of personal data which, by their nature, may pose a risk to the data subjects when processed and need enhanced protection. Such data are subject to a prohibition principle and there are a limited number of conditions under which such processing is lawful (EU Agency for Fundamental Rights and Council of Europe 2018: 96). Within the framework of the GDPR, the following categories are considered sensitive data: personal data revealing racial or ethnic origin; political opinions, religious or other beliefs, including philosophical beliefs; trade union membership; genetic data and biometric data processed for the purpose of identifying a person; and, personal data concerning health, sexual life or sexual orientation. Since digital ballots reveal political opinions (they contain the political preferences of voters), they must be considered sensitive data. As a matter of fact, research conducted by Duenas-Cid et al. (2020) concludes that it was precisely the processing of political opinions as a special category of personal data that motivated an audit in the Åland Islands.

In both the Åland Islands (Scytl 2019: 11) and in France, votes are encrypted and sealed in encrypted envelopes (directly on the voter's computers). The encrypted vote is then digitally signed (also in the voting device). Since votes are digitally signed, only the votes cast (and signed) by eligible voters are verified and stored in the voting server (i.e., the digital ballot box) (Scytl 2019: 38). In the case of Åland, the system also provided individual verifiability (cast-as-intended and recorded-as-cast verifiability). In practice, it means that after casting their vote, voters could log into the voting service to check that their vote had reached the voting server unaltered (TechLaw 2019: 8).

Data processing: The Role of Data Controllers and Data Processors. 'Data processing' concerns any operation performed on personal data. According to the GDPR, "processing of personal data [...] shall mean any operation [...] such as collection, recording, organisation, structuring, storage, adaptation or alteration, retrieval, consultation, use, disclosure by transmission, dissemination or otherwise making available, alignment or combination, restriction, erasure or destruction" (art. 4.2).

Whoever determines the means and purposes of processing the personal data of others is a controller under data protection law. If several persons take this decision together, they may be joint controllers. A 'processor' is a natural or legal person that processes the personal data on behalf of a controller. If a processor determines the means and purposes of data processing itself, they become a controller. Any person to whom personal data are disclosed is a 'recipient' (EU Agency for Fundamental Rights and Council of Europe 2018: 101). Any person other than the data subject, the controller, the processor and persons who are authorised to process personal data under the direct authority of the controller or processor is considered a 'third-party'.

The most important consequence of being a controller or a processor is a legal responsibility for complying with the respective obligations under data protection law. In the private sector, this is usually a natural or legal person. In the public sector, it is usually an authority. There is a significant distinction between a data controller and a data processor: the former is the natural or legal person who determines the purposes and the means of processing, while the latter is the natural or legal person who processes the data on behalf of the controller, following strict instructions. In principle, it is the data controller that must exercise control over the processing and who has responsibility for this, including legal liability (EU Agency for Fundamental Rights and Council of Europe 2018: 101). Yet, processors also have an obligation to comply with many of the requirements which apply to controllers[5]. Whether a person has the capacity to decide and determine the purpose and means of processing will depend on the factual elements or circumstances of the case.

As has been already seen, according to the Council of Europe's Recommendation it is "[t]he electoral management body in charge of organising e-voting [who] identifies such data and should be able to explain what are the underlying legal provisions and considerations that render them necessary" (Council of Europe 2017b: 65) In a similar vein, the GDPR clearly states that the processor may only process personal data on instructions from the controller, unless the EU or Member State law requires the processor to do so (art. 29). According to the GDPR, if the power to determine the means of processing is delegated to a processor, the controller must nonetheless be able to exercise an appropriate degree of control over the processor's decisions regarding the means of processing. Overall responsibility lies with the controller, who must supervise the processor to ensure that their decisions comply with data protection law and their instructions (EU Agency for Fundamental Rights and Council of Europe 2018: 108).

For the sake of clarity and transparency, the details of the relationship between a controller and a processor must be recorded in a written contract (GDPR, art. 28.3 and .9). The contract between the controller and the processor is an essential element of their relationship, and is a legal requirement (GDPR, art. 28.3). It must include, in particular, the subject matter, nature, purpose and duration of the processing, the type of personal data and the categories of data subjects. It should also stipulate the controller's and the processor's obligations and rights, such as requirements regarding confidentiality and security. Having no such contract is an infringement of the controller's obligation to provide written documentation of mutual responsibilities, and could lead to sanctions (EU Agency for Fundamental Rights and Council of Europe 2018: 109). Yet, in the

---

[5] Under the GDPR, "processors must maintain a record of all categories of processing activities to demonstrate compliance with their obligations under the regulation" (art. 30.2). Processors are also required to implement appropriate technical and organisational measures to ensure the security of processing (art. 32), to appoint a Data Protection Officer (DPO) in certain situations (art. 37), and to notify data breaches to the controller (art. 33.2).

case of the Åland Islands the DPA criticized, precisely, "the lack of clarity of contracts between the Government, ÅDA and Scytl" (Krimmer et al. 2019: 11). In France, the CNIL's updated Recommendation specifically provides that "the processing of personal data, including the voting systems, must in principle be subject to a data protection impact assessment (PIA) when meet at least two of [several] criteria". Among these, this project seems to include, indeed, at least two of these criteria, i.e.: processing of sensitive data (i.e., political opinions) and large-scale processing of personal data. Thus, such an assessment is required in internet voting in France.

Anonymisation, Pseudonymisation and (Sensitive) Personal Data. Data are anonymised if they no longer relate to an identified or identifiable individual (EU Agency for Fundamental Rights and Council of Europe 2018: 83). Pseudonymisation is a measure by which personal data cannot be attributed to the data subject without additional information, which is kept separately. The 'key' that enables re-identification of the data subjects must be kept separate and secure. Data that have undergone a pseudonymisation process remains personal data (EU Agency for Fundamental Rights and Council of Europe 2018: 83). The principles and rules of data protection do not apply to anonymised information. However, they do apply to pseudonymised data (EU Agency for Fundamental Rights and Council of Europe 2018: 83).

The process of anonymising data means that all identifying elements are eliminated from a set of personal data so that the data subject is no longer identifiable (GDPR, Recital 26). In its Opinion 05/2014, the Article 29 Working Party analysed the effectiveness and limits of different anonymisation techniques. It acknowledged the potential value of such techniques, but underlined that certain techniques do not necessarily work in all cases. To find the optimal solution in a given situation, the appropriate process of anonymisation should be decided on a case-by-case basis. Irrespective of the technique used, identification must be prevented, irreversibly. This means that for data to be anonymised, no element may be left in the information which could, by exercising reasonable effort, serve to re-identify the person(s) concerned (GDPR, Recital 26). The risks of re-identification can be assessed by taking into account "the time, effort or resources needed in light of the nature of the data, the context of their use, the available re-identification technologies and related costs" (EU Agency for Fundamental Rights and Council of Europe 2018: 94). When data have been successfully anonymised, they are no longer personal data and data protection legislation no longer applies. On the other hand, pseudonymisation means that certain attributes (such as name, date of birth, sex, address, or other elements that could lead to identification) are replaced by pseudonym. EU law defined 'pseudonymisation' as 'the processing of personal data in such a manner that the personal data can no longer be attributed to a specific data subject without the use of additional information, provided that such additional information is kept separately and is subject to technical and organisational measures to ensure that the personal data are not attributed to an identified or identifiable natural person' (GDPR, art. 4.5). Contrary to anonymised data, pseudonymised data are still personal data and are therefore subject to data protection legislation. Although pseudonymisation can reduce security risks to the data subjects, it is not exempt from the scope of the GDPR (EU Agency for Fundamental Rights and Council of Europe 2018: 94). The GDPR recognises various uses of pseudonymisation as an appropriate technical measure for enhancing data protection, and is specifically mentioned for the design and security of its data processing (GDPR, art. 25.1). It is also an appropriate safeguard that could be used to process personal data for purposes other than for which they were initially collected.

Based on these provisions, it is clear that both anonymisation and pseudonymisation techniques were used in these two projects. However, most of the time the data processed is pseudonymised, not anonymised. Since it is always possible to relate the encrypted data to a pseudonymous, which in turn can be related to the actual voter identity[6], it is difficult to argue that no element has been left in the information which could, by exercising reasonable effort, serve to re-identify the person(s) concerned[7]. In Åland, and since multiple voting is supported (Election Act for Åland, Section 61), it is necessary to keep the link between the encrypted vote and the VoterID to cleanse those online votes cast by voters who have cast more than one i-vote, as well as those who have also cast a postal vote or an advanced one in polling stations. In France, it is necessary to prevent i-voters from casting a paper vote in polling stations on election day[8]. In order to prevent a voter from casting a second vote, the voter rolls need to be updated. More specifically, at the end of the internet voting period, a mark is included by the side of the name of those voters who have already voted, i.e.: a list of voters having voted (*liste d'émargement*) is generated. The main implication here is that pseudonymous data remain personal data and must be processed as such.

Yet, it is also possible to talk about anonymised data. In the two projects we can find "both technological and procedural guarantees" (Scytl 2019: 41) in place to break the link between the vote and the voter's pseudonymous identifier (VoterID). In the case of Åland, during the counting phase a mix-net removes the connection between the identity of the voter and their vote (TechLaw 2019: 8). According to Scytl (2019: 12), this "cryptographic mixing process shuffles the encrypted votes and re-encrypts them at the same time. In this way, any correlation between the original encrypted votes and the re-encrypted ones is broken". Once mixed, it is no longer possible to link a vote with the identity of the voter who has cast it. In France, on the other hand, homomorphic tallying is used. In homomorphic tallying, the different options (whether selected or not) are encrypted separately, aggregated, and then decrypted anonymously. When the voter issues their vote, the voting client generates as many cyphertexts as possible options. Therefore, the encrypted vote is represented as an array of as many individual cyphertexts as possible voting options there are within the ballot. During the counting phase, the digital ballot box is exported from the online component of the voting system and imported in the offline one. In the offline environment, all the cyphertexts from all the votes corresponding to the same voting options are aggregated (multiplied), which allows for the computation of a unique aggregated cyphertext for each option. In both cases, the private key used for decryption is protected by a cryptographic secret-sharing scheme

---

[6] Which is necessary to "to guarantee that all votes have been cast by eligible voters and that only the appropriate number of remote electronic votes per voter gets counted" (Scytl 2019: 38).

[7] Recital 26 of the GDPR explicitly includes a scenario where it is foreseeable that further data recipients, other than the immediate data user, may attempt to identify the individuals (EU Agency for Fundamental Rights and Council of Europe 2018: 91).

[8] Contrary to good practice (Council of Europe 2017c: 9.b), in France once a voter has cast an i-vote, they cannot cast a second vote in person to cancel it.

(Shamir) that requires the collaboration of several members of the electoral commission to reconstruct the key before decryption. Thus, to decrypt these results, it is required that a minimum number of their members meet to reconstruct the election private key: i.e., three out of five persons in Åland (Election Act for Åland, Section 61) and four out of the eight members of the Bur*eau de vote électronique* (BVE) in France (Code *électoral*, R177-5).

Post-election: The Destruction of Data, Universal Verifiability and Public Access to Personal Data. The CNIL's Recommendation (2019a) states that all supporting files of an election (such as copies of the source and executable codes of the programs and the underlying system, voting materials, signature files, results' files, backups) must be kept under seal until the channels and deadlines for litigation are exhausted. This conservation must be ensured under the supervision of the electoral commission under conditions guaranteeing the secrecy of the vote. Obligation must be made to the service provider, if necessary, to transfer all of these media to the person or to the third party named to ensure the conservation of these media. When no contentious action has been taken to exhaust the time limits for appeal, these documents must be destroyed under the supervision of the BVE. This requirement is not new, and already in 2012 various audits were conducted on data destruction in the context of the parliamentary elections (OSCE/ODIHR 2012bb: 13). Along these lines, the Council of Europe's Recommendation also provides, in its Explanatory Memorandum, that "[t]he duration of processing, storing etc. [of personal data] also depends on legal requirements, namely those related to appeals". While these measures may be necessary to ensure the preservation of data protection in the long term, they may prevent the election data from being audited or universally verified[9]. Notwithstanding, the Election Act for Åland (Section 99) requires that "after confirming the result of the election, the ballot papers and a copy of the combined list of candidates or a copy of a list of presidential candidates is placed in a container, which shall be sealed as islaid down by the Ministry of Justice. These are to be kept until the next corresponding elections have been conducted"[10].

Overall, there is a growing realisation of the importance of government transparency for the functioning of a democratic society (EU Agency for Fundamental Rights and Council of Europe 2018: 62). The right to receive information, which forms part of freedom of expression, may come into conflict with the right to data protection if access to documents would reveal other's personal data. Art. 86 of the GDPR clearly provides that personal data in official documents held by public authorities and bodies may be disclosed by the authority or body concerned in accordance with EU or Member State's law to reconcile public access to official documents with the right to data protection (EU Agency for Fundamental Rights and Council of Europe 2018: 63). Balancing between data protection and access to documents requires a detailed, case-by-case analysis. Neither right can automatically overrule the other. The CJEU has had the chance to interpret the right to access to documents containing personal data in two cases (EU Agency for

---

[9] Universal verifiability refers to "tools which allow any interested person to verify that votes are counted as recorded" (Council of Europe 2017b: 56).

[10] That is so even if an "appeal shall be sent to a competent Provincial Administrative Court within 14 days from the confirmation of the election results" (Election Act for A°land, Section 102).

Fundamental Rights and Council of Europe 2018: 65). According to these judgements, interference with the right to data protection in the context of access to documents needs a specific and justified reason. Furthermore, according to the principle of storage limitation, data must be kept 'in a form which permits identification of data subjects for no longer than is necessary for the purposes for which the personal data are processed' (GDPR, art. 5.1.e). For internet voting, it seems advisable that this information is kept at least until the next election has taken place (and not, as it is provided in the CNIL's recommendation, until the channels and deadlines for litigation are exhausted). Consequently, data would have to be erased or anonymised if a controller wanted to store them after they were no longer needed and no longer served their initial purpose (EU Agency for Fundamental Rights and Council of Europe 2018: 63).

4 Conclusion

The entry into force of the EU's GDPR has set new requirements for the implementation of internet voting in Europe. Yet, no general guidance has yet been provided on how it impacts this kind of projects specifically. In this context, we have aimed at identifying some critical aspects in the implementation of GDPR's requirements in online voting, to understand how they have been translated into practice, and to comprehend how they have impacted the implementation of i-voting projects.

Two sorts of conclusions can be inferred from this research. First, the requirements for personal data processing in remote electronic voting projects are independent of secret suffrage and cannot be subsumed by this latter principle. Personal data protection is broader than the principle of secret suffrage since any processing of personal data is subject to appropriate protection. Thus, data that may not fall under the scope of secret suffrage, such as personal data about candidates, is also covered by the GDPR. Second, our account of the internet voting experiences in the Åland Islands and in France has allowed us to identify some critical aspects related to the GDPR in the implementation of internet voting projects, namely: the categories of personal data processed (both about voters and candidates), as well as the processing of special categories of personal data (i.e., the votes, which are personal data that reveal political opinions); aspects related to the role played by data controllers (normally, electoral authorities) and processors (usually, technology vendors and services' providers); the use of pseudonymisation techniques for the processing of 'sensitive data'; and, the post-election processing of personal data, including its destruction, as well as possible limits to (universal) verifiability and public access to personal data. As we have seen, all these aspects could benefit from more guidance, be it by the national regulator or at the wider EU-level.

Acknowledgments. This work has received funding from the European Commission under the auspices of PROMETHEUS Project, Horizon 2020 Research and Innovation action (Grant Agreement No. 780701).

References

Act on the Autonomy of Åland (2010)

Åland Data Protection Authority: DNR T1-2019 (2019a). https://www.di.ax/anslagstavla/dnr-t1-2019. Accessed 03 Aug 2020

Åland Data Protection Authority: Resultat och beslut av den beslutade Dataskyddstillsynen gällande personuppgiftsbehandling i Lagtingsvalet, särskilt fokus I-valet Dnr T1-2019 (2019b). https://www.di.ax/anslagstavla/dnr-t5-2019. Accessed 03 Aug 2020

Åland Data Protection Authority: Rapport om Säkerhetsåtgärder i E-valet samt svar från Scytl (2019c). https://www.di.ax/anslagstavla/rapport-om-sakerhetsatgarder-e-valet-samt-svar-fran-scytl. Accessed 03 Aug 2020

Article 29 Data Protection Working Party: Opinion 4/2007 on the concept of personal data (2007). https://www.clinicalstudydatarequest.com/Documents/Privacy-European-guidance.pdf. Accessed 03 Aug 2020

Article 29 Data Protection Working Party: Opinion 05/2014 on Anonymisation Techniques (2014). https://ec.europa.eu/justice/article-29/documentation/opinion-recommendation/files/2014/wp216_en.pdf. Accessed 03 Aug 2020

Court of Justice of the EU: Scarlet Extended SA v Société belge des auteurs, compositeurs et éditeurs SCRL (SABAM) (2011)

CNIL: Délibération n° 2010-371 du 21 octobre 2010 portant adoption d'une recommandation relative à la sécurité des systèmes de vote électronique (2010). https://www.legifrance.gouv.fr/affichTexte.do?cidTexte=JORFTEXT000023124205&categorieLien=id. Accessed 03 Aug 2020

CNIL: Sécurité des systèmes de vote par internet: la CNIL actualise sa recommandation de 2010 (2019a). https://www.cnil.fr/fr/securite-des-systemes-de-vote-par-internet-la-cnil-actualise-sa-recommandation-de-2010. Accessed 03 Aug 2020

CNIL: Délibération n° 2019-053 du 25 avril 2019 portant adoption d'une recommandation relative à la sécurité des systèmes de vote par correspondance électronique, notamment via Internet (2019b). https://www.legifrance.gouv.fr/affichTexte.do?cidTexte=JORFTEXT000038661239. Accessed 03 Aug 2020

Code électoral, France (2019)

Council of Europe: Recommendation CM/Rec(2017)5 of the Committee of Ministers to member States on standards for e-voting (2017a). https://search.coe.int/cm/Pages/result_details.aspx?ObjectId=0900001680726f6f. Accessed 03 Aug 2020

Council of Europe: Explanatory Memorandum to Recommendation CM/Rec(2017)5 of the Committee of Ministers to member States on standards for e-voting (2017b). https://search.coe.int/cm/Pages/result_details.aspx?ObjectId=0900001680726c0b. Accessed 03 Aug 2020

Council of Europe: Guidelines on the implementation of the provisions of Recommendation CM/Rec(2017)5 on standards for e-voting (2017c). https://search.coe.int/cm/Pages/result_details.aspx?ObjectId=090000168071bc84. Accessed 03 Aug 2020

Duenas-Cid, D., Krivonosova, I., Serrano, R., Freire, M.., Krimmer, R.: Tripped at the finish line: the Åland Islands internet voting project. In: Krimmer, R., et al. (eds.) Electronic Voting. Fifth International Joint Conference, E-Vote-ID 2020. Springer, Cham (2020)

Election Act for Åland (2019)

EU Agency for Fundamental Rights and Council of Europe: Handbook on European data protection law - 2018 edition (2018). https://fra.europa.eu/sites/default/files/fra_uploads/fra-coe-edps-2018-handbook-data-protection_en.pdf. Accessed 03 Aug 2020

European Commission: Free and Fair elections. Guidance Document. Commission guidance on the application of Union data protection law in the electoral context (2018). https://ec.europa.eu/commission/sites/beta-political/files/soteu2018-data-protection-law-electoral-guidance-638_en.pdf. Accessed 03 Aug 2020

International Covenant on Civil and Political Rights (1966)

International IDEA: International Obligations for Elections. Guidelines for Legal Frameworks (2014). https://www.idea.int/sites/default/files/publications/international-obligations-
for-elections.pdf. Accessed 03 Aug 2020

Krimmer, R., Duenas-Cid, D., Krivonosova, I., Serrano, R., Freire, M., Wrede, C.: Nordic Pioneers:
facing the first use of Internet Voting in the Åland Islands (Parliamentary Elections 2019) (2019).
https://doi.org/10.31235/osf.io/5zr2e. Accessed 03 Aug 2020

Lécuyer, Y.: Le droit a des élections libres. Council of Europe, Strasbourg (2014)

OSCE/ODIHR: Republic of France Parliamentary Elections, 10 and 17 June 2012. Needs
Assessment Mission Report (2012a). https://www.osce.org/files/f/documents/7/5/90763.pdf.
Accessed 03 Aug 2020

OSCE/ODIHR: Republic of France Parliamentary Elections, 10 and 17 June 2012. Election
Assessment Mission Final Report (2012b). https://www.osce.org/files/f/documents/7/7/93621.
pdf. Accessed 03 Aug 2020

OSCE/ODIHR: France Presidential and Parliamentary Elections, 2017. Needs Assessment Mission Report (2017c). https://www.osce.org/files/f/documents/0/8/311081.pdf. Accessed 03 Aug
2020

Protocol (no. 1) to the Convention for the Protection of Human Rights and Fundamental Freedoms
(European Convention on Human Rights, ECHR) (1952)

Regulation (EU) 2016/679 of the European Parliament and of the Council of 27 April 2016 on
the protection of natural persons with regard to the processing of personal data and on the free
movement of such data, and repealing Directive 95/46/EC (General Data Protection Regulation,
GDPR) (2016)

Sénat: Rapport d'information fait au nom de la commission de lois constitutionelles, de légisation,
du suffrage universel, du Règlement et d'administration générale (1) sur le vote électronique
(2014). https://www.senat.fr/rap/r13-445/r13-4451.pdf. Accessed 03 Aug 2020

Sénat: Rapport d'information fait au nom de la commission de lois constitutionelles, de légisation,
du suffrage universel, du Règlement et d'administration générale (1) sur le vote électronique
(2018). http://www.senat.fr/rap/r18-073/r18-0731.pdf. Accessed 03 Aug 2020

Scytl Secure Electronic Voting, S.A.: Åland's I-voting Project. Clarification of the Audit Report by
the Åland Data Protection Authority (2019). https://www.di.ax/sites/default/files/attachment/
pinboard-message/data_protection_audit_clarifications_v3.0.pdf. Accessed 03 Aug 2020

TechLaw Sweden AB: Granskning av säkerhetsåtgärder hos Scytl (2019). https://www.di.ax/
sites/default/files/attachment/pinboard-message/rapport-aland-scytl-190916_0.pdf. Accessed
03 Aug 2020

Universal Declaration on Human Rights (1948)

The Oxymoron of the Internet Voting in Illiberal and Hybrid Political Contexts

Bogdan Romanov[1] and Yury Kabanov[2(✉)]

[1] University of Tartu, Tartu, Estonia
romanovbogdan4@gmail.com
[2] National Research University Higher School of Economics, St. Petersburg, Russia
ykabanov@hse.ru

Abstract. This paper explores the phenomenon of e-voting, in particular, new i-voting technologies, within the context of hybrid and authoritarian political regimes. While e-voting and i-voting are not particularly widespread, more and more illiberal countries are implementing these innovations, which has been overlooked in the academia so far. The paper attempts to fill in this gap. Firstly, we provide a general overview of the problem and identify the key features of non-democracies adopting e-voting and i-voting. Secondly, we explore the case of Russia, a hybrid regime, which may become a role model for other countries in the near future. The research exposes the potential of e-voting, and in particular, i-voting as a tool for the regime stability and provides some avenues of the future research.

Keywords: I-voting · E-voting · Autocracies · Hybrid regimes

1 Introduction

While the impact of the Internet on authoritarian politics is an emerging topic [1], little attention in this context has been given so far to e-voting technologies. This is partly due to the fact that unlike online repressions [2] and even e-participation [3], the use of e-voting is not so widespread among hybrid and authoritarian political regimes [4].

At the same time, this situation might change soon. The capacity of non-democracies to utilize the Internet is rapidly increasing [1, 5]. Moreover, the COVID-19 pandemic may give another powerful impetus for new practices of voting [6]. In this regard, it becomes vital to explore the possible causes and effects of such innovations, considering the social and political contexts in which they are implemented.

This paper attempts to preliminarily address this issue and answer the question as to whether e-voting technologies can be embedded into the resilience strategies of hybrid and authoritarian regimes. The study mostly deals with Internet voting, or i-voting, when a person casts a vote via the Internet or a mobile device [7, 8]. Yet, some of the conclusions can be applicable to other e-voting practices and *new voting technologies* [8].

© Springer Nature Switzerland AG 2020
R. Krimmer et al. (Eds.): E-Vote-ID 2020, LNCS 12455, pp. 183–195, 2020.
https://doi.org/10.1007/978-3-030-60347-2_12

To answer the question, we first overview the general trends of e-voting and i-voting diffusion in non-democracies, to see if there are certain clues to understand when and why such countries introduce these innovations. Secondly, we explore the case of Russia, a hybrid regime, which is quite active in promoting Internet voting from 2019 onwards. We outline what happened during the 2019 elections for the Moscow State Duma and present some insights into the future development of i-voting in the country.

The ultimate goal of this paper is to provoke the discussion on the functions e-voting and i-voting may play in different social and political contexts. Furthermore, the paper overviews a preliminary framework to analyze future initiatives of that kind in authoritarian and hybrid political regimes.

2   E-Voting and I-Voting: Not So Democratic Anymore?

2.1   Patterns of Diffusion

The implications of ICTs within political regime dynamics heavily depend on the position we take within the debate between the Internet optimists and pessimists. The former claim that the Internet has a democratizing potential, as it creates new opportunities for free communication and political mobilization [9–11]. From this viewpoint, e-voting technologies increase the effectiveness of elections by reducing the human factor and making them more accessible for citizens [8, 12, 13].

Yet, there is more evidence to support the pessimistic view, claiming that the Internet has been successfully incorporated into authoritarian strategies of survival and governance [1, 2]. For example, autocrats use e-participation to get information and boost legitimacy [4, 14, 15], whilst the democratizing effects of the Internet are hindered by restrictions and prohibitions [2, 16].

E-voting and i-voting are rarely discussed in this context. However, scholars have recently started to pay more attention to the political and social context, in which new technologies are introduced [17, 18]. Cheeseman et al. note that "even the most advanced forms of technology depend on human input to no lesser extent than manual election management and are in certain cases actually more vulnerable to manipulation. Significantly, this risk is exacerbated by the difficulty of monitoring "black box" digital processes, especially in counties in which the ruling party is able to exert control over the electoral commission" [19, p. 1411]. This observation is in line with Oostveen and van den Besselaar, who suggest that "e-voting could possibly and relatively easily be used to reinforce control by the ruling party" [20, p. 19].

This viewpoint is further amplified by several case studies, tracing the experiments with e-voting and i-voting in hybrid and authoritarian regimes, including Russia [4], Pakistan [21], Oman [22], the UAE [23] and Kazakhstan [24]. Though these practices are still rare, such countries are no less interested in new electoral technologies.

Why do such countries implement e-voting (i-voting)? There are different answers to this question, and each state might have its own rationale. A possible factor that would obviously facilitate e-voting (i-voting) is an institutional one. For instance, explaining the Internet elections of 2012 in Russia, Toepfl argued that since the elections had been practiced for a long time in the country, "[a]n additional flurry of semi-competitive Internet votes to fill advisory bodies to the government was thus, apparently, not perceived as a major threat" [4, p. 969]. In other words, new technologies are to be expected in the *electoral authoritarian regimes*, accustomed to voting procedures and familiar with the methods of electoral manipulations [25, 26].

Of course, other regime types may also benefit from Internet voting. For example, monarchies, as shown by Kneuer and Harnish [27], are counterintuitively active in promoting new participatory technologies. This can be explained by the fact that their political structure lacks institutionalized participation channels [27]. By analogy, i-voting seems a safe and easy to control alternative to collect citizens' preferences.

Another possible factor of e-voting (i-voting) adoption is the legitimacy quest. Cheeseman et al. argue that digital electoral technologies are often associated with the idea that they "boost the process's legitimacy – and hence that of the elected government" [19, p. 1398]. This idea falls into the emerging research area on legitimation as a source of authoritarian stability [28–30]. There are different legitimation strategies that autocrats may use. For instance, von Soest and Grauvogel [31] distinguish between six types of legitimacy claims: *foundational myth, ideology, personalism, procedures, performance, international engagement*, and measure the values of such claims for various types of non-democracies. Their findings suggest that certain legitimacy claims (e.g. *performance*) are of equal importance to most of the regime types. This methodology has been refined in the new *Varieties of Democracy* dataset [32, 58], where the classification encompasses four types of legitimation strategies: *performance, rational-legal, ideology* and *the personality of the leader*. In this regard, it can be speculated that i-voting will become more widespread within the countries that actively employ procedural legitimation strategies, "based on the carrying out of elections and other rule-based mechanisms for handing over power through 'orderly' process" [31, p. 291].

There is not enough evidence so far to prove these propositions, but the data we have demonstrate their plausibility. As shown in Table 1, different e-voting technologies can be found in both hybrid regimes and consolidated autocracies. According to the IDEA,[1] there are 10 multi-party and 2 monarchy regimes currently using e-voting, including 4 countries that use i-voting. This indeed suggests that e-voting can be easily adapted by the states already holding elections, but not exclusively, as other regimes may use ICTs to expand their regime resilience repertoires. It is notable that both monarchies use i-voting, in line with what has been said previously. The situation with legitimation is more complicated since many countries employ multiple strategies. Yet, again, most of the countries score 3 and higher on more "democratic" legitimation, like the *rational-legal* and *performance* legitimation [32].

Here we may conclude that while the topic of e-voting (i-voting) in non-democracies is new, the emerging studies and new empirical cases suggest that this issue should be taken seriously. Like other IT-enabled and digital tools, voting technologies are being adapted and utilized by authoritarian and hybrid countries. Our preliminary analysis suggests that the regime institutional configurations and legitimation strategies are promising variables to explain this trend. However, it requires further testing using more rigorous techniques.

---

[1] https://www.idea.int/data-tools/data/icts-elections.

Table 1. E-voting and i-voting in non-democracies

Country[a]	Regime type[b]	Legitimation strategies[c]			
		Rational – Legal	Performance	Leader	Ideology
Armenia*	Multi-party	2.66	**3.24**	2.46	1.13
Bangladesh	Multi-party	0.76	**3.45**	3.82	3.33
Bhutan	Multi-party	**3.62**	**3.12**	2.24	2.61
Congo, DR	Military	1.53	1.5	2.8	1.34
Fiji	Multi-party	**3.3**	**3.52**	3.19	3.06
Honduras	Multi-party	2.83	**3.21**	0.63	2.37
Iran	Other	2.19	2.38	3.62	3.92
Iraq	Multi-party	2.13	1.21	3	3.29
Kyrgyzstan	Multi-party	**3.19**	**3.36**	0.85	0.93
Oman*	Monarchy	**3.19**	2.77	3.73	3.18
Pakistan*	Multi-party	**3.63**	**3.63**	1.72	1.81
Russia**	Multi-party	**3.29**	2.82	3.76	2.78
UAE*	Monarchy	**3.02**	**3.51**	3.28	3.27
Venezuela	Multi-party	1.15	3	2.96	3.65

Sources

[a]Countries currently using e-voting. Source: ICTs in Elections Database. IDEA. URL: https://www.idea.int/data-tools/data/icts-elections.

[b]Typology of regimes by Wahman et al. [33], data for 2014.

[c]Legitimation strategies from the Varieties of Democracy Project, data for 2018 [32, 58].

*Countries, using i-voting, according to the IDEA Database

**Russia introduced the opportunity for i-voting in 2020

2.2 Effects

The question of what impact e-voting (i-voting) has on the regime dynamics is hard to answer empirically so far. Evidently, the effect will depend on which technology is used. For example, some e-voting applications, for instance, optical scan voting systems, were reported to prevent some falsifications [34]. Regardless, they are unlikely to provoke any democratization, since when the technology is fully controlled by the incumbent, it will rather *reinforce* existing power relations [35].

To know what effects new voting technologies may have on non-democracies, we need to understand why they organize them in the first place. Although there are various explanations, their basic functions are, first, to show the strength and legitimacy of the regime, and secondly, to obtain information about citizens' preferences [36, 37]. These goals may be contradictory, as they require different degrees of electoral manipulation and fairness of the results [38]. And here the emerging i-voting technologies, in comparison to paper-based and even other e-voting options, appear to be more valuable in maintaining authoritarian practices, especially when it comes to *remote voting* [7].

First, Internet voting is assumed to increase turnout, since citizens may take part in elections from wherever they are [7, 39]. This assumption has found little support in reality, but it is still very popular with researchers and policymakers [40–43]. In non-democracies, where the academic discourse towards e-voting is more positive [20], this claim can be even more profound.[2] This feature of i-voting may be of particular relevance to those regimes employing the high turnout strategy that "confers legitimacy, demonstrates the regime's invincibility, and allows the regime to gather information on societal grievances" [44, p. 1].

At the same time, in usual circumstances this strategy may be risky in various ways [44, p. 28], leading, for example, to the increase of votes for the opposition [45]. We argue that unlike traditional voting practices, i-voting may substantially reduce such risks, if the technology is fully controlled by the incumbent. Even in democracies, remote i-voting raises concerns about proper voters' authentication, absence of coercion and accurate votes' calculation in i-voting are raised in democracies [39]. As put by Goos et al., "there is no technical solution available which would guarantee transparency, accessibility, resistance to intimidation and vote selling and, last but not least, resistance to fraud or errors" [7, p. 136]. It is clear that authoritarian or hybrid regimes can demonstrate more instances of such malpractice.

If the general principles of i-voting *end-to-end verification* [46] are violated, the incumbents may substantially increase their capacity to control the elections at any stage. They, first, may benefit from the high turnout to legitimize their rule (naturally or by cheating). Secondly, as the votes do not need to be falsified when cast (it can be done in the later stages of votes' tallying or publication), the incumbents may get rather objective information about citizens' preferences.

3   Internet Voting in a Hybrid Regime: The Case of Russia

3.1   Framework: Electoral Authoritarianism Goes Digital

There are different frameworks allowing the estimation of the integrity of i-voting, but most of them deal with technical questions of verifiability, privacy, secrecy etc. [46] Such problems occur rather often [47, 48] and they should not necessarily be regarded as a move away from democracy. What may potentially make them a repeated practice of non-democratic politics is the social and political context in which they happen. Thus, several additional theoretical frameworks will be of use.

Firstly, the development of Internet voting in a non-democratic country heavily depends on the level of control a government has over the online space. The Internet still poses a threat to authoritarian survival [49], and those risks should be mitigated before new technologies are introduced. As the literature suggests, many Internet-savvy dictators follow a *double strategy*: by developing online participatory tools they simultaneously strengthen their censorship, filtering, or other repressive capacities [3]. Such policy usually refers to as the *networked authoritarianism*, i.e. "[w]hen an authoritarian

---

[2] Krivonosova I.: E-voting in Moscow: A Gratuitous Gimmick—RIDDLE. (n.d.). Retrieved June 2, 2020, from https://www.ridl.io/en/e-voting-in-moscow-a-gratuitous-gimmick/.

regime embraces and adjusts to the inevitable changes brought by digital communications" [16, p. 33]. Thus, to understand the perspectives of i-voting, we need to look at the general *capacity* of a country to control the Internet for regime resilience [5].

Secondly, we need to explore the whole electoral process – from defining the positions to be filled in with elections, to the validation of results. As shown by the research on electoral authoritarianism, at every stage of the process, dictators have a variety of tools to manipulate the choice, which are by no means limited to falsification of results. Here we use the framework developed by Schedler, who proposes a *menu of manipulation* across seven steps of elections: (1) *the object of choice*; (2) *the range of choice*; (3) *the formation of preferences*; (4) *the agents of choice*; (5) *the expression of preferences*; (6) *the aggregation of preferences*; (7) *the consequences of choice* [25, p. 39].

These frameworks help to describe what we may call the *digital electoral authoritarianism*, i.e. one that utilizes online repression and electoral manipulations to hold i-voting for regime resilience.

3.2 2019 Moscow City Duma Elections and Beyond

Russia seems to be a good case to analyze the transformation of i-voting in a hybrid regime. On the one hand, it is usually referred to as *competitive* or *electoral authoritarianism*, which "employs unfair electoral practices to an extent that deprives elections of their primary functions of political choice and elite circulation, and reduces them to a mere tool of legitimization and mobilization of support" [50, p. 623]. This set of practices is changing over time, shifting to more subtle manipulations, like changing electoral formulae [51] or denying oppositional candidates of registration [52].

On the other hand, it is usually emphasized that the government control over the Internet is increasing over time in the country, including various types of control and legal regulations [53, 54]. The country falls into a *double strategy* [3]: despite restrictive measures on the Internet, the government actively promotes e-government and e-participation to engage citizens into public policymaking [55]. One of the first initiatives in e-participation was the *Russian Public Initiative* e-petitions portal [56], followed by more successful regional portals, like the *Our Petersburg* portal in St. Petersburg [57] or the *Active Citizen* in Moscow, which have not only become important consultative instruments [4], but also have prepared the ground for further policy innovations.

Both factors – the developed stage of the *network* and *electoral authoritarianism* – make Russia an obvious candidate to introduce Internet voting. Although, e-voting in the country had already been operational in other formats,[3] for many years it was not the case for Internet voting, as such practices were rare and related only to advisory bodies [4]. Yet, from 2019 this agenda became profound in relation to Moscow City Duma (MCD) elections. However local this case is, as will be shown further, it may be also considered either a rehearsal for a massive introduction of i-voting or a model of how such online elections can be held in the future.

---

[3] Krivonosova I.: E-voting in Moscow: A Gratuitous Gimmick—RIDDLE. (n.d.). Retrieved June 2, 2020, from https://www.ridl.io/en/e-voting-in-moscow-a-gratuitous-gimmick/.

Internet elections in Moscow were held on September 8, 2019, as an experiment, which was initially proposed by a liberal journalist Alexey Venediktov and then formulated as a federal bill by the State Duma deputies.[4] Eventually, only three electoral constituencies were included in the experiment.[5]

There were different opinions regarding the purpose of i-voting implementations. The explanation of the state officials was quite in line with the *procedural legitimation*. For example, Valentin Gorbunov, the chair of the Moscow Electoral Commission, emphasized that i-voting was a consequent step of the digital economy, which "creates additional circumstances for the realization of active suffrage".[6] Apparently, the increase of turnout became the most important goal, as many Muscovites were used to "solves all their issues via smartphone" (see Footnote 6). Alexey Shaposhnikov, the chair of the MCD, made it rather explicit: "Everyone supposes that the larger turnout is, the more legitimate the elections are. I think that the option of distant voting allows raising the turnout tremendously."[7]

Unlike the government, the so-called *non-system opposition* did not perceive that innovation as a positive step, claiming that it would become another instrument of electoral manipulation for the ruling party.[8] Many experts were also concerned about i-voting integrity. For instance, Dmitry Oreshkin, a political scientist, argued that "when the electronic voting is introduced, you do not have any observers. There will even be no primary protocols… The disappearance of voting results can be now justified by even a short circuit".[9] Other experts were also skeptical about the capacity of the government to ensure the integrity, secrecy and privacy of the procedure.[10]

---

[4] V Gosdumu Vnesli Zakonoproekt o Testiro-vanii Elektronnogo Golosovaniya v Moskve – Vedomosti. (n.d.). Retrieved June 2, 2020, from https://www.vedomosti.ru/politics/news/2019/02/26/795201-elektronnogo-golosovaniya.

[5] Moskvichi s 3 po 9 iyunya smogut vybrat' okruga dlya provedeniya elektronnogo golosovaniya—Moskva—TASS. (n.d.). Retrieved June 9, 2020, from https://tass.ru/moskva/6489105.

[6] Cel' eksperimenta po vnedreniyu distancionnogo elektronnogo golosovaniya na vy-borah v Mosgordumu – sozdat' dlya moskvichej dopolnitel'nye vozmozhnosti realiza-cii aktivnogo izbiratel'nogo prava. (n.d.). Retrieved June 9, 2020, from https://duma.mos.ru/ru/34/news/novosti/tsel-eksperimenta-po-vnedreniyu-distantsionnogo-elektronnogo-golosovaniya-na-vyiborah-v-mosgordumu-sozdat-dlya-moskvichey-dopolnitelnyie-vozmojnosti-realizatsii-aktivnogo-izbiratelnogo-prava.

[7] A. Shaposhnikov: Elektronnoe golosovanie pozvolit kolossal'no podnyat' yavku na vyborah deputatov Mosgordumy—Agentstvo gorodskih novostej «Moskva»—Informacionnoe agentstvo. (n.d.). Retrieved June 7, 2020, from https://www.mskagency.ru/materials/2884983.

[8] Aleksej Naval'nyj—Oficial'no: U nas est' to, chego byt' ne dolzhno. «Elektron-noe golosovanie» polnost'yu skomprometirovano. (n.d.). Retrieved June 9, 2020, from https://navalny.com/p/6234/.

[9] Dnevnoj fal'sifikat. Dmitrij Oreshkin ob"yasnyaet, kak vvedenie elektronnogo go-losovaniya pomozhet vlastyam vyigriyvat' vybory. (n.d.). Retrieved June 9, 2020, from https://novayagazeta.ru/articles/2020/05/14/85376-dnevnoy-falsifikat.

[10] «Okej, golosujte bumazhno» Aleksej Venediktov otvetil na kritiku internet-vyborov v Mosgordumu. My poprosili ekspertov proverit' ego zayavleniya—Meduza. (n.d.). Retrieved June 7, 2020, from https://meduza.io/feature/2019/07/01/okey-golosuyte-bumazhno.

In terms of Schedler, concerns related to i-voting arose not only with the technologies *per se*, but also with the political context in which such technologies were introduced. For instance, there was an issue with the *range of choice*, as several oppositional candidates had been denied registration, which caused a series of public protests.[11] Though this is an "offline" issue, the rules of registration are applicable to all candidates, hence denial of access might also limit the choice for voters. The same "offline" problem was with the *formation of preferences*, as the candidates from the ruling party were competing as independent candidates without any party affiliation.[12] In terms of *expression* and *aggregation of preferences*, the problems with i-voting included the issues with the *end-to-end verification*,[13] as well as cases of the system malfunction, during which voters could not cast their votes or their votes were not counted.[14]

Regardless of the technical and organizational issues, the major goal set by the policymakers seems to have been achieved. First, the majority of votes in all three districts was given to the independent candidates, affiliated with the *United Russia* party (see Footnote 14). Though the general turnout was rather average (20–25%), the i-voting turnout was much higher: out of 11 228 registered voters, about 92% have cast their votes.[15] It is not clear whether the introduction of Internet voting has contributed to the victory of any candidates, but there were expert accounts that although the level of manipulation had been low in general, "experimental districts … have turned out to be much more pro-government, than in Moscow generally".[16]

The fact that the experiment was considered rather successful by the elites can be also indirectly proved by the decision to continue and expand this practice. In 2020, during the COVID-19 pandemic, the government decided to hold the Internet voting on the constitutional amendments in two regions – Moscow and Nizhegorodskaya oblast.

---

[11] Eksperty prokommentirovali otkaz v registracii kandidatov na vyborah v MGD - RIA Novosti. 31.07.2019. (n.d.). Retrieved June 9, 2020, from https://ria.ru/20190731/1557026300.html.

[12] «Edinaya Rossiya» ne vydvinula ni odnogo kandidata v Mosgordumu No frakciya edinorosov v stolichnom parlamente vse ravno budet —Meduza. (n.d.). Retrieved June 8, 2020, from https://meduza.io/feature/2019/06/13/edinaya-rossiya-ne-vydvinula-ni-odnogo-kandidata-v-mosgordumu.

[13] Meriya Obeshchala Prozrachnoe Internet-Golosovanie v Moskve. V Itoge Ona Mozhet Opublikovat' Lyubye Rezul'ta-ty, i Proverit' Ih Nikto Ne Smozhet — Meduza. (n.d.). Retrieved June 2, 2020, from https://meduza.io/feature/2019/09/06/meriya-obeschala-prozrachnoe-internet-golosovanie-v-moskve-v-itoge-ona-mozhet-opublikovat-lyubye-rezultaty-i-proverit-ih-nikto-ne-smozhet.

[14] Onlajn-Golosovanie v Moskve Dvazhdy Priostanavlivali Iz-Za Sboya - Novosti – Politika – Kommersant. (n.d.). Retrieved June 2, 2020, from https://www.kommersant.ru/doc/4086901.

[15] V Moskve Podveli Itogi Eksperimenta s Elektron-nym Golosovaniem — Rossijskaya Gazeta. (n.d.). Retrieved June 1, 2020, from https://rg.ru/2019/09/09/reg-cfo/v-moskve-podveli-itogi-eksperimenta-s-elektronnym-golosovaniem.html.

[16] Urnoterapiya. Poluchiv psihologicheskuyu travmu god nazad, vlast' stala otsekat' negativnye scenarii na dal'nih podstupah k uchastkam. CHto iz etogo vyshlo. (n.d.). Retrieved June 9, 2020, from https://novayagazeta.ru/articles/2019/09/10/81915-urnoterapiya?utm_source=tg&utm_medium=novaya&utm_campaign=matematik-sergey-shpilkin-proanalizirova.

As of 15 June 2020, about 548 thousand people have registered to vote online.[17] What is even more important, in May 2020 a federal law was introduced, allowing the citizens to vote by mail or online in the elections and referendums of all levels.[18] It is possible that i-voting will be used in several regions in September 2020 for the additional elections for the State Duma, with the goal to increase turnout and raise their popularity.[19]

Of course, technical issues with elections may happen, especially during an experiment, and they *per se* do not prove the intention of the government to increase the control over electoral process. But there are enough facts to conclude that this experiment will continue and become a full-fledged practice. This, in turn, will require thorough analysis of its causes and effects.

In sum, several conclusions can be drawn. First, Russia, being a hybrid regime that is based on electoral institutions, and to a larger extent on a *procedural legitimation*, with a vast repertoire of the reactive and proactive Internet controls, can be considered a perfect example of the general trend that we have previously outlined. What is more, the Russian case can become a role model for other countries that either update their electoral rules or introduce elections from scratch. Secondly, the case of 2019 MCD elections reveals a set of issues with the use of the i-voting, which are not necessarily related to the technologies, but also to the broader social and political context.

4 Discussion and Conclusion

This paper is a preliminary attempt to explore the issue of e-voting and, especially, i-voting diffusion in the countries other than liberal democracies. Having reviewed some recent events occurring in the world and Russia, in particular, we argue that there might be a new trend of emerging online voting technologies in the context of authoritarian and hybrid political regimes, which, in turn, will question the status of e-voting and i-voting as a purely democratic innovation. Non-democracies that have suitable institutional configurations and relevant legitimation strategies, may become more interested in these innovations in the near future, thus opening the agenda of authoritarian e-voting (i-voting), like it was a couple of years ago regarding e-participation [3]. Whereas China is considered one of the leaders in online consultations [1, 14], Russia has all the potential to become a role model in the case of Internet voting. The COVID-19 pandemic may also contribute to this trend [6], being a stimulus, or a "window of opportunities" to justify the changes in electoral rules.

---

[17] Bolee 548 tysyach chelovek podali zayavki na uchastie v onlajn-golosovanii—Parlamentskaya gazeta. (n.d.). Retrieved June 7, 2020, from https://www.pnp.ru/social/bolee-548-tysyach-che lovek-podali-zayavki-na-uchastie-v-onlayn-golosovanii.html.

[18] Federal'nyj zakon ot 23 maya 2020 g. N 152-FZ "O provedenii eksperimenta po organi-zacii i osushchestvleniyu distancionnogo elektronnogo golosovaniya v gorode federal'nogo znacheniya Moskve"—Rossijskaya gazeta. (n.d.). Retrieved June 7, 2020, from https://rg.ru/2020/05/25/fz-o-golosovanii-v-moskve-dok.html.

[19] Elektronnoe golosovanie na dovyborah v Gosdumu projdet v Kurskoj i YAroslavskoj oblastyah. (n.d.). Retrieved June 13, 2020, from http://actualcomment.ru/elektronnoe-golosovanie-na-dov yborakh-v-gosdumu-proydet-v-kurskoy-i-yaroslavskoy-oblastyakh-2007271358.html?fbclid= IwAR0UdmWrTsGKVDB8x4_ycnwRBOuz_KH4GNPQWYuIcHkC0wzuTCRgQZXnyxQ.

We are of the opinion that the questions highlighted in this paper should become an important item of the *E-Voting Studies* research agenda in several respects. In the first place, more attention should be drawn to the importance of "offline" social and political context in which e-voting technologies are employed [20]. Modern Political Science and comparative authoritarianism offer a wide range of frameworks which may well complement the existing approaches that deal with the technical issues related to e-voting and i-voting *per se*. While our paper was working mostly with rationales and possible outcomes of e-voting, we have intentionally overlooked the technical aspect of online voting in non-democracies. However, this lacuna might be easily filled in by the theoretical framework, constituted by Heiberg et al. [46], in which the authors pinpoint core principles of verifiable elections in Estonian case—this potential projection would once again emphasize the contrast between e-voting in different contexts.

Secondly, while this paper proposes some clues to the factors that drive e-voting (i-voting) innovations in non-democracies (namely, institutional structures and legitimation strategies), more elaborate research techniques should be utilized to explore the determinants and incentives of e-voting adoption at the state and individual level. Here, both the large-N comparisons and deep case studies will be important.

Finally, as this issue is relatively new, it is rather early to estimate the possible effects of such innovations in terms of democratization and autocratization of adopting countries. Yet, this line of research will also be of great value, as the volume of empirical evidence continues to grow.

References

1. Keremoğlu, E., Weidmann, N.B.: How dictators control the internet: a review essay. Comp. Polit. Stud. (2020). https://doi.org/10.1177/0010414020912278
2. Rød, E.G., Weidmann, N.B.: Empowering activists or autocrats? The Internet in authoritarian regimes. J. Peace Res. **52**(3), 338–351 (2015)
3. Karlsson, M.: Carrots and sticks: internet governance in non–democratic regimes. Int. J. Electron. Gov. **6**(3), 179–186 (2013)
4. Toepfl, F.: Innovating consultative authoritarianism: internet votes as a novel digital tool to stabilize non-democratic rule in Russia. New Media Soc. **20**(3), 956–972 (2018)
5. Christensen, B.: Cyber state capacity: a model of authoritarian durability, ICTs, and emerging media. Govern. Inf. Q. **36**(3), 460–468 (2019)
6. Krimmer, R., Duenas-Cid, D., Krivonosova, I.: Debate: safeguarding democracy during pandemics. Social distancing, postal, or internet voting—the good, the bad or the ugly? Public Money Manage. 1–3 (2020)
7. Goos, K., Beckert, B., Lindner, R.: Electronic, internet-based voting. In: Lindner, R., Aichholzer, G., Hennen, L. (eds.) Electronic Democracy in Europe, pp. 135–184. Springer, Cham (2016). https://doi.org/10.1007/978-3-319-27419-5_4
8. Krimmer, R.: A structure for new voting technologies: what they are, how they are used and why. In: Bergener, K., Räckers, M., Stein, A. (eds.) The Art of Structuring, pp. 421–426. Springer, Cham (2019). https://doi.org/10.1007/978-3-030-06234-7_39
9. Berman, J., Weitzner, D.J.: Technology and democracy. Soc. Res. **64**(3), 1313–1319 (1997)
10. Calingaert, D.: Authoritarianism vs. the internet. Pol. Rev. 14 (2010)
11. Diamond, L.: Liberation technology. J. Democr. **21**(3), 69–83 (2010). https://doi.org/10.1353/jod.0.0190

12. Grider, M.: Securing the vote: electronic voting in theory and practice. 9 (2018)
13. Vassil, K., Solvak, M., Vinkel, P., Trechsel, A.H., Alvarez, R.M.: The diffusion of internet voting. Usage patterns of internet voting in Estonia between 2005 and 2015. Gov. Inf. Q. 33(3), 453–459 (2016). https://doi.org/10.1016/j.giq.2016.06.007
14. Kornreich, Y.: Authoritarian responsiveness: Online consultation with "issue publics" in China. Governance 32(3), 547–564 (2019). https://doi.org/10.1111/gove.12393
15. Truex, R.: Consultative authoritarianism and its limits. Comp. Polit. Stud. 50(3), 329–361 (2017). https://doi.org/10.1177/0010414014534196
16. MacKinnon, R.: Liberation technology: China's "networked authoritarianism". J. Democr. 22(2), 32–46 (2011)
17. Herrnson, P.S., et al.: Early appraisals of electronic voting. Soc. Sci. Comput. Rev. 23(3), 274–292 (2005). https://doi.org/10.1177/0894439305275850
18. Kshetri, N., Voas, J.: Blockchain-enabled e-voting. IEEE Softw. 35(4), 95–99 (2018). https://doi.org/10.1109/MS.2018.2801546
19. Cheeseman, N., Lynch, G., Willis, J.: Digital dilemmas: the unintended consequences of election technology. Democratization 25(8), 1397–1418 (2018)
20. Oostveen, A.M., van den Besselaar, P.: The academic debate on electronic voting in a socio-political context. In: E-Vote-ID 2019. 17 (2019)
21. Binte Haq, H., McDermott, R., Taha Ali, S.: Pakistan's internet voting experiment. arXiv: 1907.07765 (2019)
22. Al Siyabi, M., Al Jabri, N., Al-Shihi, H., Al-Khod, A. K.: The uptake of voting participations in oman through e-voting. In: The International Information Systems Conference (iiSC) 2011 Sultan Qaboos University, Muscat, Sultanate of Oman (2011)
23. Al-Khouri, A.M., Authority, E.I., Dhabi, A.: E-voting in UAE FNC elections: a case study. Inf. Knowl. Manage. 2(6), 25–84 (2012)
24. Kassen, M.: Politicization of e-voting rejection: reflections from Kazakhstan. Transform. Gov. People Process Policy 14, 305–330 (2020)
25. Schedler, A.: Elections without democracy: the menu of manipulation. J. Democr. 13(2), 36–50 (2002)
26. Schedler, A.: The Politics of Uncertainty: Sustaining and Subverting Electoral Authoritarianism. OUP, Oxford (2013)
27. Kneuer, M., Harnisch, S.: Diffusion of e-government and e-participation in Democracies and Autocracies. Global Policy 7(4), 548–556 (2016)
28. Dukalskis, A., Gerschewski, J.: What autocracies say (and what citizens hear): proposing four mechanisms of autocratic legitimation. Contemp. Polit. 23(3), 251–268 (2017)
29. Gerschewski, J.: The three pillars of stability: legitimation, repression, and co-optation in autocratic regimes. Democratization 20(1), 13–38 (2013)
30. Gerschewski, J.: Legitimacy in autocracies: oxymoron or essential feature? Perspect. Polit. 16(3), 652–665 (2018)
31. von Soest, C., Grauvogel, J.: Identity, procedures and performance: how authoritarian regimes legitimize their rule. Contemp. Polit. 23(3), 287–305 (2017)
32. Tannenberg, M., Bernhard, M., Gerschewski, J., Lührmann, A., Von Soest, C.: Regime Legitimation Strategies (RLS) 1900 to 2018. V-Dem Working Paper. 86 (2019)
33. Wahman, M., Teorell, J., Hadenius, A.: Authoritarian regime types revisited: updated data in comparative perspective. Contemp. Polit. 19(1), 19–34 (2013)
34. Bader, M.: Do new voting technologies prevent fraud? Evidence from Russia. In: 2014 Electronic Voting Technology Workshop/Workshop on Trustworthy Elections (EVT/WOTE 2014) (2014)
35. Dutton, W.H., Danziger, J.N.: Computers and Politics: High Technology in American Local Governments. Columbia University Press, New York (1982)

36. Brancati, D.: Democratic authoritarianism: origins and effects. Annu. Rev. Polit. Sci. **17**, 313–326 (2014)
37. Gandhi, J., Lust-Okar, E.: Elections under authoritarianism. Ann. Rev. Polit. Sci. **12**, 403–422 (2009)
38. Ananyev, M., Poyker, M.: Do Dictators Signal Strength with Elections? (2018). SSRN 2712064
39. Gibson, J.P., Krimmer, R., Teague, V., Pomares, J.: A review of e-voting: the past, present and future. Ann. Telecommun. **71**(7–8), 279–286 (2016)
40. Goodman, N., Stokes, L. C.: Reducing the cost of voting: an evaluation of internet voting's effect on turnout. Br. J. Polit. Sci. 1–13 (2018). https://doi.org/10.1017/S0007123417000849
41. Vassil, K., Weber, T.: A bottleneck model of e-voting: why technology fails to boost turnout. New Media Soc. **13**(8), 1336–1354 (2011)
42. Solvak, M., Vassil, K.: Could internet voting halt declining electoral turnout? New evidence that e-voting is habit forming. Policy Internet **10**(1), 4–21 (2018)
43. Germann, M., Serdült, U.: Internet voting and turnout: evidence from Switzerland. Electoral. Stud. **47**, 1–12 (2017)
44. Reuter, O.J: Political Participation and the Survival of Electoral Authoritarian Regimes. http://ojreuter.com/wp-content/uploads/Turnout_Paper.pdf
45. Frantz, E.: Voter turnout and opposition performance in competitive authoritarian elections. Electoral. Stud. **54**, 218–225 (2018)
46. Heiberg, S., Martens, T., Vinkel, P., Willemson, J.: Improving the verifiability of the Estonian Internet Voting scheme. In: Krimmer, R., et al. (eds.) Electronic Voting. International Joint Conference on Electronic Voting, pp. 92–107. Springer, Cham (2017). https://doi.org/10.1007/978-3-319-52240-1_6
47. Springall, D., et al.: Security analysis of the Estonian internet voting system. In: Proceedings of the 2014 ACM SIGSAC Conference on Computer and Communications Security, pp. 703–715 (2014)
48. Bull, C., Gjøsteen, K., Nore, H.: Faults in Norwegian internet voting. In: E-Vote-ID 2018 Proceedings, pp. 166–169 (2018)
49. Ruijgrok, K.: From the web to the streets: internet and protests under authoritarian regimes. Democratization **24**(3), 498–520 (2017)
50. Golosov, G.V.: The regional roots of electoral authoritarianism in Russia. Europe-Asia Stud. **63**(4), 623–639 (2011)
51. Turchenko, M.: Electoral engineering in the russian regions (2003–2017). Europe-Asia Stud. **72**(1), 80–98 (2020)
52. Ross, C.: Regional elections in Russia: instruments of authoritarian legitimacy or instability? Palgrave Commun. **4**(1), 1–9 (2018)
53. Maréchal, N.: Networked authoritarianism and the geopolitics of information: understanding Russian Internet policy. Media Commun. **5**(1), 29–41 (2017)
54. Nocetti, J.: Russia's' dictatorship-of-the-law' approach to internet policy. Internet Policy Rev. **4**, 1–19 (2015)
55. Maerz, S.F.: The electronic face of authoritarianism: e-government as a tool for gaining legitimacy in competitive and non-competitive regimes. Gov. Inf. Q. **33**(4), 727–735 (2016)
56. Chugunov, A.V., Kabanov, Y., Zenchenkova, K.: Russian e-petitions portal: exploring regional variance in use. In: Tambouris, E., et al. (eds.) Electronic Participation. International Conference on Electronic Participation, pp. 109–122. Springer, Cham (2016). https://doi.org/10.1007/978-3-319-45074-2_9

57. Kabanov, Y., Chugunov, A. V.: Electronic "pockets of effectiveness": e-governance and institutional change in St. Petersburg, Russia. In: Janssen, M., et al. (eds.) Electronic Government. International Conference on Electronic Government, pp. 386–398. Springer, Cham (2017). https://doi.org/10.1007/978-3-319-64677-0_32

58. Coppedge, M., et al.: V-Dem [Country–Year/Country–Date] Dataset v10. Varieties of Democracy (V-Dem) Project (2020). https://doi.org/10.23696/vdemds20

Effective Cybersecurity Awareness Training for Election Officials

Carsten Schürmann$^{(\boxtimes)}$, Lisa Hartmann Jensen,
and Rósa María Sigbjörnsdóttir

IT University of Copenhagen, Copenhagen, Denmark
carsten@itu.dk, lisaha85@gmail.com, rosa.sigbj@gmail.com

Abstract. Cybersecurity awareness training has a bad reputation for being ineffective and boring [21]. In this paper, we show the contrary, namely that it is possible to deliver effective cybersecurity awareness training using e-learning. We provide a general methodology on how to create cybersecurity awareness training and evaluate it based on Kirkpatrick's model of evaluation [22]. We have conducted a pilot study of the methodology in context of the European Parliament election 2019.

Keywords: Cybersecurity awareness training · E-learning · Human factors · Attack trees · Election officials

1 Introduction

Organizations rely on their staff for protection of their assets. No matter how many security polices are put in place, security always comes down to how the individual employee behaves. In March 2016, for example, the personal Google mail account of John Podesta, a former White House chief of staff and chair of Hillary Clinton's 2016 U.S. presidential campaign, was compromised in a data breach accomplished via a spear-phishing attack allegedly carried out by foreign Nation State. Allegedly, Podesta's assistant, following the advice of a security technician, complied and followed the instructions contained within the phishing mail [20].

Therefore, to protect an organization from security breaches, it is vital to protect the technical and organizational infrastructure including sensitive data *and* prepare users, employees, consultants, and guests to recognize and defend against cyberattacks. In this paper, we focus on the human factor. Social engineering attacks, where an adversary exploits human traits, such as modesty, altruism, empathy, and diligence of a victim to gain access to restricted resources, steal secrets, or causes other kinds of havoc. It seems natural that the only way to protect an organization against this kind of attack is by sharpening a user's common sense and the ability to recognize, react, and mitigate an imminent attack, and to install a designed behavior in connection with security [15]. Therefore, education is an important part of creating a security culture in organizations [6]. However, cybersecurity awareness training has the reputation of being ineffective [2].

© Springer Nature Switzerland AG 2020
R. Krimmer et al. (Eds.): E-Vote-ID 2020, LNCS 12455, pp. 196–212, 2020.
https://doi.org/10.1007/978-3-030-60347-2_13

Not wanting to accept this conclusion, we set out in this work to demonstrate that cybersecurity awareness training for short-term retention of knowledge, for example for election officials, *can be made* effective. The hypothesis of our work is that one of the reasons for the perceived ineffectiveness is that cybersecurity training is often unspecific, explaining concepts abstractly, such as confidentiality, integrity, and availability that are good to know, but often not directly relevant and difficult to translate into practice. Instead such training must be methodologically relevant, consistent, role-based and continuously adopted to an ever-evolving threat landscape [21].

As a corollary, effective cybersecurity awareness training can only take place, after a rigorous security analysis of the attack surface, the entire security context, and the security background of the target audience, i.e. users and course participants, has been conducted. These findings must inform the learning objectives of the cybersecurity awareness training, not more and not less. Concretely, in this paper, we develop a methodology consisting of a few easy to follow steps to prepare tailored security training for a particular target group to be deployed in a well-defined security context.

We evaluate this methodology empirically, in the context of the European Parliament election 2019, held in Denmark. In close cooperation with Copenhagen municipality, we conducted a security analysis of the voter identification system, deployed in each of the 53 polling stations in Copenhagen, and prepared an e-learning course for 53 election officials, the digital election secretaries, responsible for all technical equipment used in the polling station. The course was organized in modules, each tailored to the security needs of the election officials. All participants had to take an entry exam before the training and a final exam after the training. We could demonstratively measure a significant increase in cybersecurity preparedness for this limited target group election officials.

The cybersecurity awareness training was administered as part of the general training of election officials, who are recruited within the municipality, some having served in this role already several times before. Election officials have to undergo training before each election, and the knowledge gained in the training is usually necessary only for the day of the election. In general, election officials were grateful to have the opportunity to learn about the attack surface. Long-term retention of knowledge was not measured. To our knowledge this is the first systematic study of e-learning with the short-term retention of cybersecurity knowledge.

The literature [21] defines three levels of security awareness: perception, comprehension, and projection. Perception is to be aware of that there are potential security risks. Comprehension is to understand and assess the dangers of security risks. Projection is to be able to anticipate future situations and how to act on potential security attacks. Based on our pilot training and the evaluative statistical analyses we conclude that cybersecurity awareness training for short-term retention delivered on all three levels of security awareness.

This paper is structured as follows. In Sect. 2, we discuss human factors in cyber security. In Sect. 3, we then design a methodology for designing cybersecurity awareness training to be delivered through e-learning. Next, we present a pilot study for the European Parliament election 2019 and an evaluation in Sect. 4 before we conclude and assess results in Sect. 5.

2   The Human Factor

The attack surface of any system includes technical as well as human components. No system is stronger than its weakest component [5], and arguably, human performance is recognized as a critical part of securing critical infrastructure [5]. Depending on the adversary's objective, social engineering will always be considered as one way to achieve the goal: As opposed to technical cyberattacks that exploit vulnerabilities and always leave traces in log files or other media, social engineering is considered a viable alternative which allows adversaries to break a perimeter and operate somewhat undetected. In general, it is also more difficult to attribute a social engineering attack to an adversary. Therefore, measures to prevent or decrease the negative impacts of cybersecurity breaches must include all processes, policies and actors involved [7]. Technology alone cannot create a secure environment, since human factors are an integral part of any system, for example, during configuration, operation, or use. According to 2020 Verizon Data Breach Report social attacks are used in 22% of all cases recorded. These attacks are almost evenly split into phishing and pretexting attacks [4].

There are many factors that influence the security behavior of users i.e. the user's respective rank in an organization, their respective personal values, and their common sense regarding security [15]. Users are often not aware or do not consider the vulnerabilities in an organization, they make mistakes or are tricked into giving away sensitive information [1]. Therefore, common sense regarding security in an organization must be taught [15] and training in cybersecurity awareness is an important part of creating a security culture [1].

However, there seems to be a problem with existing cybersecurity awareness training as it does not change behavior as expected [2]. There are several reasons that this is the case. Firstly, cybersecurity awareness training is often designed as too general without a clear target group in mind, leading to users not finding it relevant. Secondly, incorrect assumptions about the targeted users and their skills and motivation tend to make cybersecurity awareness training too general.

3   Training Design Methodology

Next, we describe a methodology for how to create cybersecurity awareness training that avoids the above mentioned factors by tailoring training to a well defined target group and focusing the training content on what the target group need to know and nothing else. The methodology consists of five steps, which are summarized in Fig. 1.

1. Target group
   − Define the target group, target setting, tasks, and responsibilities
2. Risk assessment
   − Define the adversarial environment
   − Define assets, including physical and logical, and processes
3. Threat modeling and risk analysis
   − Model the entire socio-technical system using CORAS/attack trees
   − Derive and prioritize potential attacks
   − Derive the attack surface and tailor it for the target group.
4. Training materials
   − Base training on knowledge gained from (1.-3.)
   − Create an e-learning platform
   − Consider using videos, audio, games as part of the training
5. Evaluate training

Fig. 1. Training design methodology

3.1 Target Group

The first step of creating good cybersecurity awareness training is to identify and characterize the target group, the target setting, and the target group's tasks and responsibilities in this setting. This can be achieved by ethnographic studies, long-time observation of work practices, and study of available procedures and documents. Usually, it is not sufficient to base this analysis only on printed materials, as common work practices often deviate from the described processes. A target group must be homogeneous, meaning all members should be assigned the same tasks and the same responsibilities. Heterogeneous target groups are not considered in this paper.

3.2 Risk Assessment

The next step is to identify assets and processes that are at risk, and define the security policies that should be enforced [3]. A good starting point for the risk assessment is to explore notions such as confidentiality, integrity, and availability, and refine them on demand. It is absolutely crucial that the target group identifies with this assessment. The cybersecurity training must be perceived as relevant by the target group for it to be effective.

A part of the risk assessment is the attack surface of the infrastructure, for which cybersecurity assessment training is to be offered. This presupposes a clear picture of the adversary's capacity and the adversary's objective. The attack surface includes all aspect of the infrastructure to be protected, including technology, networked computing equipment, air-gapped equipment, access control, cryptographic key distributions, physical access etc.

With the risk assessment in place, the next step is then to identify the weak points in the infrastructure that an adversary could exploit and to define the role of the human to detect attacks and protect assets and processes. These insights and this knowledge form the basis of understanding of the infrastructure and feeds into the design process of the training materials, of which attacks participants should learn to spot, and which procedures they should learn follow to neutralize threats effectively.

3.3 Threat Modeling and Risk Analysis

In our experience, modern threat modeling tools, such as CORAS [16], attack trees [17] or even attack-defense trees [14] are useful tools to explore the threat model of any socio-technical system in a systematic and complete way. The CORAS method is a defensive risk analysis approach where the Unified Modeling Language (UML-diagrams) is used to model the target of the analysis. Unwanted behaviors are drawn as threat scenarios. The CORAS method comes with tool support, in particular, there exists a tool that supports drawing and analyzing diagrams. Alternative ways of conducting security analyses and modeling threats are described in this survey article [11]. In this paper, however, we focus on attack trees as a modeling tool.

An attack tree is a mathematical tree-like structure that organizes threats and attacks against a system. The root of the tree comprises the goal for the adversary, and the leaf nodes denote the different actions an adversary can execute to achieve this goal. Each node in a tree can be seen as a subgoal. The disjunctive "OR"-node represents alternatives, i.e. if *one* of the subtrees is successful then so is the subgoal. In contrast, the a subgoal rooted in a conjunctive "AND"-node is successful if an only if *all* subtrees are successful. There are also other variants of attack trees, that could in theory be considered, for example those supporting sequential conjunctions. The methodology presented here applies as well. The visual representations of "OR"-nodes, "AND"-nodes and leaf-nodes are depicted in Fig. 2.

Fig. 2. Explanation of nodes in attack tree

Attack trees are known for their ability to express socio-technical systems and model human factors. We will be using them as well in our pilot study for securing polling stations during the European Parliament election 2019 that we describe in the Sect. 4.

3.4 Training Materials

Next, we identify the critical elements of the analysis and translate the attack tree into suitable training materials. We proceed in four steps, tagging, normalizing, prioritizing, and finalizing.

Tagging: When normalizing an attack tree, all information about the structure of the inner nodes, i.e. OR and AND nodes is lost. In practice, however, it is useful, to tag such inner nodes with keywords that help structure the content of the training materials, and collect them during the normalization procedure. Possible tags include, for example, social engineering attacks, man in the middle attacks, attacks against air-gapping, SQL-injection attacks, cross-site scripting attacks, buffer overflow attacks, and so on. An example of tagging can be seen in Fig. 3.

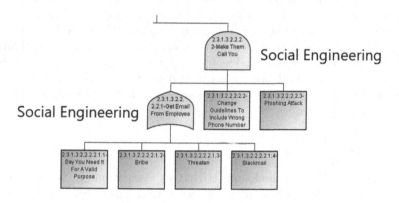

Fig. 3. Example of tagging sub-trees

Normalizing: Hereafter, the attack tree is normalized as to create a list of attack-chains in plain text. Attack-chains only include leaf nodes. Correspondingly the normalization procedure is augmented, to derive an additional tag-chain, of all of the tags that were encountered while constructing the attack chain. Below A and T are normalized attack-chain/tag-chain pair displaying the fragments derived from the attack tree depicted in Fig. 3:

$A = \{ \ldots$
    Say You Need It For A Valid Purpose,
    Change Guidelines To Include Wrong Phone Number,
    Phishing Attack
    $\ldots \}$
$T = \ldots,$ Social Engineering, $\ldots$

The above step should result in a number of attack/tag-chains pairs. Duplicate attack chains should be removed while their tag-chains should be merged.

Prioritizing: Next, we identify precisely the topics that should be covered in the training materials. We therefore correlate the attack-chains with the tasks the target group is in charge of to determine what parts of the attack-chain, if not all, need to be included. It is critical for the training to be effective to educate the target group exactly in the topics they need to know - nothing more and nothing less. We use the tag chains as a guide to structure and organize the material.

Finalizing: In this last step, we create new or update existing training materials to create a consistent product. Recall that the success of effective training is to make sure the target group attains three levels of awareness of security risks, namely perception, comprehension and projection [21]. We propose to use e-learning as platform for the training, since interactive and adaptable material i.e. videos, also called hyper media-based material, can lead to effective cybersecurity training [21] and motivation for learning through such a platform tends to be high. Prior research has shown that video-based training is preferred over other methods and yields better results [1, 18]. The length of the video is important to get the participants engaged, and a study shows that videos that are 0–3 minutes have the highest engagement [9]. The training videos developed should train the target group to observe, identify, react, and defend against the individual steps laid out in the attack chains. Training material can be rearranged and reused for other target groups.

3.5   Evaluating E-learning

The final step of our methodology is that of evaluation. It is good practice to document the effects of security awareness training, to analyze the training objectively, and to measure the efficiency and effectiveness of it. Evaluation can help create a common understanding about the human factor defense capabilities, which areas of understanding among the target group are sufficient, and identify weaknesses that need to be strengthened [8].

Choosing an evaluation model to evaluate e-learning is dependent on the scale and the time frame of the e-learning. The state of the art is described in an article by Tripathi et al. [23] where four different evaluation models are described in depth. We found that more models could be used in our case, and many of the models don't differ that much when measuring short-term effects, as we do. If we had to measure long term, we would have to go back and look at the evaluation models again. The two best models for our purpose are CIRO or Kirkpatrick's model of evaluation.

The CIRO model does not take the behavior of the learners into account and is, therefore, thought to be better suited for management focused training rather than for people working on lower levels of organizations [23,24], therefore we chose to use Kirkpatrick's model of evaluation.

Kirkpatrick's model of evaluation was introduced in 1959. The model evaluates outcomes of training programs at four levels: reaction, learning, behavior and results. *Reaction* addresses how the participant felt and reacted to the training experience. *Learning* measures to which extent knowledge has increased and how intellectual capability has changed from before the training. *Behavior* measures how the participant has changed behavior and applied the learning. *Results* addresses how the improved performance of the participant affect organizations [13].

Kirkpatrick's model is applied after training. The model is popular and still widely used among organizations. The main strength of the model is the focus on behavioral outcomes of the participants [13, 23].

Quizzes can be used to measure learning in Kirkpatrick's model. A quiz can be thought of as a survey, i.e. a quantitative method to collect data. The quiz, which must be taken both before and after training, consists of closed-ended questions. Participants can choose from a set of answers, where either one or more are correct. Participants can answer closed-ended questions fast and they can get instant feedback when they have taken the quiz. Another reason for using this type of question is that it is easy to analyze [19]. The quiz must be constructed in such a way that it measures the three levels of security awareness.

A survey can also be used to measure reaction in Kirkpatrick's model. The survey to measure this level consists of questions answered by a likert-scale and open questions. The likert-scale questions should give an indication of how relevant the participants find the e-learning. The open questions can help to discover unforeseen findings, and are essential to understand how the target group perceive the training [19].

4   Pilot Study: Digital Election Secretaries in the Election Context

In connection with the European Parliament election conducted in Denmark on 26th May, 2019, a group of election officials employed by Copenhagen municipality, called digital election secretaries, partook in cybersecurity awareness training. The staff at each polling station includes one *digital election secretary*, who is responsible for all computer equipment that is used in a polling station, that is, a digital voter identification system and a digital results transmission system. In Denmark, ballots are not interpreted and stored digitally, only the result of precinct-level tabulation is. The scope of our pilot was limited to cybersecurity awareness training with respect to the digital voter identification system. It was the first time that election officials had received any role-based cybersecurity training to recognize and act on attacks happening at the polling stations. The objective of our pilot study was to measure the improvement of their cybersecurity awareness.

4.1   Target Group

Copenhagen municipality has 53 digital election secretaries, one for each polling station. The main responsibilities of this group is to secure the equipment at the polling station and the electoral register including all the data in the above mentioned register. The digital election secretaries are recruited within the workers of the municipality and differ in age and background. Some have served in the role of digital election secretary several times before. Despite the demographic differences, the group is highly homogeneous in the tasks they perform on election day. They will spend election day in similar environments, the different polling stations, and work with the same kind of election technologies, including the electoral register.

4.2   Risk Assessment

We conducted a detailed risk assessment of the processes connected with the digital election secretaries on election day, and identified a set of potential objectives of a hypothetical adversary. We consider confidentiality, integrity, and availability in turn.

Confidentiality: We consider an attacker who aims to get unauthorized access to information. If published by the attacker, it would weaken the trust in the security of the election and violate this security goal. It is the digital election secretaries' responsibility to protect voters' data at the polling stations and will, therefore, be considered in our cybersecurity awareness training.

Integrity: We consider an attacker who could try to violate election integrity by voting multiple times with the goal to change the election result in his or her favor. This is very difficult achieve given the organization of a Danish national election as several checks and balances were put in place for this not to happen. For example, every voter receives a voting card in the mail which they will have to bring to the polling station. All voting cards will be kept until the end of voting day and then counted to validate the number of votes cast. Once a voter is identified in the polling station, the physical poll book or in the electoral register will be updated, the former only if the electoral register fails. However, it is the digital election secretary's responsibility to ensure that no one voted more than once, and will hence be considered in our cybersecurity awareness training.

Availability: The attacker's objective could be to weaken public confidence in the voting process, by trying to make headlines in the press or on social media. To succeed, the attacker would have to break one or more security goals, for example, by rendering the electoral register at a polling station unavailable/unusable. To protect this asset, again, lies within the responsibilities of the digital election secretary and will hence be considered in our cybersecurity awareness training.

4.3   Threat Modeling

Based on the analysis in the previous section, we focus on all security goals, in particular an attacker's intent to weaken public confidence. We exclude insider attacks from our threat model. To succeed, the attacker would have to break one or more security goals, and it does not matter which one(s). With this objective

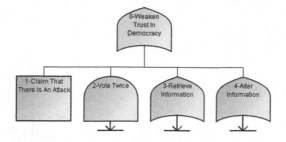

Fig. 4. Root and first level of the attack tree (Color figure online)

in mind, we develop an attack tree of the election system from the vantage point of a digital election secretary.

Together with election experts from Copenhagen municipality, we identified 88 possible attack scenarios leaving us with an attack tree too large to include in this paper. The full attack tree can be found on the project's homepage[1]. Figure 4 depicts the top two levels of the attack tree. The leftmost singleton subtree (shaded in grey) states that a possible attack would be an attacker crying wolf and claiming that the election is under attack. Clearly, the digital election secretaries cannot stop people from lying, but still, such circumstances may arise, and the digital election secretary would need to know how to react. Hence, this must be a part of the cybersecurity awareness training.

The other three subtrees, describe ways on how an attacker could conceivable vote twice, gain access to privileged information, or alter the information stored in the electoral register. In the interest of space, we comment only the second subtree that is depicted in Fig. 5. In our estimation, this attack is highly hypothetical and very difficult to execute. The nodes of the subtree are largely self-explanatory, except perhaps the unit that is called PCA, which refers to the laptop named "A" that contains the binding version of the digital electoral roll. In general, the polling place consists of several (through wired Ethernet) networked laptops. This network is not connected to other networks including the Internet during operation, but has been during configuration.

4.4   Training Materials

In our pilot study, we considered the entire attack tree[1], tagged the inner nodes, normalized to obtain attack/tag-chain pairs, prioritized them, and used this knowledge as input for the design of training materials. The training materials, which were created throughout a two months period, consist of an e-learning website with several modules and videos. The course page is online an can be accessed under https://valgsikkerhed.dk.[2] All 53 digital election secretaries were

---

[1] See https://www.demtech.dk/training/.

[2] The website is online, and anyone interested can make an account and access the teaching materials. Note, that the website is only in Danish.

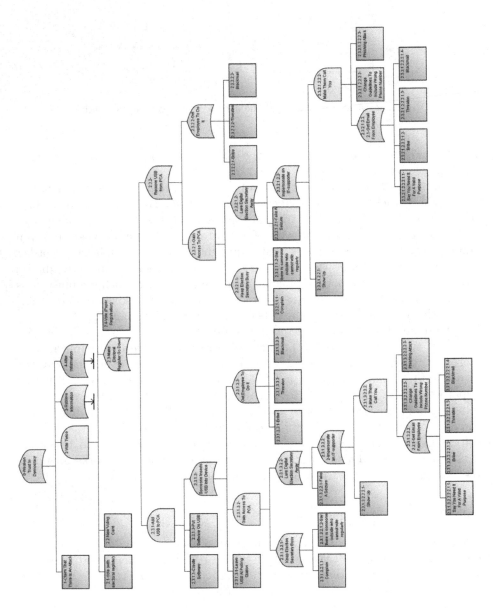

Fig. 5. Subtree 2: vote twice

invited to complete the e-learning course at their own pace and in their own time. Participating in the training was not mandatory.

All potential attacks are based on social engineering techniques aiming to coerce employees to retrieve desired confidential information or execute an attack on behalf of the adversary. Some potential attacks include also elements of man-in-the-middle attacks. Our training material therefore includes modules aimed to explain both, social engineering and man-in-the-middle attacks. The video on man-in-the-middle discusses devices that should not be present at polling stations, and how to react if they are spotted. The social-engineering videos focus on attacks that could be conducted before election day or at polling stations, i.e. exploiting common human traits resulting in that employees give access to confidential information to people with authority, follow instructions in phishing e-mails or gain access to any of the networked PCs in particular PCA, by creating a distraction. The training materials even include guidelines on how to calm worried voters in the case of an imminent cyberattack.

4.5   Evaluating E-learning

Learning Outcome. To evaluate if the digital election secretaries had gained cybersecurity awareness, they were tested both before and after the training with the same questionnaire.

The questionnaire was designed in such a way that each level of awareness was covered by more than one question. It is designed with reaction and learning levels from Kirkpatrick's model in mind. Since we are not measuring long term effects, there is no reason to evaluate the participants changed behavior nor how their changed behavior affect the organizations they work for.

77.4% of the target group signed up to the platform but only 71.7% completed the e-learning training. That means that 92% of those who started the e-learning finished it. The distribution of the grades can be seen in Fig. 6.

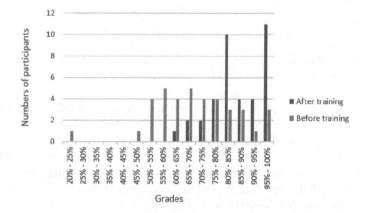

Fig. 6. Distribution of the grades before and after training.

A paired t-test can be used to check if the learning is effective by comparing before and after observations. This is done to show that there is statistical evidence that the difference of the means between the paired samples is significantly different from zero [12].

In order to do a paired t-test on this small data set, one need to make sure that the data is normally distributed. This was tested with a Q-Q Plot, that can be seen in Fig. 7. It shows that the data is, indeed, normally distributed.

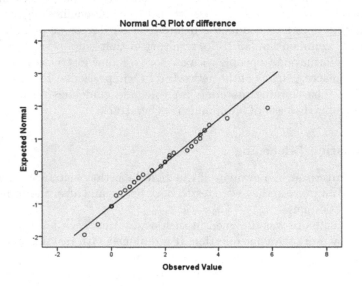

Fig. 7. Q-Q plot of data.

The t-test is run with the following hypotheses:

$$H_0 : \mu_d = 0 \tag{1}$$

$$H_1 : \mu_d \neq 0 \tag{2}$$

In other words, H_0 assumes that the security awareness training has no effect on the mean and the alternative hypothesis, H_1 assumes that there is a difference.

The grades before and after were used to run the paired t-test. Since the participants can also score less than before we do a two-tailed test.

SPSS is a widely used statics application created by IBM [10] and was used to run the paired t-test. The test was run with $\alpha = 0.05$. The result of the test is shown in Fig. 8. As can be seen in the figure the digital election secretaries score, on average 1.6 points higher in the latter quiz. It also shows that the Sig. (2-tailed), also called the p-value, is much smaller than α. This means that we can reject the null-hypothesis.

Paired Samples Test

		Mean	Std. Deviation	Std. Error Mean	95% Confidence Interval of the Difference Lower	Upper	t	df	Sig. (2-tailed)
	Paired Differences								
Pair 1	before - after	-1.59789	1.50898	.24479	-2.09388	-1.10191	-6.528	37	.0000001217

Fig. 8. Paired t-test results

To evaluate the awareness layers, as mentioned in [21], they are translated to this specific context. Perception is getting the digital election secretaries recognizing and understanding potential security risks in an election. Comprehension is to teach them to take in information from multiple sources, interpret them and be able to pass on information that can help others actors in the election. Projection is for them to be able to prevent future attacks.

The results in Table 1 shows that all the three levels of successful security awareness training was reached for the election officials that participated in the e-learning training.

Table 1. Table of scores for the three levels of security awareness

Awareness level	Before	After	t(37)	p
Perception	M = 1.45, SD = 0.57	M = 1.64, SD = 0.49	−2.113	0.041
Comprehension	M = 2.24, SD = 0.75	M = 2.237, SD = 0.41	−4.112	0.00209
Projection	M = 3.3, SD = 0.89	M = 4.15, SD = 0.59	−5.929	0.0000007835

An analysis on the time spent on the quizzes, shows that the participants spend on average 4 min less on the latter quiz. However, we can not draw any conclusion by that in itself as we decided to give the participant the freedom to do the training at their own pace. Hence we have not measured the individual questions in the quizzes and, therefore, do not know how which questions they spend less time on in the latter quiz. We leave this to future work.

Participant Evaluation. 52.6% gave feedback on their experience of the e-learning. 85% said that they felt they had either gained new knowledge or refreshed knowledge they already had. 85% also said that they thought the content of the e-learning was good and relevant for their duties as digital election secretaries.

5   Conclusion

This paper provides a methodology for designing and delivering cybersecurity awareness training for short-term retention. The methodology was tested on 53 digital election secretaries who were deployed to 53 polling stations in Copenhagen municipality during the European Parliament election in 2019. We have evaluated the training using Kirkpatrick's model of evaluation found it to be effective. We are certain that our methodology carries over directly to the other 97 Danish municipalities, as their elections are organized in a manner similar to those in Copenhagen. We also believe that it is applicable beyond Denmark, as other European countries use digital voter identification and results transmission systems. The training material must be updated and adjusted to the respective target audiences and the specific technologies in use in a particular location.

Through understanding of the target group, the adversarial environment and the attack surface it was possible to create training materials tailored toward the job of the digital election secretaries. The training was delivered through a custom-made e-learning platform, containing short videos to deliver individual modules derived from potential attacks identified using attack trees. After training, we demonstrated that the target group reached all levels of successful security awareness: perception, comprehension and projection. In addition, a training evaluation showed that (1) the digital election secretaries perceived the training to be both good and relevant for their work on election day and (2) they also felt that they gained or at least refreshed their cyber security knowledge.

In future work, we would like to collect more evidence that this is a sustainable methodology to design and conduct cybersecurity awareness training. Firstly, we would like to compare a group that has been trained with a group that has not been trained to identify the difference, if any. Secondly, it would be interesting to analyze time spent on each task and correlate with retention of the concepts associated with each task. Hence do a more granular evaluation of the cyber security awareness training. Thirdly, we would like to conduct similar awareness training with the same group of digital election security at future elections to identify trends in the evaluation data. Fourthly, we would like to broaden the pilot to the whole of Denmark to examine if we can reproduce our results. Lastly, we believe that it would be interesting to apply the same methodology to elections in other countries and/or broaden cybersecurity awareness training beyond the elections to other sectors as well to study the robustness of the methodology.

Acknowledgments. We would like to thank the employees Copenhagen municipality's election office, the Ministry of Social and Internal Affairs, and KL, the association and interest organization of the 98 Danish municipalities.

References

1. Abawajy, J.: User preference of cyber security awareness delivery methods. Behav. Inf. Tech. **33**(3), 237–248 (2014)
2. Bada, M., Sasse, A.M., Nurse, J.R.: Cyber security awareness campaigns: Why do they fail to change behaviour? arXiv preprint arXiv:1901.02672 (2019)
3. Basin, D., Schaller, P., Schläpfer, M.: Applied Information Security: A Hands-on Approach. Springer, Heidelberg (2011). https://doi.org/10.1007/978-3-642-24474-2
4. Bassett, G., Hylender, C.D., Langlois, P., Pinto, A., Widup, S.: 2020 verizon data breach report (2020)
5. Boyce, M.W., Duma, K.M., Hettinger, L.J., Malone, T.B., Wilson, D.P., Lockett-Reynolds, J.: Human performance in cybersecurity: a research agenda. In: Proceedings of the Human Factors and Ergonomics Society Annual Meeting, vol. 55, pp. 1115–1119 (2011)
6. Dhillon, G.: What to do before and after a cybersecurity breach? American University, Washington, DC, Kogod Cybersecurity Governance Center (2015)
7. Dutton, W.H.: Fostering a cybersecurity mindset. Internet Policy Rev. **6**(1), 110–123 (2017)
8. Eminağaoğlu, M., Uçar, E., Eren, Ş.: The positive outcomes of information security awareness training in companies-a case study. Inf. Secur. Tech. Rep. **14**(4), 223–229 (2009)
9. Guo, P.J., Kim, J., Rubin, R.: How video production affects student engagement: an empirical study of mooc videos. In: Proceedings of the First ACM Conference on Learning@ Scale Conference, pp. 41–50. ACM (2014)
10. Hinton, P.R., McMurray, I., Brownlow, C.: SPSS Explained. Routledge, London (2014)
11. Hussain, S., Kamal, A., Ahmad, S., Rasool, G., Iqbal, S.: Threat modelling methodologies: a survey. Sci. Int. (Lahore) **26**(4), 1607–1609 (2014)
12. Kent State University: SPSS tutorials: Paired samples T test (2019). https://libguides.library.kent.edu/spss/pairedsamplesttest
13. Kirkpatrick, D., Kirkpatrick, J.: Evaluating Training Programs: The Four Levels. Berrett-Koehler Publishers, San Francisco (2006)
14. Kordy, B., Mauw, S., Radomirović, S., Schweitzer, P.: Foundations of attack-defense trees. In: Degano, P., Etalle, S., Guttman, J. (eds.) FAST 2010. LNCS, vol. 6561, pp. 80–95. Springer, Heidelberg (2011). https://doi.org/10.1007/978-3-642-19751-2_6
15. Leach, J.: Improving user security behaviour. Comput. Secur. **22**(8), 685–692 (2003)
16. Lund, M.S., Solhaug, B., Stlen, K.: Model-Driven Risk Analysis: The CORAS Approach. Springer, Heidelberg (2010). https://doi.org/10.1007/978-3-642-12323-8
17. Mauw, S., Oostdijk, M.: Foundations of attack trees. In: Won, D.H., Kim, S. (eds.) ICISC 2005. LNCS, vol. 3935, pp. 186–198. Springer, Heidelberg (2006). https://doi.org/10.1007/11734727_17
18. Merkt, M., Weigand, S., Heier, A., Schwan, S.: Learning with videos vs. learning with print: the role of interactive features. Learn. Instr. **21**(6), 687–704 (2011)
19. Neuman, W.L., Robson, K.: Basics of social research: qualitative and quantitative approaches. Power **48**, 48 (2007)
20. Sciutto, J.: How one typo helped let Russian hackers. In: CNN, 27 June 2017

21. Shaw, R.S., Chen, C.C., Harris, A.L., Huang, H.J.: The impact of information richness on information security awareness training effectiveness. Comput. Educ. **52**(1), 92–100 (2009)
22. Topno, H.: Evaluation of training and development: an analysis of various models. J. Bus. Manage. **5**(2), 16–22 (2012)
23. Tripathi, J., Bansal, A.: A literature review on various models for evaluating training programs. IOSR J. Bus. Manage. **19**(11), 1 (2017)
24. Warr, P., Bird, M., Rackham, N.: Evaluation of management training: a practical framework, with cases, for evaluating training needs and results. Gower Press, London (1970)

Does Vote Verification Work: Usage and Impact of Confidence Building Technology in Internet Voting

Mihkel Solvak$^{(\boxtimes)}$ (iD)

Johan Skytte Institute of Political Studies, University of Tartu, Ülikooli 18,
51003 Tartu, Estonia
mihkel.solvak@ut.ee

Abstract. The paper examines cast-as-intended verification usage in Estonia by looking at who verifies votes, how they do it and what is the effect on perceptions of election integrity. Using anonymized log and survey data a typical use case of verification is established - younger, Linux using male voting late at night - which suggest verification is used by more cyber risk aware users. Vote verifiers, when re-voting, are also more likely to change the voting environment compared to those re-voters who do not verify their vote, indicating verification is not simply used to check one's own mistakes in candidate selection. The effects of verifying on confidence in the vote being correctly taken into account are substantial - vote verifiers show a stronger belief in the election integrity. Overall, verification technology seems to be building confidence in the system and being used by the more risk aware voting population.

Keywords: Internet voting · Cast-as-intended verification · Voter confidence

1 Introduction

Remote Internet voting gives voters a convenient location independent way of casting the vote. Though still not widely used in national elections, various theoretical and practical aspects of it have been examined over the years by computer science, behavioral and legal scholars, see for example [1–5]. One particularly interesting aspect of this is *individual vote verification*. Definitions of what is and what is not a verifiable voting system are presented below, but it suffices to say that the need for vote verification has seen a resurgence with Internet voting. There is more agreement on what constitutes individual verification. It should allow individual voters to verify that their vote was indeed *cast as intended* - the voting application correctly recorded the voters will - as well as *recorded as cast* - the vote was accepted into the virtual ballot box - or even *tabulated as recorded* - the vote was correctly tabulated. Though this is a disputable feature as it gives the voter final proof of their vote being counted, which compromises vote secrecy and might lead to electoral integrity problems.

© Springer Nature Switzerland AG 2020
R. Krimmer et al. (Eds.): E-Vote-ID 2020, LNCS 12455, pp. 213–228, 2020.
https://doi.org/10.1007/978-3-030-60347-2_14

Research on verification from the end user point of view has been so far more theoretical, as not many real-life applications - i.e. actual use cases in elections - are available. This paper addresses that gap by using observational data on verification from Estonia to examine if the findings from the literature on verification being hard to comprehend by the average voter and being used for non-intended purposes do hold in an actual election settings as well.

Estonia introduced internet voting in 2005 and after a proof-of-concept vote manipulating malware demonstration in 2011 also introduced individual vote verification in 2013 which allows voters to check if the vote was cast as intended and recorded as cast. The ability of verify should in theory add to the voter's confidence that a technology intensive and hard to understand voting system is indeed performing as foreseen, is free from malicious manipulation and is overall trustworthy. All this of course presumes that the technology is actually used, used by those for whom the above mentioned features are important and that it truly functions as a trust building technology in an environment of increased cyber threats against the privacy and secrecy of the individual vote.

This research examines in detail the actual usage patterns of Internet vote verification and its effect on/or correlation with beliefs in the integrity of Internet voting itself. It will do so by examining two data sources, anonymized Internet voting logs from the 2019 Estonian parliamentary elections and survey data on Internet voting from the period between 2013–2019. The paper will proceed as follows, first it discusses potential explanations of usage and formulates hypotheses based on theses followed by an explanation of the data and design, and finally examines the empirical evidence from log and survey data on usage and attitudes to determine if the hypotheses hold and concluded by a discussion.

2   Theory

What defines if elections are end-to-end verifiable has not been fully agreed on and different authors list different features of such systems, one can however be certain that individual verification of cast as intended and recorded as cast is a subset of any such definition [6]. How exactly these features are implement might differ and cast-as-intended verification proposals are plentiful [7–11,13]. The common feature is that the voter should be in a position to verify that the voting application has correctly recorded his or her will in the form of the candidate/party number or name for whom she wanted to vote for and that this vote has been also recorded as cast, meaning correctly placed into the ballot box. Given this it is surprising that verification usage or willingness to use it tends to be rather low in reality. This suggests risk awareness and the desire to protect one's vote against it can be presumed to be rather low. Kulyk et al. propose to explain low verification usage with a "lack of awareness, lack of concern, lack of self-efficacy, lack of compulsion and lack of perseverance" [14] when faced with security and privacy risks of internet voting. Lets dub it the "five-lacks" explanation. They can be divided into three larger categories, one being risk perceptions, the second usability of the technology and third security practices. Lack of awareness and concern refer to inability to imagine potential risks or a perception that theses "won't affect me". Lack of self-efficacy suggests a inability to use verification either due to being unable to grasp its function or overly complex design for the average voter. Finally, lack of compulsion and perseverance explain low usage through verification being an optional feature in voting as well as voters not adopting their other online risk mitigating practices when it comes to electronic voting.

The "five lacks" are in line with what has been observed in studies on voter perceptions of security in the voting context. Olembo et al. [15] for example find that the most prevalent mental model used when faced with verification system is, first either extending the trust they usually hold towards paper voting also to the electronic voting system, which is mistaken as the risks differ considerably in their nature (deemed the *trusting* mental model) or second, simply not being able to imagine how the integrity of the voting process could be compromised in the first place and how verification could be used to counter that (deemed the *no knowledge* mental model). In sum, taking the reverse of explanations why verification usage tends to be low points to an expectation that verification user should be a clear non-random subgroup of voters with higher risk awareness. Therefore one can posit a hypothesis on likely users:

H1: Vote verifiers have a distinct profile with traits typical for more risk aware users

Usability studies of cast-as-intended verification solutions point towards other expectations when turning from user profiles to actual verification practices. Design of the verification procedure could for example feed into the voter's perception that verification guards foremost against his/her own mistake in picking the correct candidate rather than actual malevolent actions by a third party [14,16]. This leads to possible interesting expectation in the Estonian situation. To mitigate voter coercion threats Internet voters can re-vote, multiple times if needed, so as to leave the potential coercer unable to ensure the coerced vote will stand. This should particularly help against so called "over-the-shoulder coercion" [12] i.e. when the immediate voting environment is somehow insecure or the vote privacy is under threat. The voter can simply change the environment and re-vote later on. However, if verification is simply used to check against mistakes made by the voter in picking a correct candidate as suggested above, and not to ensure against malicious vote manipulation, then upon noticing the mistake in candidate selection the voter would likely re-vote again immediately without any change in the environment. This leads to a hypothesis on verification practice:

H2: Vote verification correlates with re-voting in the same environment

An alternative to this hypothesis is of course the intended use case of verification, i.e. verifying to make sure that the correct vote arrived at the authorities and security risks have not materialised. The corresponding hypothesis reads the following:

H3: Verification is more likely when voting environment is not private and/or deemed less secure

This hypothesis rests on the conditions under which the vote is given, if it is more open to risks or presumed to be so by the voter, then verification should give an additional guarantee that the risks did not come true. While we do not know the outcome of the verification, it could be additionally posited that voting under such conditions should lead more likely to re-voting as well.

The potential effects of verification on voter perceptions should be intuitive. Because of the particular logic of the *cast-as-intended* and *recorded-as-cast* verification logic we can further narrow down what part of the election process integrity should be solidified in the eyes of the voters - namely the belief that their vote was indeed correctly taken into account by the voting system. Even though this might already seem as part of the *tabulated as recorded* verification, which many verification features in fact do not allow to check, I doubt that the average voter makes this minute distinction. It is more likely that he presumes the cast-as-intended verification to show that the vote indeed is now safely cast and will be correctly taken into account. This leads to the fourth and final hypothesis:

H4: Vote verifiers are more likely to believe that their vote was correctly taken into account

It is clear that the belief in election integrity is influenced by a multitude of factors. Survey research has shown that voter perceptions are influenced by personal experiences on election day [17], voting for election losers [18], party affiliation [19] or even the propensity in general to believe in conspiracies [20]. The confidence level in electoral fairness also shows significant variation cross-nationally, which suggest cultural and institutional influences play a role [21]. Due to scope and space limitations I will however not attempt a comprehensive explanation of perceived electoral integrity but focus currently only in identifying if verification shows a tangible effect on belief in integrity while keeping other things constant. Next the data and design of the study are examined in more detail.

3   Data and Design

The hypotheses are examined using two different dataset. First the verification patterns and the typical verifier profile are examined through the analysis of anonymized Internet voting logs from the 2019 parliamentary election. This dataset holds information on 247 232 Internet vote outer envelopes and contains the voter age, gender, identification type (ID smart card, Mobile ID or Digi ID), operating system of the computer used for voting, anonymized public IP and timestamps on when the vote was cast and if it was verified. Examining the verifier's profile will allow to evaluate hypothesis 1.

Hypothesis 2 and 3 will also be examined with log data. For hypothesis 2 the voting environment is defined through the anonymized IP, operating system and ID type of the voter. A change of any of these between two votes by the same voter would indicate some change in the immediate voting environment. Though these are mere proxies they do allow to see if something changed between casting the second vote. Changing locations will mean the IP has changed, a changed operating system will mean another computer was chosen to vote again and a change in eID type could in theory reflect a reaction to a vote manipulating coercer who has access to or control of the voter's credentials. In the extreme this could mean a vote could be cast in the voters name [11]. In the Estonian case this would mean having access to the signing key stored inside the eID tool (smart card or Mobile-ID) [12]. A change in ID type would hence indicate that the voter has some issue with one type of ID and feels the need to vote again using another identification tool. If verification is however simply used to check one's own mistakes in candidate selection then none of the above described should be taking place and upon seeing the mistake the voter would simply re-vote after verifying the first vote without making any changes to the environment.

For hypothesis 3 I'll examine if verification is more frequent when the vote is cast using an IP that is shared meaning multiple votes are cast from a internet network that has the same public IP, indicating the same internet connection and most likely a shared office or home with another voter. In addition I'll examine if verification is more likely when the vote is given outside of Estonia as voting from abroad could lead to a additional need to reassure the voter that the vote indeed has successfully "travelled" across border or due to voting from a hotel or other internet connection they have not full confidence in compared to home networks.

Finally, hypothesis 4 is examined with survey data from the Estonian Internet voting survey 2005–2019, only data from the period 2013 2019 is included in this study as this covers the time when verification was possible. Therefore six post-election cross sectional surveys with questions on voting, usage of verification, attitudes and sociodemographics are utilized. The surveys included a question of election integrity, asked as: "How confident are you that your vote was counted as intended in the elections?". With a 4 category Likert scale from very confident to not at all confident. The same questions is asked about the confidence that votes by others were counted as intended. These questions will allow to examine if the vote verifiers show higher confidence levels in the elections as they have used the cast-as-intended and recorded-as-cast features of verification. The sample size in all surveys is roughly 1000 respondents and the full database consists of approximately 6000 survey interviews.

4   Results

4.1   Who Verifies the Vote

Verification usage rates are displayed in Table 1. It is clear that verification is not used widely and there is no discernible increase in usage over the years. The share fluctuates between 3 to 5% out of all cast Internet votes. For the 2019 parliamentary election this translates into roughly 13 000 verified votes.

Figure 1 shows verification frequency according to age and gender, extracted from the logs. We see that a comparatively larger share of ivotes are verified

Table 1. Internet vote verification percent (2013–2019)

Election	Share of verified votes
Local 2013	3.4
EP 2014	4.0
Parliamentary 2015	4.3
Local 2017	4.0
Parliamentary 2019	5.3
EP 2019	4.1

Source: National Electoral Committee

by young males. Interestingly there seems almost a constant verification rate of 8–10% among males between 18–45 years of age, after which the share drops significantly as age increases further. No such plateau among female voters is observable. The substantial gender difference in verification frequency disappears only among voters in their late 60's. On average men are about two times more likely to verify the vote compared to female voters. Women in Estonia nowadays make up a majority among ivoters with a share in the 2019 parliamentary election of 55%. The gender difference among ivote verifiers is however in the reverse direction, with males making up 61%.

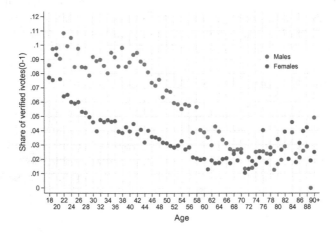

Fig. 1. Share of ivotes verified by age and gender

Examining the typical verifier further we see that verification share is clearly higher during late voting hours. Figure 2 shows that verification share starts to increase when ivotes are given after 8 pm and peaks at 3 pm night-time. Time of course does not influence verification probability, it simply shows that the ivoters who vote at these hours are a somewhat distinct user group.

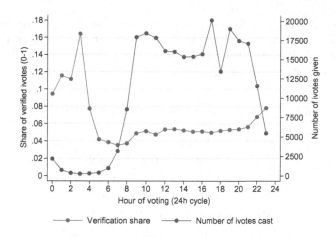

Fig. 2. Verification share and number of votes by time of day

Finally an examination of the other variables available in the logs (Table 2) shows verification to be more prevalent among Linux users with every 5th vote being verified compared to every 20th verified among Windows users. Also, Mac using voters are likely verifiers with a share that is twice that of Windows using voters. For ID types (Table 3) voters using Mobile-ID are much more likely to verify. This is explainable by the fact that they already have the smart device that can be used for verification at hand as they use it to authenticate themselves and digitally sign the vote.

Table 2. Verification rate by operating system used for ivoting

Op. system	Verified the vote		
	No	Yes	Total
Windows	215 612	10 923	226 535
	95.18%	4.82%	100.0%
Mac	22 941	2 127	25 068
	91.52%	8.48%	100.00%
Linux	1 552	417	1 969
	78.82%	21.18%	100.00%
Total	240 105	13 467	253 572
	94.69%	5.31%	100.00%

To sum up the profiles on can say that when the average ivoter is a 45 year old woman, but the average verifier a 40 year old male. Taking into account the very high verification share among males between 18 to 40, the disproportionate presence of Linux users as well as the voting hours it is safe to say that the

ivote verifiers are clearly distinct from average ivoters, let alone voters. The
verifier profile fits a more technology and computer literate user description.
A logical conclusion from this is also that they are above average when it comes
to awareness of the privacy and security risks connected to Internet voting.

Table 3. Verification rate by ID means used for ivoting

eID	Verified the vote		
	No	Yes	Total
ID-card	168 095	7 136	175 231
	95.93%	4.07%	100.00%
Mobile-ID	68 205	6 155	74 360
	91.72%	8.28%	100.00%
Digi-ID	3 805	176	3 981
	95.58%	4.42%	100.00%
Total	240 105	13 467	253 572
	94.69%	5.31%	100.00%

4.2   How Is Verification Used

Let us move from a typical user to more concrete usage patterns of verification.
Figure 3 examines the paths voters took depending on whether they verified the
vote or not and how did their voting environment changed in relation to that. A
couple of interesting aspects appear. As a sidenote, the total figures differ from
previous tables which included re-votes by the same voters, in Fig. 3 only paths
of unique voters are shown.

First, most of the 12 077 who verified left it at that and did not re-vote, the
percentage is almost the same among verifiers (97.5%) and non-verifiers (97.9%).
Out of the ones who did vote a second time a majority did not change either the
setting (change of IP), the device (change of operating system) or eID mode used
for voting. But the same is apparent for those who did not verify. Changing the
voting environment is however more likely among the verifiers compared to the
non-verifiers, which runs counter to hypothesis 2. It is also apparent that once
you verified the first vote you are also more likely to verify subsequent re-votes
regardless of the change in environment as verification is the modal category for
both (path 2 and 4) while not verifying the second vote is the modal category
when you also did not verify your first vote (path 6 and 8). But lets examine time
between the votes for the paths in Fig. 3 as well before we conclude anything.

This is done in Fig. 4. In both cases, for those who verified their first vote
and for those who did not, the second vote is cast comparatively faster than
among the group who actually changed either the IP, operating system or ID
means. The IP change indicates a change of location and the operating system

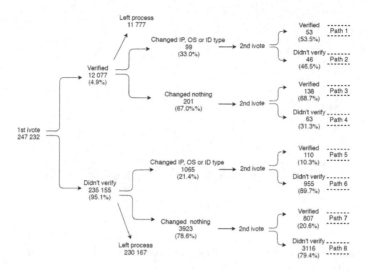

Fig. 3. Change patterns for those who voted second time (everyone included)

change means a change of the device used for voting. In other words, the second vote is given comparatively faster by those who leave everything unchanged. This is of course to be expected, if you vote from another network later on or purposefully move to another network to re-vote, there is bound to be more time between your two votes. The question is if this pattern supports the verification to "self-check and vote again" hypothesis (H2). A detailed look at the cumulative distributions shows that those who do not verify and simply vote again using the same setting do so substantially faster when compared to those who verify and then vote again using the same setting. Even zooming into the really fast re-voters, i.e. those who do so within 5 min after the first vote, we see that they make up 24% among the former group and only 11% among the latter. In fact, for every time period - be it 5, 10, 30 or even up to 720 min between two ivotes - the share is larger in the former group compared to the latter by a factor of two.

All in all the evidence does not seem to support H2. Verification compared to non-verification actually leads more likely to changing the environment and voting again, while it does not lead to a faster re-vote compared to non-verifying re-voters. And finally verifying your second vote is much more likely among voters who verified their first vote. All this does not seem to support the expla- nation that verification is used to simply checking if you did not make a mistake in candidate selection yourself.

Turning now to evidence for H3 leaves a final aspect to examined from the logs - is verification usage due to a possible vote secrecy and privacy concerns. Again, I have to employ a proxy for this in the form of a shared public IP, i.e. if two or more votes from separate voters share a public IP. This means they have voted from the same internet connection as some other voter. The logic being

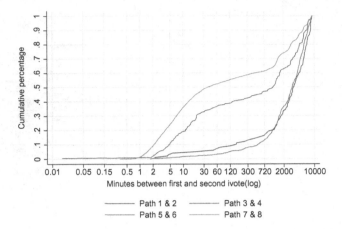

Fig. 4. Cumulative distributions of time between two ivotes for separate vote and verification paths in Fig. 3

that voting in a setting that is perceived as not so private - shared network - leads more likely to verifying the vote. Figure 5 shows that this is not the case. Casting a vote from an IP from which more than one was cast does not lead to a higher share of votes being verified. Figure 5a shows that most ivotes are given from a public IP that is shared by two voters, but Fig. 5b shows that verifying is most prevalent when voting from an IP that is not shared with any other voter. So voting from a network shared with others does not lead to more likely verification, the opposite is true. The caveat is of course that votes per IP does not tell us if it is a network indeed used only by one person, it merely shows no-one else used it for voting, it could still be some public work network. But this is the best proxy I have and it does not support H3.

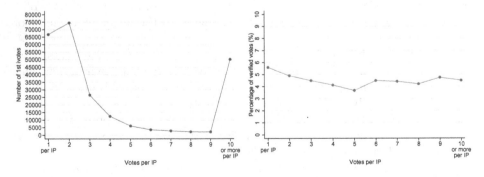

(a) Number of votes given from shared IPs   (b) Share of verified votes

Fig. 5. Number of 1st ivotes and share of verifying depending on how many votes were given from shared IPs

Another proxy for perceived security could be the location were the vote is cast from. If a vote is given abroad then the voter might need additional proof that the vote has made it safely "home" across the borders or that a unknown hotel/public/office network or computer used for voting can be trusted, something which verification can provide. This is done in Fig. 6. We see that comparatively more ivotes are indeed verified if they are given abroad. This does suggest a need for further confirmation of the integrity given voting happens in a foreign country. In 2019 ivotes were cast from more than 140 countries across the globe and on average verification rate of votes from abroad was clearly higher when compared to the roughly 5% of verified votes in Estonia.

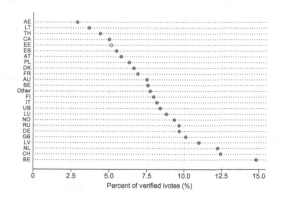

Fig. 6. Verification share by country (Estonia marked red) (Color figure online)

All in all. The data shows that voting from an IP that is shared by some other voter, a proxy for a shared location and presumably less private voting environment, does not translate into a higher probability to verify the vote. Voting from abroad however is indeed clearly connected to a higher verification usage frequency.

4.3   Effect of Verification

Finally, lets examine also the connection between verification usage and belief in election integrity with the help of survey data. Confidence in the integrity of one's own vote is shown in Fig. 7a and in other votes in 7b. Without bringing verification in yet Fig. 7 shows that 87% are somewhat or fully confident that their vote has been correctly taken into account and 89% think so of the votes by other voters. But once this is broken down according to knowing about and using verification (Fig. 8) we see that confidence in one's own vote is clearly higher for voters who are either aware of the verification option (Fig. 8a) or who have also used it (Fig. 8b).

This difference in confidence for those who know compared to those who don't know about the verification option persists after controlling for gender,

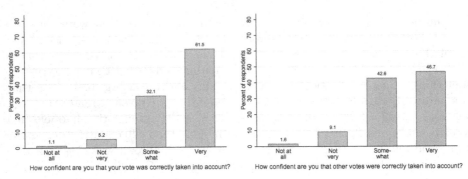

(a) Own vote was taken into account   (b) Other votes were taken into account

Fig. 7. Confidence vote was correctly taken into account

age, income, education, computer literacy level and internet usage frequency in an ordered logistic regression model with standard errors clustered by election. Table 4 displays the average marginal effect of knowing about it as well as using verification extracted from the regression model. We see that even after controlling for other covariates that affect confidence, people who know about verification being available have a 17% points higher probability in being very confident that their vote was correctly taken into account, while less likely to be somewhat or not very confident in this. As for actually using verification the effect on confidence is borderline non-significant.

Though this is not enough to claim that verification itself increases confidence as this data is cross sectional and post-election i.e. post-usage, one can clearly state that awareness of the verification option being available and the actual user experience correlate with a clearly heightened belief in integrity, so the cast-as-

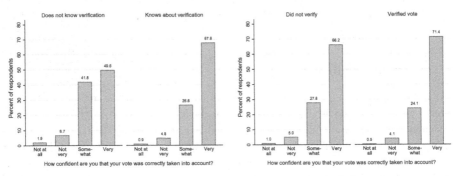

(a) Knowing verification and confidence (ivoters only)   (b) Using verification and confidence (ivoters who know about verification only)

Fig. 8. Confidence own vote was correctly taken into account according to knowledge and usage of individual verification

intended and recorded-as-cast features of verification seem to be producing the expected results in voter confidence.

Moving to the belief in the integrity of other votes we see somewhat surprisingly that people actually aren't overly confident that these were also correctly taken into account, as shown by Fig. 9. The pattern in the figures is however the same as already seen above, verification awareness and usage correlates with a higher belief in the integrity of other votes. Again, the average marginal effects in Table 4 confirm these associations to be robust to controls.

Table 4. Average marginal effects on confidence that votes were taken into account (standard errors in parentheses)

	Confident your vote taken into account			
	Not at all	Not very	Somewhat	Very
Knows of verification	−0.011	−0.039***	−0.117***	0.167***
(ref: does not know)	(0.006)	(0.010)	(0.027)	(0.040)
Verified vote	−0.004	−0.015	−0.056	0.076
(ref: did not verify)	(0.002)	(0.010)	(0.029)	(0.039)
	Confident other votes taken into account			
	Not at all	Not very	Somewhat	Very
Knows of verification	−0.012***	−0.059***	−0.095**	0.166***
(ref: does not know)	(0.001)	(0.014)	(0.021)	(0.034)
Verified vote	−0.002	−0.008	−0.021	0.030
(ref: did not verify)	(0.003)	(0.012)	(0.032)	(0.047)

$^{*}p < 0.05$, $^{**}p < 0.01$, $^{***}p < 0.001$

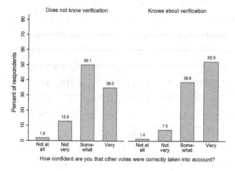

(a) Knowing verification and confidence (ivoters only)

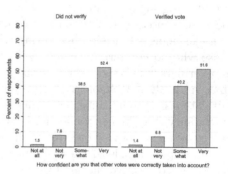

(b) Using verification and confidence (ivoters who know about verification only)

Fig. 9. Confidence that other votes were correctly taken into account according to knowledge and usage of individual verification

5 Discussion

In light of the evidence above the hypotheses can now be re-examined. The first hypothesised that verifiers have a specific profile that might show higher risk knowledge. The second posited that verification might be used to simply check ones own mistake and re-vote without changing much and not to guard against security risks or vote manipulation. The third hypothesised a contrary option that privacy concerns might lead to verification. The evidence is clearly supporting the first hypothesis, verifiers are younger male and Linux user with verification rate especially high in the 18 to 40 age group. Leaving out gender this is surely not a profile of a typical ivoter, let alone a voter, but does conform with a profile of a person who is more computer and technology literate and hence probably also more aware of potential privacy and security risks when it comes to Internet voting. As for the second hypothesis the data does not support it, verification leads actually more likely to changing the settings of the voting session for the re-vote and the data does not show that verifiers re-vote quickly after the initial self-check, the fastest re-voters are actually those who do not verify the first vote. I'm inclined to conclude that verification is indeed more likely used to check against cyber risks rather than voter made mistakes, at least the proxy measures suggest a pattern that is more in line with this. As for the third hypothesis the evidence is again somewhat mixed, while voting from a network that is shared with other voters does not lead to more verification, voting from abroad clearly does so. The fourth hypothesis proposed that cast-as-intended verification leads more likely to higher confidence in the integrity of the form of being certain that ones vote was taken into account. This was clearly backed up by the data.

All in all cast-as-intended and recorded-as-cast verification does correlate with having higher confidence in the integrity of the vote. It does seem to be more likely used by the more risk aware subgroup of voters, who are more likely to make changes to their when voting environment before a re-vote compared to those who do not verify the vote, even though a large majority of verifiers and non-verifiers who re-vote do so without changing the setting. All this indicates that verification technology is fulfilling its intended purpose - being used to mitigate risks around Internet voting by the one's who are more risk aware. Its availability gives higher confidence in the vote integrity even without necessarily using the technology, knowledge of the possibility seems to suffice.

On a practical level these findings suggest a simple way how to increase the observed positive effects of verification. Raising awareness about this option would not only increase usage numbers, but also belief in the integrity of elections among the non-users. Those who have concerns or who are more risk-aware seem to be using it to mitigate the perceived risks. Those who are not so risk-aware as to be converted into using seem to be clearly more confident in election integrity if they know that the opportunity to verify is in principle available. Even though they choose to trust internet voting rather than verify, evidence at hand shows having the liberty to rely on trust with the option to exercise some verification clearly already boosts belief in election integrity.

The question raised in the title can be answered in the affirmative - verification works.

References

1. Krimmer, R., et al. (eds.): E-Vote-ID 2019. LNCS, vol. 11759. Springer, Cham (2019). https://doi.org/10.1007/978-3-030-30625-0
2. Krimmer, R., et al. (eds.): E-Vote-ID Proceedings, Austria. TUT Press (2018)
3. Krimmer, R., Volkamer, M., Braun Binder, N., Kersting, N., Pereira, O., Schürmann, C. (eds.): E-Vote-ID 2017. LNCS, vol. 10615. Springer, Cham (2017). https://doi.org/10.1007/978-3-319-68687-5
4. Krimmer, R., Krimmer, R., et al. (eds.): E-Vote-ID 2016. LNCS, vol. 10141. Springer, Cham (2017). https://doi.org/10.1007/978-3-319-52240-1
5. Haenni, R., Koenig, R.E., Wikström, D. (eds.): VOTELID 2015. LNCS, vol. 9269. Springer, Cham (2015). https://doi.org/10.1007/978-3-319-22270-7
6. Popoveniuc, S., Kelsey, J., Regenscheid, A., Vora, P.: Performance requirements for end-to-end verifiable elections. In: Proceedings of the 2010 International Conference on Electronic Voting Technology/Workshop on Trustworthy Elections, pp. 1–16. USENIX Association, Berkeley (2010)
7. Allepuz, J.P., Castelló, S.G.: Internet voting system with cast as intended verification. In: Kiayias, A., Lipmaa, H. (eds.) Vote-ID 2011. LNCS, vol. 7187, pp. 36–52. Springer, Heidelberg (2012). https://doi.org/10.1007/978-3-642-32747-6_3
8. Morales-Rocha, V., Soriano, M., Puiggali, J.: New voter verification scheme using pre-encrypted ballots. Comput. Commun. 32, 1219–1227 (2009)
9. Helbach, J., Schwenk, J.: Secure Internet voting with code sheets. In: Alkassar, A., Volkamer, M. (eds.) Vote-ID 2007. LNCS, vol. 4896, pp. 166–177. Springer, Heidelberg (2007). https://doi.org/10.1007/978-3-540-77493-8_15
10. Clarkson, M., Chong, S., Myers, A.: Civitas: toward a secure voting system. In: IEEE Symposium on Security and Privacy, pp. 354–368 (2008)
11. Juels, A., Catalano, D., Jakobsson, M.: Coercion-resistant electronic elections. In: WPES, Alexandria, Virginia, USA, pp. 61–70 (2005)
12. Krips, K., Willemson, J.: On practical aspects of coercion-resistant remote voting systems. In: Krimmer, R., et al. (eds.) E-Vote-ID 2019. LNCS, vol. 11759, pp. 216–232. Springer, Cham (2019). https://doi.org/10.1007/978-3-030-30625-0_14
13. Kulyk, O., Teague, V., Volkamer, M.: Extending Helios towards private eligibility verifiability. In: Haenni, R., Koenig, R.E., Wikström, D. (eds.) VOTELID 2015. LNCS, vol. 9269, pp. 57–73. Springer, Cham (2015). https://doi.org/10.1007/978-3-319-22270-7_4
14. Kulyk, O., Volkamer, M.: Usability is not enough: lessons learned from 'human factors in security' research for verifability. In: Krimmer, R., et al. (eds.) E-vote-ID Proceedings, Austria, pp. 66–81. TUT Press (2018)
15. Olembo, M.M., Bartsch, S., Volkamer, M.: Mental models of verifiability in voting. In: Heather, J., Schneider, S., Teague, V. (eds.) Vote-ID 2013. LNCS, vol. 7985, pp. 142–155. Springer, Heidelberg (2013). https://doi.org/10.1007/978-3-642-39185-9_9
16. Schneider, S., Culnane, C.: Focus group views on Prêt à voter 1.0. In: International Workshop on Requirements Engineering for Electronic Voting Systems, REVOTE 2011, Trento, Italy (2011)

17. Kerr, N.: Election-day experiences and evaluations of electoral integrity in unconsolidated democracies: evidence From Nigeria. Polit. Stud. **66**, 667–686 (2018)
18. Karp, J., Nai, A., Norris, P.: Dial 'F' for fraud: explaining citizens suspicions about elections. Electoral Stud. **53**, 11–19 (2018)
19. Bowler, S., Donovan, T.: A partisan model of electoral reform: voter identification laws and confidence in state elections. State Polit. Policy Q. **16**, 340–361 (2016)
20. Norris, P., Garnett, H.A., Grömping, M.: The paranoid style of American elections: explaining perceptions of electoral integrity in an age of populism. J. Elections Public Opin. Parties **30**, 105–125 (2020)
21. Birch, S.: Electoral institutions and popular confidence in electoral processes: a cross-national analysis. Elect. Stud. **27**, 305–320 (2008)

Correction to: Electronic Voting

Robert Krimmer[iD], Melanie Volkamer[iD], Bernhard Beckert[iD],
Ralf Küsters, Oksana Kulyk, David Duenas-Cid[iD],
and Mihkel Solvak

Correction to:
R. Krimmer et al. (Eds.): *Electronic Voting*, LNCS 12455,
https://doi.org/10.1007/978-3-030-60347-2

The original version of the cover and book was revised. The seventh editor name has been updated.

The original version of this chapter "A Unified Evaluation of Two-Candidate Ballot-Polling Election Auditing Methods" contains the following errors which have been now corrected:

Page 117:

- "It can be continuous, discrete, or neither." should read "It can be continuous, discrete, or a combination of the two."

Page 118:

- "...is *risk-maximizing*: for such a prior, limiting the upset probability to α also limits the risk to α." should read "...is *risk-maximizing*. For such a prior, limiting the upset probability to v also limits the risk: for the specific type of Bayesian audits considered by Vora [11], the risk limit is v; however, for the Bayesian audits described here (see below), the risk limit is $\frac{v}{1-v} > v$."
- "The upset probability, $\Pr(H_0 \mid Y_n)$, is **not** the risk, which we write informally as $\max_{H_0} \Pr(\text{certify} \mid H_0)$." should read " The upset probability, $\Pr(H_0 \mid Y_n)$, is **not** the risk, which is $\Pr(\text{certify} \parallel p_T)$."
- "For risk-maximizing priors, taking $h = \frac{1-\alpha}{\alpha}$ yields an audit with risk limit α." should read "For risk-maximizing priors, taking $h = \frac{1}{\alpha}$ (which is equivalent to a threshold of $v = \frac{\alpha}{1+\alpha}$ on the upset probability) yields an audit with risk limit α."

Page 119:

- "$\Pr(Y_n \mid p_1)$" should read "$\Pr(Y_n \parallel p_1)$" (3 instances).
- "$\Pr(Y_n \mid p_0)$" should read "$\Pr(Y_n \parallel p_0)$" (1 instances).

The updated version of the book can be found at
https://doi.org/10.1007/978-3-030-60347-2
https://doi.org/10.1007/978-3-030-60347-2_8

Author Index

Printed in the United States
by Baker & Taylor Publisher Services